STROKES OF GENIUS

STROKES

A HISTORY OF SWIMMING

OF GENIUS

ERIC CHALINE

REAKTION BOOKS

Lifelong friendships
To M-H, Sue, Rohan & Anne and Nathalie

Published by Reaktion Books Ltd
Unit 32, Waterside
44–48 Wharf Road
London N1 7UX, UK
www.reaktionbooks.co.uk

First published 2017
Copyright © Eric Chaline 2017

Printed and bound in Great Britain by Bell & Bain, Glasgow

A catalogue record for this book is available from the British Library

ISBN 978 1 78023 819 7

Contents

Introduction

Pleasure beckons at the water's edge. Whether it's the lazy, sensual slide into the shallow end of the pool, or the invigorating shock of the dive into deeper water, our connection with swimming is first and foremost an embodied one. Full immersion entails a transition to another state of awareness, in which the usual balance of our senses is upset: sight and hearing make way for touch, smell and taste. In water, we become buoyant as we could never be while rooted by earth's gravity; a strong kick sends us gliding, weightless above the tiled chequerboard of the swimming pool or the ocean's sandy, rock-strewn depths.

Of the four elements, water alone opens up to welcome us, drawing us into its liquid embrace. We cannot soar through the air like birds, burrow down into the earth like moles or walk salamander-like through fire, but we can swim with the fishes. Transformed into mermaids and Tritons in garish Lycra, we are freed from our terrestrial clumsiness and mundane worries, and cleansed of our earthly sweat and sins. Swimming is much more than the application of strokes mechanics to water resistance and displacement, because it engenders in us powerful feelings of physical, mental and spiritual well-being.

From my earliest childhood memories, I have always been enamoured of the water and swimming. My preference for sun-and-sea holidays has always won out. In that, I seem to be in a comfortable majority in the chilly north, whose population yearly decamps for two weeks of brine-soaked summer sun in the south.

If I pass an inviting body of water on a warm day, my thoughts will quickly turn to the practicalities of taking a dip. For leisure and fitness, I have spent years of my life ploughing up and down a pool, but if I were to walk the same 25- or 50-m course back and forth for an hour, it would seem absurd to any reasonable person; so why isn't it absurd in a pool?

This book sets out to discover what connects us to swimming and explain why many of us enjoy it so much. Is it a relatively recent love affair born of affluent, leisured lifestyles dating back to Victorian prosperity, or does the connection go much further back to the origins of our species? Why do we swim at all? Apart from dogs, which we have taught to swim, other habitually terrestrial mammals will not enter the water willingly, and most will probably avoid it altogether other than in the direst need. The only exceptions to this generalization are our cousins the primates, several of which are known to take a dip from time to time, often with every sign of enjoyment. Does that mean we are hard-wired to find pleasure in an aquatic excursion? To answer this question, I have had to go much further back than I had originally envisaged to an as yet unresolved controversy about the evolution of hominin lineage.

Water Worlds

Close to half the world's population lives and works in coastal regions, which are also the world's preferred warm-weather holiday destinations. When we do not have ready access to natural bodies of water, we spend millions on equipping our cities with state-of-the-art aquatic facilities. And one of the main activities that we do in the 'water worlds' we live by, visit or recreate is 'swim', which, for the purposes of this book, is defined as moving on or beneath the surface of the water under our own motive power. While this includes scuba (self-contained breathing apparatus), it excludes the classic nineteenth-century diving suit (Standard Diving Dress) – the combination of waterproofed canvas suit, heavy spherical copper helmet linked to the surface by an air hose, and oversized metal boots that allowed the diver to stagger along the sea bottom. Nor does this include any means of artificial underwater propulsion, such as underwater scooters, manned torpedoes and wet subs, though they will feature as the story of swimming unfolds.

Most of us associate swimming with recreation or fitness training in a pool or at the seaside, or with competitions in four of the five aquatic disciplines,[1] but the range of activities that involve swimming, both historically and in the present day, covers all aspects of human activity, in addition to recreation and sport: hunting, farming, work, commerce, warfare, health and fitness, religion, science and the arts. In order to cover them all, this book will document long-forgotten, past water worlds, reveal the existence of little-known contemporary ones and look to future water worlds, as well as feature those that are more familiar to us, outlining their origins and evolution through time, culture and place.

But beyond the task of descriptive history, one of my aims in writing this book is to explore the origins of our ancient and enduring emotional, psychological and cultural relationship with swimming. The evidence of this attachment is to be found not just in the huge infrastructure of coastal resorts and swimming pools but in much more subtle ways, both positive and negative: in language, for example, which features a number of swimming-related expressions, such as 'being in the swim of things', 'swimming against the tide' and 'things going swimmingly', or less benignly, 'treading water', 'going under' and 'being out of one's depth', all associating our progress through life with swimming, and all used by people who might have little or no personal connection with or lived experience of the practice of swimming. According to Sigmund Freud, our connection with swimming goes deep into our subconscious. In *The Interpretation of Dreams* (1899), he described swimming as a symbolic representation of emotion, the unconscious and sexuality – areas of our psyche that are beyond the scrutiny or control of our higher conscious, rational self. How do we explain this link – stronger, I would argue, than that with much more commonplace human activities, such as walking and running, which we practise far more often than swimming? In order to find the answer, we need to go far back to our individual origins, as foetuses 'swimming' in our mother's womb; and much, much further back into the past to the origin of our species, in the evolution of our earliest ancestors, who lived in Africa between 5 and 7 million years BP (Before Present), when our line diverged from that of the great apes.

The Swimmer's Ascent

A cartoon of Charles Darwin had his head attached to the body of a great ape in order to ridicule the notion that men were descended from 'lower animals'. But this was a gross misrepresentation of Darwin's theory of evolution through natural selection as he never argued that we are descended from apes, which are, in fact, our closest living relatives in the animal world. Although we are closely related to chimpanzees, gorillas and orang-utans, our last common ancestor (LCA) is believed to have lived between 5 and 7 million years BP, when the lineages split, giving rise to the great apes and our own early ancestors.

Until the last quarter of the twentieth century, scientists had widely differing views as to where and when the first representatives of the genus *Homo*, who would become modern-day humans, had evolved. With each new fossil and artefact discovery, the picture became more complex and confused, with possible early ancestors discovered first in Europe, then in Asia. Matters were not helped by national pride in claiming to 'own' the first human ancestor and also biased by racist theories that placed the genesis of modern humans in the regions of the planet occupied by Caucasians. The problem with our evolutionary tree is that while it has a number of branches – possible candidates as our early ancestors – not one is universally recognized by all researchers in the field, and though we have an ancestral tree, quite a lot of its trunk and key sections of several major branches are missing, in particular during the several million years between the human-ape LCA and the first universally accepted members of the genus *Homo*, *Homo habilis* ('handy man'), who first appeared around 2.3 million years BP.

In 1924, anthropologist Raymond Dart (1893–1988), working at Taung, near Kimberley, South Africa, made one of the most significant discoveries of the twentieth century when he discovered the fossilized skull of a juvenile hominin showing traits common to both apes and humans, but most significantly an upright bipedal gait and a comparatively large brain. The Taung Child was the first recorded discovery of a representative of *Australopithecus*, a genus of presumed human ancestors who lived in East Africa 4.2–1.2 million years BP. In the intervening ninety years, many other specimens have been discovered, and the australopithecines have been subdivided into several species. Their discovery reduced the gap between the human-ape LCA and the first proto-humans by between 1 and 3 million years. At present there are several fossil candidates to be the 'missing links' that might close the remainder of the gap, but none that are yet generally accepted.

What is particularly significant about this gap in the fossil record is that it includes the key evolutionary steps that led to later hominids becoming fully bipedal and increased the size of their brains. In the film *2001: A Space Odyssey* (1968),[2] primitive ape-like creatures encounter an alien artefact – the sinister black 'Monolith' – that turns them from peaceful apes into killer humans (so much for the Kubrick-Clark view of human evolution). Although it is extremely unlikely that it was a single artefact, alien or otherwise, that nudged apes to evolve into humans, in the present state of knowledge it is just as good a theory as any that has been put forward. We still do not know, nor can we explain beyond reasonable doubt, why our lineage began to evolve at that moment in time in the way it did.

The standard model of human evolution is that a move from an arboreal to an open savannah environment prompted bipedalism, larger brains, hairlessness and the host of other physical and behavioural changes that differentiate us from the great apes. But it is only a theory, and in 1960 an alternative was put forward that at some point between the human-ape LCA and the australopithecines, early hominins had an aquatic interlude that explains many modern human features. These distant ancestors did not turn into 'mermen' and 'mermaids', with fish tails like seals or dolphins – other mammals that returned to the sea and whose lower limbs fused together in a tail and whose upper limbs became flippers – but it might explain why they lost their fur and began to walk upright on two legs. This intriguing possibility was put forward most forcefully during the 1970s and '80s by a non-scientist, Elaine Morgan, which explains why, for decades, the theory was ignored, ridiculed or flatly rejected by the scientific establishment. It is only in the past 25 years that scientists have begun seriously to evaluate the claims of the 'aquatic ape hypothesis' (AAH).

While it is beyond the scope of this book (and the capacity of the author) to confirm or deny the claims of the AAH, these will be presented in full in Chapter One as an intriguing piece of evidence that might explain our powerful attachment to the practice of swimming – one that might go a very long way indeed in the collective unconscious memory of our species. Even if there never was an aquatic or semi-aquatic human ancestor, there is evidence to suggest that some of our most recent predecessors, the Neanderthals, who lived between 250,000 and 30,000 years BP and shared the planet with us, were at home in the water, and not just paddlers in the shallows foraging for food, but strong open-water swimmers who managed to swim to offshore islands.

The first *Homo sapiens*, who first appeared in Africa around 200,000 BP, would have had a similar relationship with bodies of water: sometimes as valuable sources of easily obtainable food, at other times as obstacles to their progress across an uncharted and untamed landscape, and probably sometimes as dark, dangerous places infested with monstrous predators. Swimming would have developed very early as a survival skill among our prehistoric ancestors. Although we cannot say how and when we first learned to swim, we might be able to reach some tentative conclusions by studying the lifestyles of the pre-industrial peoples who made aquatic environments their homes.

Swimming into History

The first urban civilizations of the Old World, Egypt, Mesopotamia, the Indus Valley and China, flourished along the banks of rivers where swimming would have been practised both as a survival skill and a pastime. Like their nomadic ancestors, settled humans swam and dived to collect food resources from seas, lakes and rivers, but as civilization became more complex and hierarchical, the products that might previously have been found and brought back by chance or as mere curiosities along with the daily catch became the main aim of the hunt: pearls, bright shells and corals to make into gems to adorn the bodies of the Bronze Age elites and to glorify their gods. Swimming as work, therefore, came into existence with civilization itself.

Later, as humans took to the seas, leading to the creation of the great seaborne empires of the Greeks, Carthaginians and Romans, swimming was a skill deemed invaluable to the sailor and soldier, and it was practised in natural bodies of water and increasingly in manmade pools. The Romans, in particular, were great exponents of the art of swimming for both peaceful and military ends. But with the passing of the classical world, and changing attitudes to the body brought by medieval Christianity, many turned their backs on antiquity's water worlds and forgot how to swim. Instead of a world of wonder, practical use and recreation, aquatic environments became the fearful haunt of monsters to be avoided at any cost.

In the West, the return to the water was a slow process that took centuries. Not only did attitudes have to change about the body and about the safety of the water, but men had to leave their landlocked cities and go back to former and new water worlds. The first was accomplished during the Renaissance and with the rediscovery of ancient texts that recommended swimming as beneficial to health, as an invaluable military skill and as a pleasant pastime. The second and third came when Europeans started to explore the wider world during the Age of Exploration, not only finding a need to swim but non-Western styles of swimming.

Humans had first explored and colonized the planet in pre-history, but with the scientific and industrial revolutions, they explored it in completely novel ways. Soon they were taking to the air, and building telescopes and microscopes to reveal unsuspected and unexpected macro- and micro-worlds. But the underwater world remained unusually resistant to exploration. While diving bell technology had been in use since antiquity, diving suits linked to the surface by air hoses that allowed divers to walk on the sea bottom at shallow depths date back to the eighteenth century. This technology was perfected during the nineteenth century and continued in use until the 1950s. But not only was this technology inherently dangerous – if the air hose was cut at depth or if carbon dioxide built up in the diver's body – it was also incredibly restrictive physically. This was not so much 'flying underwater' as shambling across the murky shallows.

By the beginning of the twentieth century, scientists, the military and diving pioneers were beginning to experiment with different scuba technologies that would finally release the diver from any attachment to the surface. This culminated in the development of the Aqualung in 1942, giving the world a scuba set that offered divers much greater freedom underwater with relative safety. No longer prisoners of the surface or the sea floor, humans could explore the planet's water worlds as never before. As these developments were taking place, there was an explosion in recreational and competitive swimming in the second half of the twentieth century.

If the worst predictions of climate science come to pass, a large part of the world's surface, including most of its major cities and densely populated coastal zones, will eventually be submerged. Shall we retreat to higher ground, or shall we move into the oceans to colonize this even bluer planet? Even if the world is saved from drowning, ever increasing pressure on available land – from the competing demands of growing populations, farming and the exploitation of natural resources – may finally force us to colonize the 71 per cent of the world's surface that is covered by the oceans and which contains not only potential habitable space but vast, untapped reserves of food and natural resources. In this new world, swimming may replace walking as humanity's basic means of locomotion, and we may finally evolve into *Homo aquaticus*.

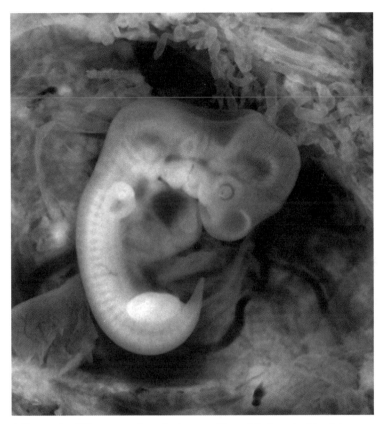

A five-week-old human embryo looks more like a fish than the bipedal primate it will grow into. Although, like other land mammals, humans are completely adapted to life out of water, they depend on it for reproduction and gestation.

1
The Aquatic Hominin

The students of the fossil record have for so long been
perturbed by the apparent sudden appearance of Man.
Where are the fossil remains that linked the Hominidae
with their more ape-like ancestors? The recent finds in
South Africa of *Australopithecus* seem to carry us a good
step nearer to our common origin with the ape stock, but
before then there is a gap. Is it possible that the gap is due
to the period when Man struggled and died in the sea?

ALISTER HARDY, 1960[1]

We are terrestrial refugees on an aquatic world. Seas and oceans
cover 71 per cent of the earth's surface – and considerably
more during periods when the climate warms and causes the ice
caps to melt. Our home planet's orbit within its solar system's
'Goldilocks' or habitable zone enabled life to develop in the oceans
around 4 billion years before the present (BP), when the land was
a barren, rocky, volcanic wasteland and the atmosphere a noxious
mixture of carbon dioxide and other gases. For the next 3.5 billion
years, Mother Nature engaged in a vast biological experiment in
earth's oceans, trying out new forms of life, until around 542 million
years BP, she hit the genetic jackpot, triggering the 'Cambrian
explosion' – 20 million years of astounding biological creativity in
earth's seas and oceans. Fifty million years later, plants had started
to colonize the land, initiating the conversion of the atmosphere
into something breathable by higher life forms. The terrestrial environment now supported plant and insect life, tempting fish and
proto-amphibians from the waters to feed and seek refuge from
predators. By around 300 million years BP – a blink in geological
time – animals had followed plants and insects and colonized the
land, severing any remaining ties with the water to become fully
adapted to terrestrial life.

'Fully terrestrial' needs to be qualified, however. All land-dwelling animals, be they reptiles, birds or mammals, need to drink water to survive, and the greater part of an animal's bodyweight is water.[2] All the body's biochemical processes take place in water, and in most mammals, its sustained absence leads to dehydration followed by death. For reproduction, too, most animals remain completely dependent on water – the amphibians, most obviously, as they have to return to the water to breed and have fully aquatic egg and larval stages. Land reptiles and birds, though they have left the water, encase their offspring in waterproof eggs that contain all the water and nutrients that they will need until they hatch. The mammalian strategy is to recreate an aquatic environment within the body. A mammalian sperm performs a 100-m (328-ft) dash to the ovum, and the foetus 'swims' in the liquid-filled maternal amnion, which is 98 per cent water. All mammals, including humans, display clear physical vestiges of their distant piscine ancestry: in its first few weeks of life the human embryo looks much more like a fish or amphibian than the upright primate it will ultimately grow into, and foetuses have folds on their necks that are vestigial gills. But unlike fish or tadpoles, mammalian foetuses do not obtain oxygen and nutrients rather from the amniotic fluid in the womb but rather from the placenta via the umbilical cord.

The human evolutionary relationship with aquatic environments, however, might be more than purely phylogenetic, and may have recurred at key points of our physiological and cultural evolution. According to the much-contested aquatic ape hypothesis (AAH), our early ancestors could have developed several key human traits during an aquatic phase, when swimming and diving could have been as or more important than walking and running. Even if the AAH, as most researchers in the field maintain, turns out to be wholly mistaken and the evolution of the human line was not shaped by water, what is not in doubt is that human facility in the water played a key role in the survival of our own genus, *Homo sapiens*, our colonization of the planet and the development of our earliest civilizations.

The Unlovely Bones

Modern humans are able and habitual swimmers. But when did humans first learn to swim? Archaeological evidence suggests that this long pre-dated the evolution of *Homo sapiens*. To help me decide how far back I should take the first chapter of the story of human swimming, I revisited my undergraduate acquaintance of palaeoanthropology – the study of Hominidae, hominin fossils and human evolution[3] – which traces the origins of the human line to between 5 and 7 million years BP, to the last common ancestor (LCA) we share with our closest living cousins, the great apes.[4] What remains of these remote human ancestors are the fossilized bones and teeth of a very few individuals that were miraculously preserved. Bones and teeth can tell us a great deal about individuals: their age and gender; whether they walked upright or on all fours; what they ate; whether they habitually climbed trees or spent most of their time on the ground; how they died – even an estimate of their cognitive abilities. But what these remains tell us little about is the topography, climate and vegetation of the environments in which our distant ancestors lived, interacted and died.

Even after the scientific community had come to terms with Charles Darwin's *On the Origin of Species* (1859) and *The Descent of Man* (1871), and the search for human ancestors had begun in earnest, palaeoanthropological research was hampered by nationalism and religious dogma and constrained by cultural and racial prejudices. The initial finds came from Western Europe, which explains why several human ancestors are saddled with unlikely *Mittel*-European names: *Homo heidelbergensis* (from Heidelberg, Baden-Württenberg, Germany) and *Homo neanderthalensis* (from Neanderthal, a river valley in North Rhine-Westphalia, also in Germany). By the late nineteenth and early twentieth centuries, the net had been cast much farther afield, and several ancient human lineages had been discovered in the Near East, Asia and Southeast Asia. But the most obvious place to seek our earliest ancestors, Africa, home to our closest primate kin, the great apes, was for many

European scientists so unpalatable that it was the last populated continent to be investigated.

All this changed in 1924, when a young Australian anthropologist, Raymond Dart (1893–1988), made a startling discovery in Taung (near Kimberley, South Africa), which turned out to be the first specimen of *Australopithecus africanus*, an early hominin that showed traits common to both apes and humans – but which most significantly walked on two legs, a mode of locomotion that is seen but is not habitual in the great apes. The australopithecines, which have since been subdivided into several species, lived in Africa

One possible reconstruction of a female *Australopithecus afarensis*, a presumed human ancestor that lived in what is now Ethiopia 3.2 million years BP. Although here closely modelled on a chimpanzee, *A. afarensis* was habitually bipedal and might have already lost its thick covering of body hair.

between 4.2 and 1.2 million years BP. One of the most complete australopithecine skeletons was discovered in Ethiopia's Afar Triangle fifty years after Dart's Taung 'child'. Nicknamed 'Lucy' and assigned to the subspecies *Australopithecus afarensis*, she was habitually bipedal but her cranium was around the same size as that of a modern great ape. This reversed the previously held belief that a larger cranium, and therefore a more intelligent hominin, had preceded habitual bipedal locomotion, which was now understood to be the trigger for other changes that had led to later human features.

Although there is now some doubt as to whether the australopithecines should be counted among our direct ancestors or are just distant cousins, they certainly figure on the human family tree somewhere between the human-ape LCA and the first representative of the genus *Homo*. Dart's claim that the australopithecines were human ancestors was immediately rejected by the palaeoanthropological establishment, until the weight of evidence and the large numbers of specimens found meant that Lucy and her kind were finally admitted into the orthodox evolutionary canon in the late 1940s. The discovery reduced the gap between the LCA and the first proto-humans by between 1 and 3 million years.[5]

When I was taught about Dart and his discovery, no mention was made of the old fogies who for twenty years had steadfastly refused to accept the African origins of mankind and had classed the australopithecines as exotic apes, yet the next generation of palaeoanthropologists were to prove to be just as conservative and resistant to a theory that did not conform to what they considered to be evolutionary orthodoxy. The theory of human evolution that I accepted as fact as an undergraduate was the 'savannah-man-the-hunter hypothesis' (SMHH), which in a much-abbreviated form goes something like this: the African climate changed; the forests were replaced by the open grasslands still seen in much of East Africa today; the as yet unidentified ancestors of the australopithecines were forced to come down from the rapidly thinning trees; their transition from arboreal to terrestrial life triggered physical changes: bipedalism, which in turn led to much greater manual dexterity, larger brains, hairlessness and a greater ability to vocalize – speech – as well as behavioural changes, such as the adoption of hunting that turned them from peaceful vegetarian omnivores into aggressive carnivorous omnivores.

At the time, I had no reason to question the idea that human evolution had been triggered by the requirements of half the proto-human population and their enthusiasm for running around, brandishing spears and killing large herbivores. Second-wave feminists, however, who were challenging all aspects of the patriarchal order, quickly homed in on those aspects of contemporary sexism whose biological 'inevitability' was underscored by ethology – the study of animal behaviour – and palaeoanthropology. They rejected the idea that male aggression and competitiveness had been the main drivers of human evolution and put forward rival theories, replacing prehistoric patriarchal bands with matriarchal lineages, and bloody competition with peaceful collaboration.

The problem facing students of evolution is that they start with modern humans and attempt to work backwards along the hominin line, but the further back they go, the sparser the links in the chain become. And even professional scientists who pride themselves on their objectivity, run the risk of incorporating the prejudices of the present into their theories, thereby remodelling the past to justify some present arrangement. For example, the SMHH could be seen as confirming a pre-feminist male-dominated social order. Another danger that we were constantly warned about as undergraduates was imposing our own experience of the world on another species. Thus, those of us who grew up in cold northerly climates where you need clothes all year around just to survive might not be best placed to imagine a very different lifestyle in the prehistoric tropics.

During my gap year, I travelled around Central America, stopping for a few weeks in the then British colony of Belize. One day, I went swimming in a lagoon a short distance up the coast from the capital, Belize City. The shallow waters were a holiday-brochure crystal-clear Caribbean blue, the beach palm-fringed and the sand a dazzling white. But what I can still recall is that there was little difference between the temperature of the air and water. I stripped off on the beach, hoping to cool down, but the water was so warm that far from being refreshing, it was more like taking a hot bath on a summer's day. If our earliest hominin ancestors had evolved in northern Europe or the northeastern u.s., they would have spent very little time in the water – even in the warmest months of the year – but in warm tropical seas, they could have spent all day fishing and foraging in the tepid, soupy waters without ever catching a chill.

The Ascent of Elaine Morgan

The feminist rejection of the smhh of human evolution must be seen, in part, in the light of the culture wars of the 1960s and '70s, when the alternative theories put forward were often mirror images of existing hypotheses: for example, the swapping of patriarchy for matriarchy. But the theory that hominins went through an aquatic phase – the aquatic ape hypothesis – during which key human traits evolved, pre-dates second-wave feminism by several decades. Its first iteration was made in 1930, by a then young marine biologist, Alister Hardy (1896–1985), who kept it secret for the next thirty years, making it public only once he had achieved his goals and when so controversial a theory could no longer damage his academic career. Even then, he publicized the theory at what he must have hoped would have been the relatively obscure public forum of an address to the British Sub-Aqua Club conference, held in Brighton in March 1960.

If Hardy had thought to slip the aah into the public domain without fuss, he was sadly mistaken. The press immediately sensationalized his address and two weeks later, he wrote his one and only outline and defence of the theory in an article entitled, 'Was Man More Aquatic in the Past?', which he published in one of the country's leading scientific journals.[6] The German biologist Max Westenhöfer (1871–1957) had reached similar conclusions in *Der Eigenweg des Menschen* (*The Unique Path to Man*). However, its publication in 1942 in Germany, when the world was engaged in another ideological conflict underpinned by a pseudoscientific theory about human ancestry, meant that his ideas did not spark the instant controversy that Hardy's did eighteen years later.

Westenhöfer died three years before Hardy's Brighton appearance, and Hardy himself, though he said he would write a book to expound the case for the AAH more fully, failed to do so before he died in 1985, appalled no doubt by the prospect of decades of bitter academic disputes were he, a marine biologist with no expertise in human evolution, to dare to challenge the serried ranks of palaeoanthropologists who championed the primacy of the SMHH. But, even now, we must be careful not to exaggerate the significance of the AAH. Hardy was no Copernicus to Westenhöfer's Galileo, and the palaeoanthropological establishment's rejection of the AAH must not be equated to the Catholic Church opposing the blindingly obvious truth of heliocentrism. The theory, which I shall review in the next section, though it has since acquired several noteworthy supporters, including noted British naturalist Sir David Attenborough (b. 1926),[7] remains one of several possible hypotheses that explain the evolution of modern humans.

What really did for the SMHH was not Hardy and Westenhöfer or feminist critiques, but the discovery that the open savannah had never dominated the ancient African landscape as the hypothesis supposed. Instead, the study of ancient climates and palaeobotany has since revealed that the australopithecines and their predecessors lived in a mixed and shifting wet-and-dry 'mosaic habitat' of forests, swamps and open grasslands.[8] The topography and climate of the Great Rift Valley of Ethiopia and Tanzania where the remains of Lucy and many of her kind were found was radically different 4 million years BP. Instead of deserts and arid savannah, there is evidence of lakes, river systems, forested areas and salt lakes. A great lake filled most of the Turkana Basin and the now bone-dry Danakil Depression was an inland sea that has long since evaporated.[9] Hence, even without the existence of AAH, the contention that our hominin ancestors had been forced to walk upright on the savannah instead of brachiating from tree to tree, and to stand on their hind legs to look over the long grass for prey and predators, was going to be displaced by completely unrelated evidence. It left mainstream palaeoanthropology with the problem of explaining what had triggered the change to bipedalism.

The Naked Hominin

With Westenhöfer long dead and Hardy cowed into silence, it was left to Welsh television screenwriter Elaine Morgan (1920–2013) to make the case for the AAH. She had come across a reference to Hardy's theory in Desmond Morris's *The Naked Ape* (1967), and she contacted the eminent marine biologist to ask his permission to write a book on the subject, which was published under the title *The Descent of Woman* in 1972. A textbook on human evolution published in 2004 gives us a flavour of the reception that Morgan's first book was given in academic circles: 'At first the idea was simply ignored as grotesque, and perhaps as unworthy of discussion because proposed by an amateur.'[10] Worse still, the book was dismissed as yet another strident feminist critique of the majority-male scientific establishment.[11] But 32 years on from Morgan's first book, the AAH has earned a degree of acceptance from members of the scientific community. She continued to refine her case in a series of books, including *The Aquatic Ape* (1982), *The Scars of Evolution* (1990), *Descent of the Child* (1995) and *The Aquatic Ape Hypothesis* (1997), arguing her case more cogently and persuasively with each new publication. She herself believed that it was only a question of time before the AAH would be fully accepted, estimating that around forty years had to elapse before so controversial a theory began to be accepted by the mainstream. Sadly, though the forty years are up, Morgan herself will never know if her one-woman crusade has succeeded or not, as she passed away in 2013.

Readers interested in Morgan's most complete and persuasive statement of the case for the AAH should read *The Aquatic Ape Hypothesis*, in which she put forward her argument with magisterial clarity, eschewing all easy polemics and point-scoring and merely laying out the evidence and asking the questions which she knew evolutionary science was unable to answer. In an earlier outing of the AAH, Morgan explained why a new theory of human evolution was needed:

> Over a hundred years have passed since Darwin wrote *The Descent of Man*. During that time, despite intense research and speculation, the major questions – why man became bipedal, lost his body hair, learned to speak, developed a big brain – have come no nearer to solution.[12]

This simple statement almost succeeds in masking an enormous gap in our knowledge. The four attributes listed sum up what make humans different from all other land mammals, though at least three are found in marine mammals. Therefore, how far-fetched is it that we, too, as Morgan, Hardy and Westenhöfer believed, for a period of several million years between the last human-ape LCA and the australopithecines, had, to quote Hardy, 'struggled and died in the sea'?

In the opening sections of her later books and articles, Morgan wasted no time in demolishing the already moribund SMHH. But she made sure that it would never rise from the grave by driving a stake through its heart and cutting off its head. If being bipedal and hairless had been such evolutionary advantages on land, she argued, why had other animals exposed to the same environmental pressures as our hominin ancestors not evolved in a similar fashion? In fact, though there exists another highly successful primate species that lives in the modern-day savannah, baboons (genus *Papio*), they have remained stubbornly quadrupeds and hirsute. In any case, as has already been pointed out, our hominin ancestors did not live in the savannah but in mosaic habitats not dissimilar to those favoured by the African great apes today. Although chimps and gorillas spend a great deal of their time on the ground and can stand and walk on two legs, by preference they 'knuckle-walk' on all fours, retain prehensile feet for climbing and, of course, they too have kept their thick fur coats.

Morgan's case did not stop there: bipedal locomotion was not just unnecessary in the habitats in which early hominins lived, its adoption would have been a costly drawback in terms of safety, the time needed to acquire it and the extra calorific expenditure it required. Most terrestrial mammals favour quadrupedal locomotion, which is stable, fast and easy to learn, and even with one limb injured, the animal can walk on three legs. In contrast, walking on two legs is unstable and time-consuming to learn and leaves the most vulnerable parts of the body – the viscera and sexual organs – exposed to attack. Additionally, it is stressful on the spine and cardiovascular system, and even after several million years of adaptation, we are still plagued by lower back and knee pains, hernias and varicose veins, which can be directly attributed to our upright stance. To borrow from George Orwell's *Animal Farm* (1945), it is definitely a case of 'four legs good, two legs bad'.

Even the SMHH's second line of argument – that bipedalism was adopted because it freed the hands for tool use and hunting – is not convincing. Not only do the great apes use simple found tools and display great manual dexterity without the need for an upright gait, they have an extra pair of prehensile feet to use when necessary.[13] Furthermore, the evidence now suggests that hominins were bipedal long before they used tools and hunted. The disadvantages of hairlessness also seem to outweigh any evolutionary advantage, especially in an arid climate. As Morgan pointed out, a covering of body hair is the first line of defence against heat, cold and UV radiation, and it can also provide camouflage. Fur is also a useful adjunct to primate mothers, as their young are able to cling on as she climbs to escape a predator or to forage for food. Humans are the only primates who have to hold their babies, having lost the body hair that a baby could easily cling on to. Hence, in some respects, losing our body hair is a distinct evolutionary disadvantage.

Bipedalism is thought to be the key to hominin evolution. And though evolutionary biologists agree that it must have appeared first, triggering a cascade of anatomical and behavioural changes, there is as yet no consensus about how it became the dominant form of hominin locomotion. Morgan suggested that there was one environment – water – in which bipedalism had a distinct advantage. She cited several primate examples that are known to frequent the

Our closest living relative, the chimpanzee, has been observed taking to the water, though not swimming. A habitual knuckle-walker on land, in water chimps are able to wade by standing on their hind limbs. Our hominin ancestors could have employed the same technique to take their first steps in the water, later developing into aquatic foragers and full swimmers.

water. The proboscis monkey (genus *Nasalis*), a resident of mosaic habitats, has been observed wading across shallow watercourses by walking on its hind legs and stabilizing itself with its outstretched arms.[14] Monkeys and apes are able to stand and walk upright, but usually in an ungainly fashion and only for short periods. Chimps and gorillas stand in displays of aggression to make themselves appear larger, but when they have to move at speed, they will revert to knuckle-walking on all four limbs.

For Morgan, wading in shallow water was a strong candidate to explain the development of bipedalism. If at some point between the human-great ape LCA and Lucy, hominins had spent 2–3 million years living in aquatic environments, they would have first learned to wade by standing on their hind legs, as a possible prelude to swimming. While in the water they would have discovered food sources that they could exploit by swimming and diving, thus improving the precision grip of their hands, while their feet, used for walking and swimming, lost their prehensile abilities, evolving into long, flat structures that were more stable when walking on land or in shallow water and that provided greater propulsion when swimming.

Our stay in the water, even if it had lasted 2–3 million years, was too short in evolutionary terms for us to become fully adapted to aquatic life like seals, manatees, dugongs, dolphins and whales – other mammals who made the transition from land back into water – whose most distinct adaptations, such as fused lower limbs and flippers, took tens of millions of years to evolve. Morgan, however, was certain that we look the way we do now because our hominin ancestors developed certain traits during an aquatic phase. Strip off and look at yourself in a mirror. When compared to any other primate, you have a streamlined silhouette that you owe to two characteristics that together are unique among terrestrial mammals: although you are covered in hair, it is mostly so fine as to be invisible, and you are also unique among the primates in having a thick layer of subcutaneous fat that gives you a rounded body shape. The only other mammals that display these two characteristics live in water. The direction of growth of our body hair is also different from that of the great apes, suggesting to Morgan that this arrangement evolved to guide water along the back, further streamlining us when swimming.

These are not the only characteristics that we share with sea mammals. Our sweat and tears contain salt, which does not have any real advantage in an arid environment like the African savannah, where it could lead to dehydration and a potentially fatal loss of essential nutrients. If you spend a lot of time in salt water, however, you need a mechanism to control your body's salt balance. Morgan argued that sweating, a mechanism that first developed as an adaptation to life in the sea, was later used for thermoregulation once our ancestors had returned to terrestrial life. The human arrangement of the larynx and voluntary breathing – meaning that unlike most terrestrial mammals, we can voluntarily suspend our breathing – is an odd halfway house between land and sea mammals. Dolphins, for example, have lost their ability to switch back to involuntary breathing and have to sleep with half their brain awake in order not to drown. It could be that speech is a by-product of our ability to hold our breath when we swim, but the argument could just as easily be turned around so that holding our breath is a product of the ability to speak. Significantly, the breath-holding reflex is present in newborn babies, who will automatically close their throats if their faces are immersed in water; babies will also make basic swimming movements with their arms and legs and seem completely at ease in the water – an ability that we unfortunately lose after a few months, meaning that, unless we remain in a semi-aquatic environment throughout infancy, we have to learn to swim and dive all over again.

There are records of island peoples in Indonesia who used to give birth in the sea. The newborn's throat-closing reflex kept it safe from drowning, and it took its first breath when it emerged from the water. Mothers and babies were more relaxed; the birth took place in salt water, which has natural antiseptic qualities; and the

Newborn babies immersed in water will automatically close their throats and make basic sculling motions with their arms and legs. Is this ability a relic of our time spent living an aquatic existence? Humans are also unique among terrestrial mammals because they are born covered in a fatty substance known as *vernix caseosa*, which Elaine Morgan suggested acted as an insulating layer for babies born in water.

umbilical cord is long enough for mothers to bring the newborn to the breast while still in the water. The Indonesian practice of water birthing, since reintroduced in the developed world in shallow birthing pools, was proscribed by nineteenth-century missionaries, who were keen to impose the norms of Victorian Europe on their Southeast Asian flocks. And as for the argument that sea water would be much too cold for newborn babies for any length of time: that does not take into account the insulating layer of a fatty substance called *vernix caseosa* that covers human newborns. As far as is known, the only other mammals who are born covered in *vernix* are seals.[15] And, of course, we are not talking of expectant mothers wading out into the surf in the seas off Margate or Kennebunkport on a brisk March morning, but in tropical seas as warm and soup-like as those of a shallow Caribbean lagoon.

Morgan presented three final pieces of evidence in support of the AAH. She agreed that we developed a precision grip because our hands were freed – not, however, because we were wandering around on land carrying stone axes and spears, but because, when we were wading or swimming, they would have been used to forage for food underwater. This also ties in with the idea that a diet richer in proteins and omega-3 fatty acids was crucial in the increase in brain size that is another key characteristic of our species. Although it was once thought that animal protein from hunting was responsible for increased hominin brain power, Morgan makes the point that the aquatic environment is even richer in the right mix of dietary chemicals to boost brain size, which for a relatively short, lightly built hominin were much easier to obtain from fish and shellfish than from large herbivores. The final piece of evidence is to be found in the way we have sex. In most terrestrial mammals, the male mounts the female from the back, while sea mammals mate face to face.

Morgan's defence of the AAH is no longer ridiculed in palaeo-anthropological circles and it is now included in textbooks as an alternative theory to explain bipedalism and hairlessness. The main stumbling block in trying to prove the AAH is finding any 'killer proof' of an aquatic phase. Lucy was found in deposits containing turtle eggs and crustaceans, but that does not prove that she or her ancestors were aquatic. She may have died close to the water's edge by chance. The AAH remains an intriguing possibility but nothing more. But if, in the future, it is to be shown to have some substance, our link to swimming would be so ancient that it would pre-date the meaningful use of the term human. For Morgan and her supporters, there would be no humanity as we know it without an aquatic interlude, but what we have to take into consideration is that any presumed aquatic inheritance would have been overlaid by the subsequent 4.2 million years of terrestrial evolution.

In 2000, human evolutionary biologist Carsten Niemitz put forward a modified version of the AAH, the 'amphibian generalist theory' (AGT), which proposed that wading was an important precursor to full bipedalism but rejected the idea that hominins had had a fully aquatic phase that led to the evolution of the other human traits Morgan cited in her books.[16] Morgan, however, never defined how 'aquatic' the human aquatic interlude actually was. She never claimed that our ancestors became 'merfolk' living exclusively in the water for 2–3 million years. Hence, the difference between Morgan's AAH and Niemitz's AGT might be a disagreement about which human traits to include or exclude – a matter of detail rather than substance.

Stone Age Swimmers

Morgan's presumed *Australopithecus aquaticus* – an aquatic hominin ancestor – may never have existed, but archaeological discoveries from the Mediterranean and Southeast Asia suggest that early members of the genus *Homo* were far more at home in and on the water than early students of prehistory ever imagined. Step back in time into a virgin world without tracks, let alone roads through its jungles, forests, deserts and open grasslands. The bands of early human ancestors who set out from Africa to colonize the earth might not have known where they were going or what lay ahead of them, but they had natural highways through the landscape that also provided them with the necessities of life: rivers were sources of fresh water and shellfish, fish and waterfowl, and their banks, lush with vegetation, also attracted a wide variety of terrestrial species. At the very least, rivers know where they are flowing to: into another larger river, a lake, marsh and ultimately the sea. When early humans came to the sea, the coast itself would have given them a direction of travel, with the sea providing them with sustenance as they moved onwards. If this hypothesis is correct, humans would have been as able swimmers as they were walkers, as they would have been constantly foraging and fishing.

Early theories about the waves of human migration that took our species out of Africa supposed that human ancestors such as *Homo erectus* and *Homo heidelbergensis* had walked off the continent, staying high and dry by crossing the Sinai Peninsula and taking advantage of the land bridges that existed during glacial periods, when the sea level was much lower than it is today, to reach the Near East, from where they dispersed via land routes to colonize the rest of the planet. Just as with the refusal to accept the AAH, there appears to be a strong terrestrial bias at work here – one that presupposes that our ancestors, when faced with a large body of water, would have been too frightened or stupid to work out how to cross it. But rather than being based on any sound archaeological evidence, this belief might merely reflect the uneasy relationship with swimming and the aquatic environment that may have afflicted many nineteenth- and twentieth-century European scholars.

The first generally accepted representative of the genus *Homo*, *H. habilis* – 'handy man', who is thought to have manufactured the earliest custom-made stone tool set – lived and died in Africa between 2.3 and 1.4 million years BP. As with the exact descent of the australopithecines, a growing number of discoveries and disagreements about the exact assignment of finds to the genus *Homo* or to a particular species or subspecies have somewhat complicated the human lineage, transforming it from a tree with a single, straight trunk into something more like a mangrove thicket. To spare the reader, I have tried to simplify the story, pruning as many dubious branches as possible. *H. habilis* was followed by *H. erectus* (1.8 million years to 70,000 years BP), whose remains have been found across Eurasia and whose easternmost range included China and the islands of Southeast Asia.

H. erectus gave rise to *H. heidelbergensis* (600,000 years to 350,000 years BP, though some researchers believe the species to be much older, first appearing 1.3 million years BP). Heidelberg man was one of the key species that moved out of Africa into Eurasia, and is believed to be ancestral to the Neanderthals (from 350,000–250,000 years until 40,000 years BP), the Denisovans (350,000–40,000 years BP) and *H. sapiens*, who first appeared around 200,000 years BP and probably left Africa in several waves of migration between 70,000 and 60,000 years BP. We can add one more name to the list: *H. floresiensis*, the so-called 'hobbit', a diminutive human who lived on the Indonesian island of Flores between 100,000 and 12,000 years BP.

As with the australopithecines, the remains of early humans consist of bones and teeth – though, of course, more numerous and much better-preserved specimens; so well preserved, in fact, that geneticists have been able to extract their DNA, allowing us to understand the relationships between different populations of extinct and extant hominins.[17] Another archaeological treasure trove is the stone tools they fashioned and used. These started as fairly shapeless lumps of rock that were used to smash, crush, pound or scrape, and developed into masterpieces of lapidary art – beautifully shaped axes, arrow- and spearheads, knives, hammers, adzes, chisels, jewellery, drills, hooks and harpoons. But what has not survived is anything made from perishable organic materials – wood and other plant materials and leather – especially if it was lost in water, where, unless preserved by very special conditions, wood will disintegrate in a few centuries. The oldest dugout canoe to have been discovered in the Mediterranean region, found in Lake Bracciano, in Lazio, northwest of Rome, is a mere 7,000 years old.[18] Clearly, *H. sapiens* had been navigating rivers, lakes and the open sea for much longer, but hard evidence is very hard to come by.

Humanity's nautical adventures are likely to be considerably more ancient than the arrival of modern humans in central Italy. *H. erectus* reached the island of Flores some 850,000 years BP or

A prehistoric dugout canoe preserved in the oxygen-poor waters of the Black Sea. Early members of the genus *Homo* could have crossed bodies of water in similar craft as they journeyed across the planet. The first generations of scholars believed that early and modern humans had colonized the earth by travelling overland, but more recent research suggests that they followed a coastal migratory route.

earlier, as evidenced by finds of stone tools on the island, and later arrivals, *H. floresiensis*, made it to the island around 100,000 years BP. There are three possible scenarios that explain how they made the crossing: they arrived on the island accidentally by floating on a log or another type of natural raft; they swam there, island-hopping until they reached Flores, Morgan's preferred hypothesis; and finally, that even as early in our evolution as *H. erectus*, our species was capable of intentionally making some kind of craft – raft or dugout canoe – all traces of which have long since perished in the sea.

Discoveries of stone tools from the Greek Aegean islands, Crete and southern Spain suggest that *H. heidelbergensis* and *H. neanderthalis* were also capable of swimming or navigating to outlying islands and across the strait that separates North Africa from Spain. The finds on Crete are particularly significant, as it has been an island for at least 5 million years, and even during periods when sea levels were much lower due to glaciation, the distance was too great for early humans to have swum south from Greece or north from Africa. The only alternative is that they had developed a fairly sophisticated boat-building technology, and that they felt quite at home not just *on* the water but also by extension *in* the water.[19]

When we look at the dispersal of our own species, conventional archaeological wisdom proposed that we reached every corner of the globe through a combination of walking across land bridges during glacial periods when sea levels dropped and crossing bodies of water, island-hopping either by swimming or with the aid of some kind of simple craft. According to the coastal migration theory, our ancestors performed a veritable dash across the planet, leaving Africa *c.* 100,000–60,000 years BP and crossing to the Arabian Peninsula, from where they hugged the Asian shoreline, reaching Australia in the south and Japan in the north in record time.

Implicit in the theory is that the migrations north and west that populated the Near East and Europe were side routes off the main transcontinental highway, which in the case of Europe would turn out to be a geographic dead end for the unfortunate future Europeans who did not realize that they were heading to an area that would be put into deep-freeze during the subsequent glaciation, while their cousins who travelled east and south were heading for a permanent subtropical summer.[20] Among the earliest *H. sapiens* seafarers were the people who island-hopped down the Indonesian archipelago to reach Australia around 50,000 years BP.[21] But even more extraordinary feats of navigation would be achieved in the past two millennia by the settlers of the Pacific islands of Micronesia, Melanesia and Polynesia, who sailed across thousands of miles of ocean without the help of navigational charts or instruments, or any certain knowledge that there was any land to discover.

Evidence from the Americas, which humans are thought to have reached around 15,000 years BP by crossing the land bridge between Asia and Alaska, suggests that they continued their southward journey as nomadic sea hunter-gatherers. They left behind them huge seashell middens, evidence of a diet that was predominantly of aquatic and not terrestrial origin.[22] We know that our

A Sama-Bajau boy swimming, with his family's houseboat in the background. The Sama-Bajau are one of a number of Southeast Asian peoples who maintain a semi-aquatic subsistence lifestyle – living on boats or over the water on houses on stilts – that gives us a clue as to how our much more distant ancestors may have travelled across the planet after they had left Africa.

ancestors also hunted terrestrial animals – horses, deer, mammoths and aurochs – from the copious remains of these animals that show the traces of human butchery and cooking, as well as cave paintings all over Western Europe depicting them. But these were creatures of colder northern climes during the last glaciation (at its height in Europe between 25,000 and 10,000 years BP), when access to aquatic resources by swimming would have been severely limited by low water temperatures and ice.

In terms of prehistoric swimming, we have evidence from, of all places, Egypt's Libyan Desert, part of the much larger Sahara Desert, now a bone-dry expanse of rock-strewn scrub and sand dunes. Around 10,000 years BP, when the caves at Wadi Sura were decorated with paintings, the Sahara was a far greener and more hospitable place, with rivers, lakes and swimming holes. As with other early cave art, the meaning and context of the images is difficult to establish, but several figures are shown doing what, as a swimming teacher, I would immediately recognize as the breaststroke, in which the body is held flat on the breast, just below the surface of the water, with the propulsion provided by a strong kick of the lower legs while the arms are held forward and circle outward in a sculling motion.

During the Age of Exploration and Discovery (fifteenth to eighteenth centuries), Europeans from Christopher Columbus to Captain James Cook were struck by the aquatic skills of the peoples they encountered, who often swam out to their ships to greet or attack them, while in Europe at the time, humans had lost their connection with the water, did not know how to swim and regarded the sea with deep suspicion and fear. Many of the native peoples of the Americas and Asia-Pacific either disappeared – as was the case with the native inhabitants of the West Indies, who became extinct through a combination of slavery, extermination policies and epidemics of European diseases – or their lifestyles changed out of all recognition after European settlement, as with the native people of Hawaii and the Maori of New Zealand. Nevertheless, several groups maintain the semi-aquatic lifestyles that facilitated our ancestors' colonization of the earth, including the Sama-Bajau people – the sea nomads of Southeast Asia – who live on boats or on houses built on stilts over the sea and live by fishing and trading the produce of the sea with their terrestrial neighbours.[23]

Are We Fish Out of Water?

I have examined the claims that at key moments in human evolution and prehistory, the aquatic environment and swimming played a key role in our physical and cultural development and survival as a species. The first and most controversial of these aquatic interludes is the one championed by Elaine Morgan. I have tried to present her thesis to the best of my ability, but it is beyond the scope of this book to confirm or deny its validity. Since Morgan's death, the AAH has not sunk without a trace; rather it has won several notable supporters. Despite the best efforts of the palaeoanthropological establishment, no killer argument has emerged to disprove the hypothesis; nor has a universally accepted alternative theory been put forward to answer all of Morgan's difficult questions about the evolution of key human traits.

For one brief moment, let us put scientific caution to one side and imagine that Morgan was right: that the journey towards humanity had begun with an aquatic phase lasting several million years. Would that explain the popularity of swimming among modern humans? Morgan admitted that the hominin aquatic moment was sandwiched between two much longer, more defining terrestrial phases. At most, it would have gifted us with the rounded, streamlined, hairless bodies that give us a facility in the water denied our angular, hirsute cousins, the great apes. Although it is true that biology and physiology can be powerful influences, these are usually trumped by material culture and social organization, as is amply demonstrated by the history of adaptation to the physical world that plays so visible a role in the continued success of our species.

Humanity's second and much better-attested aquatic moment comes with the migration of *H. erectus* out of Africa. A nomadic human hunter-gatherer, *H. erectus* reached East and Southeast Asia, and though much of his journey eastwards could have been done overland, his migration could also have been largely coastal and maritime. We have no reason to suppose that *H. erectus* avoided the water for most of the journey and when faced with the sea, suddenly learned to swim or build boats. Rather, like subsequent waves of human migrants, they were probably just as comfortable in the water as on land, and may have used whichever was the simplest method of travel depending on the environments they encountered. Similarly, *H. heidelbergensis* and *neanderthalis* are thought to have been strong swimmers and able mariners, because they reached Mediterranean islands at a time when these were cut off from the mainland.

When *H. sapiens* followed earlier migration routes out of Africa, they went much farther than their forebears, colonizing the Americas and crossing the vast expanses of the Pacific to reach Easter Island during the first millennium CE. An unexpected side effect of the colonization of the planet was the establishment of a long-lived division between northerners, who broke their connection with the water and survived the last glaciation by becoming land-based nomadic-hunters, and southerners, who enjoyed a much more comfortable existence based on the exploitation of aquatic resources by swimming and diving. It took hundreds of thousands of years for these two human worlds to reconnect. When European explorers finally reached the Americas and Asia-Pacific, they considered the cultures they encountered so alien precisely because they were so well adapted to the aquatic environments that they themselves had long ago abandoned.

When does the story of human swimming begin? The romantic in me would like to believe in Morgan's 5-million-year-old aquatic hominin, but the realist must conclude that it was the human colonization of the earth that began 1 million years ago that explains why and how humans took to the water and made the first strokes of genius.

2

Divine Swimmers

By medieval times the mermaid had developed into
a symbol with a substantial history. She was part human,
part animal, part nymph, part goddess, with traits that
were both creative and destructive.

THEODORE GACHOT, *MERMAIDS: NYMPHS OF THE SEA* (1996)[1]

The mythical being that we most commonly associate with the
aquatic environment and swimming is, of course, the mermaid.
A creature of magic and enchantment, she glides effortlessly through
the water, propelled by the powerful down-sweep of her tail, raising
little more than streams of bubbles in her wake. She easily outpaces
the fastest record-breaking Olympic swimmer whose flailing arms
and legs churn up the water like the wheels of a paddle steamer. A
Jungian anima of the aquatic sphere, she displays the speed and
ease in the water that all swimmers aspire to but can only experience
in their dreams. Although we might associate the mermaid's most
recent 'fifteen minutes of fame' with Disney's animated rendering
of Hans Christian Andersen's *Den lille Havfrue* ('The Little
Mermaid') (1837),[2] the hybrid that combines human with fish or
sea-mammal traits and that dwells in seas, lakes and rivers is a
common mythological trope that occurs in the myths of cultures
as temporally and geographically separate as the ancient Near East,
medieval Europe, the pre-Columbian Americas and contemporary
Southeast Asia.

Supernatural beings that combine fish or sea mammal and
human characteristics appear in the pantheons of every culture,
but their powers, social functions and gender have varied greatly
over the millennia. If we look at these beings in terms of their social
and cultural functions, we can make a direct link between their
prominence within a divine hierarchy and the importance of
aquatic resources to a given culture. As one would expect, the myths

This sketch of 1900 for Pre-Raphaelite painter John William Waterhouse's
A Mermaid (1900) embodies the stereotypical Western image of the human-
fish hybrid. Always female, nubile and attractive, the mermaid represents an
alluring but potentially dangerous mix of eroticism and physical otherness
whose origins can be traced back to some of humanity's earliest myths.

of pagan maritime and riparian communities are particularly rich in water divinities, who are given the starring roles in accounts of creation and of the birth of civilization. The pagan worldview personified all natural elements and forces, thereby hoping to exert some control over them through sacrifices and magico-religious rituals. But even when the multitude of pagan gods had been swept away by monotheism, there remained a need for a symbol and personification of the sea – of its resources and perils – with which humans could have some form of personal interaction. In the maritime communities of Christian Europe, though it was frowned upon by the Church, it was the mermaid, the last in a long line of human-fish hybrid beings, who played that role.

In the previous chapter I examined the possibilities that early hominins had lived through an aquatic interlude during their evolution and that early representatives of the genus *Homo* had been just as much at home in the water as they were on land. The physical evidence for the former is inconclusive, and for the latter, circumstantial. But we have another readily available source of information about our distant past in the myths that our ancestors told themselves about the creation of the cosmos, the gods and humanity, and about the emergence of civilization. For certain scholars, such as the French anthropologist and father of structural anthropology Claude Lévi-Strauss (1908–2009), myths cannot be taken at face value. The tropes that make up their narratives – the natural elements, humans and animals, magical objects and supernatural beings – should be read as universal symbols of psychic structures that are shared by all cultures: myths are coded stories that seek to explain and guide humanity's interaction with reality. For Lévi-Strauss the details of a particular myth are irrelevant and serve only to obscure the universal truths it contains.[3] Although I do not disagree that much can be learned about how humans think and interact with the world when myths are analysed in this way, they can also be read much more literally.

The myths of the ancient world acquired the set forms that we know today when they were written down, but this occurred thousands of years after they were first told by the shaman-storytellers who guided and advised the bands of hunter-gatherers that set out from Africa to colonize the planet. As myths were retold to each new generation, they were edited and elaborated, like a millennia-long game of Chinese whispers, to accommodate the new circumstances and experiences that humans encountered during their planet-wide wanderings. The genesis of the mermaid myth probably dates back to the many tens of thousands of years our species spent discovering and colonizing the planet. These early journeys would have been constant forays into the unknown, when our ancestors encountered new habitats populated by unknown animal species, giving us another possible clue to the origins of the mermaid myth. Under certain circumstances, the human imagination will seriously distort perception: for example, when it prefers to believe that a natural phenomenon or a manmade object is an extraterrestrial craft.

Did groups of our ancestors see unfamiliar sea mammals, such as seals, dugongs and manatees, and mistake them for human-fish or human-sea mammal beings? Alternatively, did more terrestrial groups of hunter-gatherers see other humans swimming, leading them to imagine that they had seen merfolk, endowing them with piscine attributes? These two streams of thought – the awe inspired by the natural world and an admiration for the abilities of animals that are far superior to our own, especially in elements such as the air and the water, and the misidentification of real sea mammals and fish or of other humans – could have come together when our ancestors started to codify their experience of the world in the first myths and came up with the idea of fish-human beings.

This kind of confusion continued well into the historical period. Upon first reaching American shores in 1492, Christopher Columbus recorded that one of his crew reported seeing

Three *serenas* who rose very high from the sea, but they were not so beautiful as they are painted, although to some extent they have a human appearance in the face. He said that he had seen some in Guinea on the coast of Malagueta.[4]

The reference to the West African coast indicates that what the sailor had actually seen were three manatees, or sea cows. Misidentification of this kind was sometimes encouraged and manufactured, as in the rather gruesome nineteenth-century hoax known as the 'Feejee Mermaid', exhibited by P. T. Barnum in New York to much acclaim and profit, which was most likely the upper half of a monkey stitched onto the rear half of a fish.[5]

City-builders and Fish-sages

Humans established permanent settlements between 11,000 years and 3,000 years BP,[6] a period known as the Neolithic Revolution that witnessed the transition from hunter-gathering to settled agricultural life, but for which we have no first-hand sources because it occurred thousands of years before the invention of writing. However, there is one very obvious physical feature that links the four oldest centres of Eurasian civilization: the river. Mesopotamia is 'the land between rivers' – the Tigris and Euphrates; ancient Egypt would not have existed without the Nile; the Harappan or Indus Valley Civilization developed along the Indus and Ghaggar-Hakra river systems; and the earliest settlements in China were built on the banks of the Yellow River and Yangtze. This should not come as a great surprise, as to be productive agriculture needs a dependable supply of fresh water for irrigation, as well as a regular inundation period when the rivers periodically flood and fertilize the fields with silt.

We can imagine a number of possible scenarios that made these areas so attractive to early humans that they became the locations of the first urban cultures. For example, a band of hunter-gatherers travelling along a riverbank might come upon an area particularly rich in edible plants, where they might decide to settle until the supply of food was exhausted. They might learn to return to the same area when it was at its most productive. By gathering seeds, fruits or tubers in one place for consumption, they might accidentally create a small area of monoculture – a proto-field – which they might expand by intentional cultivation later on. A fertile riverbank would not only provide an environment suitable for raising crops with a ready supply of water but would have also have been rich in food resources that could be hunted, fished or gathered to supplement agricultural produce: fish, shellfish, aquatic plants and waterfowl. Hence the first farmers were probably also able swimmers and free-divers. From returning to the same spot to harvest natural or semi-natural crops, it is not a great jump to settle the area permanently to care for them, increase their yield and protect them from animals and other humans.

Even when agriculture produced major surpluses, enabling the development of large urban cultures such as those of ancient Egypt and Mesopotamia, the river continued to be an important source of food. A mural from the tomb of Nebamun (second millennium BCE) shows the deceased hunting waterfowl in the marshes near Thebes, while another that depicts him spearing fish is now lost. In ancient Egypt, as it must have been in the other early centres of riparian civilization, natural food resources, such as fish, shellfish and waterfowl, played an important role in supplementing agricultural production. In the developed world, the links between agricultural communities and nearby natural resources were severed by the rapid urbanization that accompanied the Industrial Revolution. All that remains of it in post-industrial Europe and North America is the collecting of mushrooms, nuts, berries and wild fruit and vegetables, sport hunting and fishing and collecting shellfish from tidal pools and mudflats.

When investigating the initial phases of settlement and the subsequent development of urban living, we have to depend on archaeological evidence. This material, however, is often just as difficult to interpret as the hominin bones discussed in Chapter One – especially when overlaid and disturbed by millennia of later deposits. But we have another potential source of information in the myths of origin and creation that would have been transmitted orally until they were given permanent form after the invention of writing. Sumer (in southern Mesopotamia; now the area of southern Iraq just north of the port of Basra) was once believed to be the 'cradle of civilization' from which all human cultures had originated. We now know that agriculture and settlement were not the inventions of a single culture but occurred independently at different times all over the world. The Sumerians, however, can claim many firsts, including the first major cities and the first writing system. Sumer occupied a 'mosaic' zone with access to three distinct aquatic environments: the twin rivers of the alluvium, the saltwater marshes and the sea. According to Sumerian mythology, it was in the very southern part of Sumer, on the margins of the marshes, where humans built the world's first city. Known as Eridu, it had one very special feature linking it to the aquatic realm. According to Assyriologist Gwendolyn Leick:

> The city commanded its own ecosystem, since it was built upon a hillock within a depression about twenty feet below

Mural from the tomb of Nebamun (Thebes, *c.* 1350 BCE). The deceased is shown hunting about the reed beds. Another panel showing him spearing fish has now been lost. Agricultural surpluses enabled the development of Egyptian civilization on the banks of the Nile, but the exploitation of the river's natural resources continued to play an important role in the day-to-day lives of both farmers and city-dwellers.

the level of the surrounding land, which allowed the subterranean waters to collect together . . . The earliest Mesopotamian texts, from the early third millennium, underline the importance of this lagoon. In Sumerian this was known as the *abzu* . . . In the almost rainless southern regions, the most obvious and crucial manifestation of water was the *abzu*.[7]

Leick compares Eridu to the biblical Garden of Eden. However, unlike the Judaeo-Christian-Islamic tradition, which places the birth of humanity in a rural setting, she explains that in Sumerian mythology 'Eden is not a garden but a city, formed from a piece of dry land surrounded by the waters.'[8] The defining feature of Eridu is the *abzu*, a lagoon of fresh water that explains why the city was built there in the first place and why it remained a sacred site for thousands of years – a Mesopotamian version of Jerusalem, Rome and Mecca – honoured as the place where humans first learned the arts of civilization. Eridu and the *abzu* were the domain and earthly residence of the Sumerian creator god Enki, who is represented in humanoid form with streams of life-giving water issuing from his body. In many representations, carp are shown swimming within the streams, which ties in with finds of carp bones littered on the floor of the ruins of Enki's temple in Eridu, indicating that it was the location for communal feasts of the fish.[9] Enki's links to fresh water and fish amply demonstrate that the first residents of Eridu made full use of the river and its resources and probably chose the site because of the existence of the *abzu* lagoon.

Ancient myths, however, do not have to be consistent or coherent; instead they often reflect the coexistence of different traditions in the same period, or the transformation of gods and their functions as the fortunes of the cities they represented waxed and waned. In another myth, Abzu (differentiated from the lagoon by the capital letter) was a deity in his own right, representing fresh water and the lover of Tiamat, the monstrous dragon goddess of salt water. Their pairing gave rise to the elder Mesopotamian gods. When the couple decided to destroy the gods to whom Tiamat had given birth, Enki killed Abzu and placed him under his temple in Eridu in the *abzu*. Tiamat tried to avenge her lover by creating eleven monsters but was defeated and killed by Enki's son Marduk, who cut her body in two, creating the vault of heaven and the earth. The tears from her eyes became the springs of the Tigris and Euphrates. The primordial chaos of the waters represented by Abzu and Tiamat, once tamed by the gods, could now be harnessed by humanity.

Once the two primeval deities had been defeated, Enki and the younger gods created humanity to be their servants – that is, to do all the heavy lifting in the world and maintain the proper running of creation, which the gods had had to do for themselves and found boring and exhausting. Humans had one purpose: to serve the gods, and in order to do so properly, they had to be taught the arts of civilization, especially how to build and maintain the cities and temples that were the abode of the gods. To instruct humans, Enki created the Seven Sages, the Apkallu, human-fish hybrids who emerged from the sea at Dilmun, an important trading centre in the Persian Gulf (modern-day Bahrain, Qatar and Kuwait) which the Sumerians believed to be an earthly paradise.[10] The first Apkallu, Adapa, was also the first human. He served Enki as his high priest and was charged with collecting the food offerings for him. In one story, Adapa very prosaically goes to the lagoon by boat to fish for the carp for his divine master's supper, reflecting the practices of the human inhabitants of Eridu, who would have fished in the lagoon. There is such a close identification in the myth between Adapa, the ancestral human, and aquatic resources – the fish in the lagoon – that he is depicted as part human and part fish.

Unsurprisingly, water plays a central element in Mesopotamian mythology, and one of the best-known Mesopotamian myths is the story of the deluge – the flood sent by the gods to wipe out humanity. The original myth, which later appears in the Tanakh, the Hebrew Bible, is known from several Sumerian, Babylonian and Assyrian versions recorded hundreds of years apart. In cities built of mud brick, floods would have been particularly feared, and scholars believe that the flood story may have been inspired by one particularly destructive event when a combination of earthquakes and floods washed away whole cities.[11] One version of the myth comes from the *Epic of Gilgamesh* (c. 2100 BCE), a poem that recounts the adventure of the king of the Sumerian city of Uruk. In his search for a way to escape death, Gilgamesh seeks out Utnapishtim, the Mesopotamian Noah and ancestor of all humans, to whom the repentant gods had granted immortality in recognition for his having saved humanity from the flood.

Utnapishtim urges Gilgamesh to accept death as an inescapable part of the human condition, but he decides to tell the hero of a magical herb that grows in the sea that will give eternal life to anyone who eats it. In order to retrieve it, Gilgamesh ties rocks to his feet so that he can dive quickly to the bottom (a real practice that we shall return to in the next chapter) and succeeds in finding the herb. Cutting himself free from the rock ballast, he swims back up to the surface. But rather than consume the herb right away, he decides to travel back to Uruk to share it with his subjects. Tragically but rather predictably, when the hero decides to rest and bathes in a pool, a snake steals the herb, denying Gilgamesh and humanity immortality.[12] The epic is a dramatization of humanity's struggle to make sense of death, and also about the hubris of those who have reached the heights of human power and seek to emulate the gods. At the same time, it contains a very realistic description of how the early Sumerians exploited natural resources through diving and swimming.

In Sumerian myth, water is not a universal structural symbol for the human condition or some manifestation of the human psyche, but the real element in its various forms, because water and the resources it contained were vital to the survival of Sumer's cities and their inhabitants. The god Enki who dwelt in the *abzu* and the Seven Sages he conjured from the sea as humanity's teachers can be read as universal symbols about the development of civilization, but their piscine nature underscores the importance of aquatic environments and swimming to historical Mesopotamia and also records and celebrates a time thousands of years earlier when humans first settled permanently on the banks of the Tigris and

Euphrates, the marshes of southern Iraq and the shores of the Persian Gulf.

The first Eridu – little more than a small chapel built on an island in the middle of a lagoon – was born of water and survived and grew into a large cult centre and city because of the resources provided by the *abzu*. If the first generation of water gods, Abzu and Tiamat, was chaotic, unpredictable and destructive, the second, led by Enki, was benign and constructive (give or take a deluge), teaching humanity the arts of civilization that, in Mesopotamia, were inextricably intertwined with water management through canals and irrigation and the exploitation of water resources through fishing and swimming. In Mesopotamian mythology, we find the grand universal themes of life, death, human hubris, the relationship between the human and divine and the birth of civilization, but in the details of the myths, we can catch a glimpse of how the first settlers of the Land between Rivers survived as farmers, fishermen and swimmers.

Poseidon's Court

The culture of Mesopotamia, like that of ancient Egypt, endured for thousands of years, surviving domination by the Assyrians, the Persians and the Hellenistic Greeks. Usually it was the invaders who were acculturated and adopted Mesopotamian ways and beliefs. As the oldest urban culture in the Near East, it greatly influenced its neighbours, many of whom adopted cuneiform script to write their own languages. Sumerian was the language of science and religion – akin to Latin and Greek in medieval Europe – and another Mesopotamian language, Akkadian, was the *lingua franca* of the second millennium BCE, used for diplomacy and international trade, as evidenced by the discovery of large archives of cuneiform tablets written in Akkadian all over the Bronze Age world. Mesopotamian myths were reinterpreted by other Near Eastern cultures: to cite the most famous example, the myth of the Great Flood was reproduced in the Jewish Tanakh, the basis for the Christian Old Testament. Through trade or warfare, Mesopotamian culture reached the Levant, Anatolia and Ionia (now Turkey) and archaic Greece (eighth–sixth centuries BCE).[13] Although the mythological canon of ancient Greece contains much that is completely original and quintessentially Greek, there also several myths – specifically those dealing with water and water deities – that are so reminiscent of much older Mesopotamian myths that the similarities cannot be ascribed to mere coincidence.

The Mesopotamians and ancient Greeks had very different relationships to the water: the former lived by rivers on which they depended for all their needs; the latter lived on a peninsula surrounded by the sea. While both Mesopotamians and Greeks were farmers, the Greeks had much less productive land on which to grow crops and raise livestock, and thus were much more dependent on the resources of the sea to survive. By necessity, as their populations grew beyond the capacity of the Greek mainland and Aegean islands to sustain them, they became great maritime explorers, establishing colonies and trading posts all around the Mediterranean and Black Sea.

From linguistic evidence, the proto-Greeks, who moved south into the Balkans in several waves to settle in Greece between the third and first millennium BCE, are thought to have migrated from the vast open grasslands of the Pontic-Caspian Steppe.[14] If this theory is correct, they lived as nomadic pastoralists and were the first people to domesticate the horse. This could explain why Poseidon, the Greek god of the sea, is also known as the 'father of horses'.[15] As the migrants moved south, finally reaching and settling on the coasts of Greece, they learned to become swimmers, fishermen and sailors. In the pagan worldview, nature and natural forces were animate, so they co-opted one of their gods as the personification of what must have been an unfamiliar and frightening environment – the sea – thus creating a means to control and placate the sea through religious ritual.

Poseidon, along with his brothers Zeus and Hades, was worshipped in Mycenaean times (sixteenth to eleventh centuries BCE), and remained one of the principal gods through the Greek Dark Ages (twelfth to eighth centuries BCE) and during the archaic and classical periods (eighth to fourth centuries BCE), surviving until the

The sea god Poseidon, depicted in this statue of *c.* 550 BCE, headed a large pantheon of sea divinities and supernatural beings. Formerly an Indo-European Central Asian land god, he was also associated with earthquakes and horses. In his archaic and classical Greek incarnations, Poseidon reflected the complex relationship the Greeks had with the marine environment.

Christianization of Greece in the fourth century CE. Anyone who has visited the imposing Temple of Poseidon at Cape Sounion, a promontory at the very tip of Attica 69 km (43 miles) south of Athens, will appreciate the honour shown to Poseidon in the Greek world.[16] Like the Sumerian Enki, Poseidon lived underwater, though not in a freshwater lagoon under a city but in the sea in a golden palace off the island of Samothrace in the northern Aegean. Like the other Olympian gods, he was represented in humanoid form carrying his trademark weapon, the trident – a fisherman's three-pronged harpoon. In artworks from the pagan Greek, Hellenistic and Roman periods, he is represented as an exalted ruler processing to and from his underwater palace accompanied by his consort, the sea nymph Amphitrite, and a host of sea creatures and supernatural aquatic beings.

Poseidon's human-fish hybrid attendants, the Tritons, like the Seven Sages who served Enki, were all male. Originally, Triton was a god, the son of Poseidon and Amphitrite, who was said to live in Lake Tritonis in Libya, but the name was also applied to a race of mermen with a human head and torso and a single or double fishtail. Unlike the wise Apkallu, who taught humans the arts of civilization, the Tritons were the marine equivalent of satyrs and centaurs, uncivilized human-animal hybrids who lived outside the bounds of civilization and who were just as likely to harm humans as to help them. The second-century CE Greek geographer and travelogue writer Pausanias claimed to have seen the preserved bodies of two Tritons, one in Rome and the second in the Boeotian town of Tanagra. He described them as having green hair, gills behind their ears, greenish-grey eyes, a finely scaled body and a dolphin's tail. He explained that the Tanagran Triton had been killed either because he had attacked local women on a beach or because he had stolen cattle.[17]

The god Triton was one of several human-fish hybrid divinities worshipped by the Greeks. Others included Oceanus, the world-girthing ocean; Proteus, said to be the firstborn son of Poseidon; Nereus, father of the sea nymphs known as the Nereids; and Glaucus, whose myth is reminiscent of one of the stories told in the *Epic of Gilgamesh*. Unusually for a Greek god, Glaucus was born a mortal of human parents, and was not high-born but a humble fisherman. One day, while sorting out his catch on land, he found a plant that he had never seen before. He ate the plant, which immediately transformed him into a fishtailed immortal, with green hair and beard and scaly green skin. The similarity with the episode in which Gilgamesh finds the magical plant that grants immortality is striking, though the story has a different outcome. Glaucus was granted the power of prophesy, and he appears in several myths in which he helps questing heroes.[18] While there were mermen in classical mythology, there were no mermaids. Sirens – a word used to refer to mermaids in French (*sirène*) and Spanish and Italian (*sirena*) – who lured sailors to their deaths with their 'siren songs' were human-bird hybrids.[19] The sea nymphs, the Oceanids and Nereids, who come closest to the later Western conception of mermaids, were female, beautiful and eternally youthful and lived in springs, rivers, lakes and seas, but they had legs, not fishtails.

The rich and varied pantheon of sea divinities headed by Poseidon is evidence of the constructive relationship the Greeks had with the sea. It was a source of sustenance through fishing and of wealth through trade. The subsidiary sea divinities, such as Oceanus, Triton and Glaucus, may have been older local sea gods whose cults were appropriated by the Greeks, who then created

Triton, one of the children of Poseidon and Amphitrite, was represented as a human-fish hybrid, as in this statue from Hierapolis, Phrygia (Turkey), of *c.* 3rd century CE. The Tritons were also a tribe of male human-fish hybrids who were personifications of the dangers of the sea and its denizens. Like later representations of mermaids, Tritons were not benevolent beings, and were much more likely to attack humans than help them.

divine genealogies to explain their relationships to Poseidon; others, like the sea nymphs, might be even more ancient spirits of place – survivals of ancient animistic cults that endowed natural features such as rocks, trees, rivers and natural springs with spiritual powers; finally, the wild, untamed Tritons could represent the dangers, both real and imagined, posed by marine animals.

Although aware of the dangers of the sea – often explained as punishments sent by a vengeful Poseidon for some sacrilegious act – the Greeks had a largely positive relationship with the marine environment. Myths explained the perils of the sea and also provided a means to circumvent them, as angry gods could be placated by the building of temples and the offering of prayers and sacrifices. The sea, its divinities and animals sometimes came to the aid of humans, as in the tale of the poet Arion, who was saved from drowning by a dolphin who carried him back to dry land. Like the land, the sea was populated by a multitude of supernatural beings, with whom humans could enter into direct communion through religious ritual.

Mesopotamian mythology looked back to a time when swimming in rivers, lagoons and marshes was an integral part of life. In contrast, the first Greeks, whose origins were in the steppes, would have initially seen the marine environment as alien and frightening. They probably knew how to swim, as they would have encountered lakes and rivers in their travels southwards, but you do not have to have seen the film *Jaws* to feel a sense of unease when you set out from the seashore and suddenly lose sight of the bottom. Then you might imagine what monstrous sea creatures might be swimming towards you from the dark depths. But the Greeks quickly took to the sea, making it the domain of one of their own gods, Poseidon, who was a very important divinity in their terrestrial pantheon as the 'father of horses'. The Greeks clearly knew how to swim, but despite inventing competitive sport and athletic training in gymnasia, they never competed or trained in swimming.[20] One could say that they were 'at home' in the water, but not, like some other peoples, 'of the water'.

The Soulless Mermaid

In contrast to the sea gods of Greece and Rome, the god of Abraham, Moses and Jesus was the god of nomadic shepherds and goatherds who lived in the Near East's deserts and hill country, far from cities and the sea. The Old Testament does not contain any stories in which water or swimming play a positive role in the lives of humans. The story of Noah (KJV [King James Version], Genesis 6–8), which is a Hebrew retelling of a Mesopotamian original, only serves to underline water's destructive power when wielded by an angry deity. Similarly, when Jonah attempts to flee from God's command, his ship is sure to be wrecked in a storm if he does not throw himself overboard. He survives after being swallowed whole by a gigantic sea creature (KJV, Jonah 1–2). Even rivers do not get a good press in the Old Testament. When the baby Moses is cast onto the waters of the Nile, he escapes death only because God intervenes and guides his basket into the hands of the pharaoh's daughter (KJV, Exodus 1–2). And in parting the waters of the Red Sea for Moses (Exodus 14–15), God obviates the need for swimming altogether, while the pharaoh and his troops are drowned as the sea closes up again. In the New Testament, the aquatic environment fares little better. Jesus performs two miracles connected with the sea: walking on water and calming the waters, but these merely highlight the alien nature of the medium, as his miraculous powers keep him high and dry. Even when John baptizes Jesus, his immersion in the River Jordan is purely symbolic – an act of cleansing and rebirth that simultaneously foreshadows the death and resurrection to come.

The Jews and early Christians who lived in Judaea away from the coast would have had little experience of the sea. Their strongholds were inland, while the Levantine coast was occupied by idolworshipping pagans – Phoenicians, Philistines and Canaanites – who lived in cosmopolitan port cities. The religion of the Jews was forged in the hills, mountains and deserts. It would be an intriguing 'what-if' to ask what Judaism and Christianity would have been like had Moses and the Israelites not wandered in the wilderness for forty years but had been cast adrift on the sea like Odysseus,

The *c.* 1300 Hereford Mappa Mundi is a Christian representation of the earth. The oceans that cover over two-thirds of the earth's surface have almost ceased to exist on this map – they are reduced to a slim ribbon around its edge – and the Mediterranean becomes a network of narrow channels squeezed between the land masses of Africa, Asia and Europe.

or had Jesus not been a carpenter from Bethlehem who fished for men's souls but a real fisherman from the Levantine coast. But unlike Poseidon or Enki, the god of Abraham, Moses and Jesus had no direct connections with water. He dwelt in the wilds and the high places of the world – a god of storms, lightning and of fire – whose attendants, appropriately for a sky divinity, were human-bird hybrids, the angels.

The triumph of Judaeo-Christian monotheism over Graeco-Roman paganism in the late fourth century CE transformed humanity's relationship with the divine. Most directly, it relegated all pagan gods, demigods and supernatural beings, which would have included the minor sea gods, Tritons and sea nymphs, to the status of demons, monsters and succubi – servants of the Great Adversary, the fallen angel Satan, whose domain was the underworld. In Judaeo-Christian cosmography, humanity lived on a terrestrial plane sandwiched between Heaven, where God dwelt with the angels, and Hell, populated by Satan and his demons; the seas, rivers, marshes and lagoons that had been so important to the Mesopotamians, Egyptians and Greeks had no role to play in the creation or the development of civilization. Even a cursory glance at the world maps of late antiquity and the Middle Ages, as exemplified by the early fourteenth-century Hereford Mappa Mundi, shows that seas almost cease to exist as a significant geographical feature. If they are depicted at all, they become an alien space, uninhabited by either demons or angels – a sort of cosmographical blank whose only legend could be 'here be sea-monsters'.

But the changes wrought by Christianity (and later reinforced by Islam – another firmly terrestrial desert religion) did not just transform the divine realm. It also brought about a major shift in attitudes to the human body, and indirectly to the aquatic environment and swimming. The Greeks, in particular, glorified the human form, not only in the arts but in their unaffected public displays of male nudity during sporting, social and religious events.[21] The Romans, while much more prudish about public nudity, were happy to be naked in the semi-private setting of the *thermae*, their luxurious public baths. As we shall see later, Roman men were able swimmers, and it was deemed a necessary accomplishment for men of every social class, as well as for the military.

In the Christian world, nudity became associated with the sinfulness of the flesh and forbidden sexual practices that had earlier been considered normal. In the eyes of the clergy, even nudity among men was viewed with deep suspicion as it might encourage same-sex relations, defined by the Church as 'sodomy'. However, we have to make certain geographical and social distinctions here. The customs of those living inland and of the elites changed completely during the Middle Ages. The great Roman *thermae* fell into ruin in Christian Europe, and the medieval Church discouraged the use of the bath-houses that replaced them because they were often little more than brothels. For centuries, godly cleanliness was limited to the parts of the body that were visible and to external clothing. Swimming as an elite pastime or as a martial skill also disappeared. As marine anthropologist Aliette Geistdoerfer explains:

> During antiquity, in many areas cultures had established 'constructive' relationships with the sea, but after the coming

The Little Mermaid, the archetypal Western view of the human-fish hybrid being that dwells in the seas, lakes and rivers. A creature with supernatural attributes – her immortality and her voice – she lives outside the human world and is denied a soul. One of a series of tiles painted *c.* 1867 by Henry Holiday.

of Judeo-Christian ideology, the sea became 'other' and even 'infernal'.[22]

Of course, throughout the medieval period communities on the sea coasts and riverbanks continued to exploit aquatic resources. Medieval fisherman and mariners would have been just as at home on and in the water as their pagan ancestors. It is from these communities that we get many stories of mermaids – a combination of ancient myths and folktales reshaped by Christian beliefs. The defining characteristics of the Christian human-fish or human-sea mammal hybrid was that she was female, usually youthful and alluring, and often had an enchanting voice that she used to bewitch men, stealing them away to live with her under the sea or luring sailors to their doom like the sirens of antiquity. As such she personified not only the uncontrolled sexual appetites of animals – her sexual organs being in her piscine half – but the dangerous sexuality of women, who in Christian theology were blamed for the Fall of humanity. She was depicted naked but she did have two trademark accessories: a hairbrush with which to brush her long hair and a mirror to gaze at herself, both symbols of feminine vanity. As she was not fully human, however, she was denied a soul, and therefore could not be saved and go to Heaven; but as she was also immortal, neither could she be consigned to Hell. She existed in between the categories of animal, human and demon, and lived in an alien medium that to the medieval mindset was full of real and imaginary dangers.

Consideration of the archetypal mermaid story takes us back to the beginning of this chapter and Hans Christian Andersen's 'The Little Mermaid'. His original, however, is far darker and more complex than the saccharine Disney version, which like other Hollywood takes on European fairy tales insists on a happy ending in which the heroine gets her man. Having fallen for a human prince, whom she saved from drowning, the Little Mermaid yearns to win his love and become human herself. She trades her enchanting voice for legs. But the act of walking on dry land is agonizing – akin to walking on knives. She meets the prince but he does not recognize her as his saviour, and as he is already betrothed, he marries another. The Little Mermaid's only hope to regain her voice and former form is to kill the man she loves, but she is unable to do so. She throws herself into the sea and is transmuted into sea foam, but in a final religious twist, she is rewarded for her self-sacrifice by being given the chance to earn a soul through doing good deeds as a spirit of the air.[23]

'The Little Mermaid' is in a long tradition of medieval tales featuring alluring female characters who are not quite what they seem. The several versions of the story of Melusine tell of a nobleman who falls in love with a beautiful young woman he meets in the forest. She agrees to marry him as long as he promises not to enter her chamber on a particular day or when she is bathing. When he breaks his oath and discovers that on the days she hides from him, she is part human, part animal – fish, dragon or serpent, depending on the version – she vanishes.[24] This is a common trope of mermaid stories, in which a mermaid is forced or consents under certain conditions to marry a human, but when she is able to escape or the conditions she has set are broken, she abandons her husband and family and returns to the sea. A variant of this is the medieval Cornish tale of the Mermaid of Zennor, who captivates a human man with her beauty and her voice and steals him away to live with her.[25]

These stories have more to tell us about Christian theology, medieval attitudes to sex and gender and the role of women in pre-modern societies than about attitudes towards swimming. But what seems obvious is that during the Middle Ages Europeans had become alienated from aquatic environments, which at best were unknown and desolate, and at worst, infernal and murderous. Cultures that did not fall under the domination of the Abrahamic faiths did not experience such a stark alienation from the sea. According to Geistdoerfer and her colleagues, the Sama-Bajau, or sea nomads, whom we met in the previous chapter, do not have their own sea monsters but have imported them from neighbouring cultures. She goes on to explain that they are much too familiar with the marine environment to create imaginary monsters. In Sama-Bajau myth, the most dangerous region is not the sea or land, but the transitional zone of the coastline, as it is home to dangerous hybrid creatures that are neither truly aquatic nor terrestrial.[26] At the other end of the planet, in the Canadian Arctic, a prominent figure in the myths of Baffin Island is Sedna, the 'Sea Woman'. A human-seal hybrid, she is both the creator of sea mammals, which were once her fingers, and their protector from human transgressions, invoked to enforce the complex taboos that govern the hunting and exploitation of sea mammals and to protect their souls.[27] In the Arctic, seals not only have souls, but humans identify so closely with them that certain groups believe that they are descended from them.

Preserving Humanity's Aquatic Connection

In Chapter One, I explored the possibility that swimming was part of our species' DNA, as our ancestors may have had successive aquatic phases that shaped both their bodies and cultures. In the ancient Mediterranean and Near East, humanity's close, constructive relationship with the aquatic realm, mediated by a vast pantheon of water divinities, lasted until the proscription of paganism in the fourth century CE. The link with water and swimming that had endured for many millennia was severed by the teachings of the Judaeo-Christian religion, which emerged in a terrestrial setting that was completely divorced from the aquatic environment. Poseidon and his consort, sons and courtiers, the Tritons and sea nymphs, were expelled from the divine realm, but the sea was sufficiently unknown and alien that its supernatural residents were not immediately consigned to the demonic legions of Hell. Instead, a few of them continued to exist in a kind of folkloric limbo, neither fully animal nor human but spared the status of demons.

The sea gods and demigods dwindled and died after their temples were closed or converted into churches, and several of their functions were taken over by Catholic saints, who were charged with the safety of fishermen and mariners and other aquatic matters – not as divinities in their own right, of course, but as intercessors with an omnipotent God. All that remained of Poseidon's court were the human-fish hybrids, who, at some point in the early Middle Ages, changed gender. The male Tritons became female mermaids. For an explanation of how this came about we need only look at the mythologies of the regions of the far north: Scotland and its islands and Scandinavia, which were never conquered or colonized by the Romans.

The Norse, better known as the Vikings, like the Greeks before them lived in coastal settlements hemmed in by forests and mountains that forced them to look outward across the seas for new lands to colonize. They were intrepid mariners who crossed the Atlantic five centuries before Columbus and who, unlike their Christian contemporaries, did not fear the seas but had a constructive relationship with it through the intercession of sea divinities. They resisted Christianization for centuries and brought along with them to the coasts of Western Europe their sea gods and the female spirits who lived in the seas, lakes and rivers of their native lands, where they merged with half-remembered Celtic and Graeco-Roman divinities and supernatural beings, creating a being who, to quote Theodore Gachot, 'was part human, part animal, part nymph, part goddess, with traits that were both creative and destructive'.[28]

Although the medieval Church used the mermaid for its own ends, turning her into a morality tale that defined her as a soulless temptress who represented the dangers of female sexuality, in the folklore of maritime communities, she remained a symbol of the link to the sea that provided them with their livelihoods.[29] But I think that she served yet a third function for those who lived far from the sea and may have never even seen it. The beautiful, graceful mermaid who swam effortlessly through the depths embodied humanity's deep and abiding emotional connection with swimming, during a period when a large proportion of the population could not swim and had become completely alienated from the aquatic environment. This connection, which dates back to prehistoric times and was celebrated in the mythologies of the Mediterranean and Near East, survived the social, political and religious upheavals that accompanied the Christianization of the Roman Empire and its subsequent collapse in Western Europe. During the Middle Ages, the human-fish hybrid was remade into the mermaid, and through the pen of Hans Christian Andersen, she took on the form that we know today.

3
Harvesting the Treasures of the Sea

Give not that which is holy unto the dogs, neither cast
ye your pearls before swine, lest they trample them
under their feet, and turn again and rend you.

MATTHEW 7:6

After *Homo sapiens* followed earlier members of the genus on the
long trek out of Africa, it underwent two radical transformations. The first, which occurred between 100,000 and 50,000 years
BP, was the attainment of 'behavioural modernity' – a change in the
way our ancestors interacted with each other and the world, setting
them on the path that would inexorably lead to the invention of
the credit card, the TV dinner for one and the smartphone. The
second, which began between 9,000 and 8,000 years BP, was the
Neolithic Revolution, when humans established the first permanent
agricultural settlements. In the previous chapter, I sketched out how
this could have taken place on an islet in the middle of a lagoon in
southern Iraq – a scenario supported by the available archaeological evidence, as well as the mythical accounts of the origins of
Sumerian civilization. For millennia, swimming and free-diving
remained key survival skills long after humanity had made the
switch from hunter-gathering to agriculture, and they would play
a central role in the next stage of socio-economic development as
small, scattered urban communities grew larger and coalesced into
the first states and empires.

Considering that the genus *Homo* had lived quite happily without
the benefits of civilization for almost 2 million years, the suddenness
and scope of these changes is startling. And, as we know from the
history books and from our own experience, the pace of change has
never slowed, so that now you barely have time to get the latest
consumer must-have out of its packaging before its replacement is

being advertised online. The shift from nomadic to settled lifestyles was followed by the development of social hierarchies, transforming what many archaeologists believe to have been fairly egalitarian groups into increasingly stratified societies. However, as Gwendolyn Leick points out, this interpretation of early settled life in early human cultures may have more to do with present-day political bias than with historical reality.[1] What is certain is that by the Bronze Age, which began in the Near East and Egypt around 5,300 years BP, social divisions based on occupation and status were well developed.

Although the terms 'king' and 'queen' are anachronistic in the Bronze Age context, because the ancient titles thus translated had different functions from those of later European rulers, there existed high-status individuals who played leading roles in society and enjoyed a standard of living far above that of the general popula-tion.[2] And the one thing that the elites of antiquity shared with those of today was the use of conspicuous consumption as an ex-pression of status, wealth and power. In the fourth millennium BCE, however, the range and availability of luxury goods was severely limited; there was nevertheless one 'object of desire' which, because it could be used without further elaboration through smelting, carving or polishing, was among the first to be actively sought and traded: the natural fresh- or saltwater pearl.

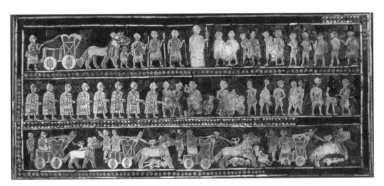

The mysterious 'Standard of Ur' – a box decorated with mosaic scenes of war and peace made of wood inlaid with shell, limestone and lapis lazuli from the Royal Cemetery of the Sumerian city of Ur (*c.* 2600 BCE) – provides evidence for the trade in aquatic products for the manufacture of high-status objects in the third millennium BCE.

Natural nacreous pearls come in a variety of shapes, sizes and colours. Early humans would have found pearls while foraging for shellfish. They were among the first non-subsistence goods to be traded because, unlike precious metals and gemstones, they needed no elaboration to be used.

Pearls were only one of several products obtained by swimming and free-diving in ancient times for use as non-subsistence commodities. The earliest were fresh- and saltwater molluscs, which are not only edible but whose shells are durable and come in a selection of useful sizes and attractive shapes, patterns and colours. Since prehistoric times, humans have used shells for personal adornment, inlays, tools, containers, games counters, currency, *materia medica* and musical instruments. Particularly sought after were shells that had an internal coating of nacre, or mother-of-pearl, not only because those shellfish produce pearls but for the mother-of-pearl itself; other products obtained from the aquatic environment were tortoiseshell, the secretions of the shellfish *Murex*, precious or red coral (*Corallium rubrum*) and natural sponges. A final 'organic' gemstone that was associated with the sea but which did not originate there was Baltic amber.[3]

The demand for non-subsistence commodities created global trading and manufacturing networks made up of aquatic specialists who harvested the original product from seas, lakes and rivers; commercial specialists who purchased, transported and traded them; and specialist craftsmen who transformed or incorporated them into finished items. If swimming had enabled humans to survive as they populated the planet, it now led to the development of a new type of economic activity. Anyone seeking the origins of today's corporate giants should look to well before the exploitation of metals to the day when a Neolithic swimmer looking for her next meal shucked an oyster and found a pearl, which she did not discard or keep for herself but decided to barter to an inland neighbour for products that she herself had no direct access to.

Once established, these networks, though they were sometimes curtailed or interrupted during periods of international unrest such as the fall of the Han Dynasty in China (220 CE) and the collapse of the Western Roman Empire (476 CE), continued to grow, develop and spread across the world. With the Age of Exploration and Discovery (fourteenth to eighteenth centuries), new sources of luxury commodities were discovered and exploited by Europeans in the Americas, Africa and Asia-Pacific region. Technologically, however, there was little progress in harvesting techniques until the advent of surface-supplied diving suits in the nineteenth century. Hence swimming and free-diving remained the principal means of recovering such commodities as pearls, corals and sponges, underlining the enormous value of these activities to the world economy. Above and beyond the economic importance of these commodities was the enduring association between something of great value – be it artistic or spiritual – and the products of the aquatic environment – emblematically, the natural pearl.

Glimmers of Modernity

Archaeologists long held that *H. sapiens* had first begun to exhibit modern traits, such as language, art, music, dance, personal adornment and religion and ritual, and achieved behavioural modernity in Europe, some 40,000 years BP. This reflects the same bias that I remarked on in Chapter One when nineteenth-century scholars sought the origins of the earliest human ancestors in Europe. Genetic data now suggests that the migration into the Near East and Europe, far from being on the main migration highway out of Africa that led eastwards towards East Asia, took place along secondary routes that led nowhere particularly interesting. Other groups of modern humans remained in Africa and migrated west and south from our species' East African birthplace. Around 100,000 years BP, one group of archaic *Homo sapiens* reached the southern-most region of the continent and took up residence in the Blombos Cave, some 300 km (185 miles) east of Cape Town. The cave remained in continuous use by humans until the first millennium BCE.

From the animal remains found in the cave, we can conclude that the occupants enjoyed a varied diet of fish, shellfish and sea mammals, which they collected by beachcombing, foraging and fishing in shallow water and swimming and diving in deeper water. The most significant finds come from the oldest levels of the cave (100,000–73,000 years BP): the perforated shells of the sea snail *Nassarius kraussianus*, which archaeologists believe were strung together into a necklace or bracelet or could have been sewn onto clothing; a no less significant discovery were seashells that had been used as containers for ochre pigment. Together these finds suggest a level of behavioural sophistication in archaic *Homo sapiens* between 35,000 to 60,000 years earlier than previously thought.[4] The link between products acquired in aquatic environments for non-subsistence uses such as ornamentation and personal adornment is a universal phenomenon that continues to this day, if we consider the seashells that most of us have picked up on a beach at one time in our lives and the mostly tacky souvenirs and jewellery sold to tourists in seaside resorts.

In periods when or parts of the world where metal was absent, rare or not worked to any degree, shells were an important part of the economic infrastructure. They were traded over vast distances to inland communities with no other connection to the sea. In Neolithic Europe, *Spondylus* shells were fished in the Aegean and made their way to Central Europe, where they were used to make different types of jewellery. A similar trade in the Pre-Columbian

Maya shell ornament, Classic period (3rd–9th century CE) showing a dignitary making an offering to the gods. Seashells were traded widely throughout Mesoamerica and were used and valued by people who had no direct connection to the sea.

Americas saw *Spondylus* shells from Ecuadorian waters traded inland to the Andean kingdoms of South America and as far north as Mesoamerica, to the Maya highlands of Yucatan and the states of the Valley of Mexico. *Spondylus* ornaments have been found in the landlocked Maya city-state of Tikal, which is some 200 km (125 miles) from the Caribbean Sea.[5] In Africa, North America and the Asia-Pacific, the cowry shell had a wide range of uses, the most famous being its use as an early form of currency unit in China before metal currency was invented; other uses included personal ornaments, badges of rank and games counters.

Imperial Fashion Statement

Shellfish furnished other valuable products in addition to their shells. One of the most expensive commodities in the ancient world was the dye known as Tyrian purple, because its main production site during classical antiquity was the Phoenician port city of Tyre (now in south Lebanon, close to the Israeli border). The dye, which depending on how it was used could produce anything from blue to very dark, almost black, purple, was, unusually for a natural stain, colourfast and, unlike most pre-industrial dyestuffs, resistant to fading when exposed to sunlight or washed. In republican Rome, the white *toga praetexta* had a broad purple border signifying senatorial rank or high public office, and with the advent of the imperial system, the dye was increasingly associated with the emperor and his immediate family.

By the Byzantine period, wearing clothes dyed dark purple was the prerogative of the imperial family, and the term *porphyrogennetos* ('born in the purple') was applied to children of the reigning emperor, partly in reference to the purple porphyry birthing chamber in the Great Palace in Constantinople but also because of the imperial prerogative to wear clothing dyed with Tyrian purple. Among the most famous representations of this exclusive imperial fashion statement are the mosaic portraits of the sixth-century CE Emperor Justinian I and his wife, the formidable Theodora, in the Church of San Vitale in Ravenna, Italy.

The dye is obtained from several species of predatory marine snail that are found in most regions of the globe. In the Mediterranean it is produced mainly from two species: *Bolinus brandaris* and *Hexaplex trunculus* (formerly both assigned to the genus *Murex*). According to ancient myth, it was Herakles' (Hercules) dog that discovered the dye. When the hero was on a Cretan beach, his canine companion ate several snails, instantly staining its maw purple. As an explanation of the discovery of the ancient world's most coveted textile dye, it lacks verisimilitude, but it is in the same vein as the myths that I examined in Chapter Two, which sought to associate certain aquatic products with cultural heroes and gods to underline their economic value. The story, however, may contain a clue as to how the dye was discovered. The flesh of the snail is edible, so it is likely that when Neolithic fishermen on Crete and the Levantine coast cooked the snails, it produced a very colourful broth that stained anything it came into contact with. The significance of the product would not, of course, have become evident until humans had developed textile yarns that they wanted to dye.

Tyrian purple was said to be worth its weight in gold and was the foundation of the wealth and power of the Phoenician cities

Detail of a mosaic panel from the Church of San Vitale in Ravenna, Italy, showing the Byzantine empress Theodora (*c.* 500–548) and her attendants. The empress wears a ceremonial silk cloak dyed with the Tyrian purple that was reserved for the imperial family. She also sports an impressive number of natural pearls on her bejewelled headdress and collar.

that produced it. It was so expensive to manufacture because each snail contains such a minute amount of the dye that many hundreds of thousands would have been needed to produce the colour of the ceremonial garments worn by Justinian and Theodora in the Ravenna mosaics. Initially the snails would have been harvested from the sea but the scale of the industry in Roman and Byzantine times meant that they were bred in captivity in large tanks and then crushed to produce the dye. It is thought that the silk yarn woven into imperial garments was double-dipped in the dye, making them not only the most exclusive garments in history but also among the most expensive.

Like many other products from the eastern Mediterranean that had once been widely available throughout Europe during the Roman period, Tyrian purple became rarer and more expensive after the Muslim conquest of the Near East, and its supply ended altogether after the conquest of the Byzantine Empire by a crusader army in the early thirteenth century and was not resumed when the city returned to Byzantine rule. Although production of the dye continued for a while in the Muslim world, Europeans were forced to turn to cheaper and less durable natural dyestuffs – yet another reason that made them want to seek alternative sources of supply, which they thought might be available from India or China.[6]

Pearl Fishers

It would be difficult to imagine the reaction of the first modern human who opened an oyster and found a natural pearl. But considering the importance of fresh- and saltwater shellfish to the diet of early humans, it must have happened many tens of thousands of years ago. Ancient shell 'middens', or waste heaps, have been found all over the world, evidence of the vast quantities of shellfish consumed by our distant ancestors. A famous example from the pre-Columbian u.s. is the Whaleback Shell Midden, created over a period of 1,000 years by Native American peoples in Maine, which is 10 m (30 ft) deep, over 500 m (1,650 ft) long and 400–500 m (1,300–1,650 ft) wide and consists mainly of oyster shells.

In antiquity the most sought-after pearl oysters were from the waters of the Persian Gulf, the Red Sea, the Indian Ocean and the South China Sea. After the conquest and settlement of Central and South America in the sixteenth century, the Spanish discovered rich pearl fisheries in the waters around the Caribbean islands of Cubagua and Margarita. Although perfectly round white pearls are particularly sought after for jewellery, they come in a variety of shapes and colours including teardrop, button, blister and baroque; among the rarest, and therefore the most valuable, are black pearls from the Pacific Ocean, but pearls are also cream, yellow, pink, gold, green and blue.

There are several misconceptions about pearls: the first and most common is that pearl formation is triggered by a piece of grit or sand that enters an oyster. Since oysters filter nutrients from seawater and spend a great deal of their time with their 'mouths' open, if something as common as sand were the real cause, by now the ocean floor would be knee-deep in pearls. In fact, pearl formation only occurs when the oyster's mantle is damaged by a predator or parasite. The oyster responds by isolating the injured area within a pearl sack, over which it deposits a layer of hard calcium carbonate ($CaCO_3$) – which in its most commonly found form is a rather uninteresting looking white mineral that is the main component of rocks, shells and eggshells.

A pearl is basic oyster first aid, and the first layer of calcium carbonate is like the human application of a sticking plaster to cover an open wound or sore. However, by one of those happy accidents of natural chemistry, the oyster produces calcium carbonate in the form of the mineral aragonite, which it mixes with an organic compound called conchiolin. These combine to produce the iridescent, rainbow-hued wonder-material that is nacre, also known as mother-of-pearl. The patient but totally brainless oyster, not satisfied with our single-layer sticking-plaster technique, spends years coating the pearl sack with layer after layer of nacre until it creates a pearl. The shape and size of natural pearls vary according to the shape and size of the original injury. Perfectly spherical pearls are extremely rare and are particularly sought after; also coveted are teardrop-shaped pearls, while irregularly shaped specimens are charitably known as 'baroque' pearls.

Common misconception number two, and another one of those great parental misdirections that I fell for as a child, was that I might find a pearl when tucking into a plate of oysters at a seaside restaurant. However, the most common edible species eaten today, the Pacific oyster, *Crassostrea gigas*, is a non-nacreous oyster, with a dull white inner shell, which is quite incapable of producing a pearl. Pearls, however, come from several varieties of oysters of the genus *Pinctada*, whose flesh is not considered appetizing by humans. The third misconception is that pearls are only found in oysters, while they in fact come from different species of fresh- and saltwater mollusc, including mussels. And the fourth and final misconception is that pearls are all nacreous. Many species of mollusc produce non-nacreous pearls of various shapes, sizes and colours, which though rare and a curiosity in their own right, lack the allure of the nacreous variety.[7]

Picking the Flowers of Immortality

When the Sumerian hero Gilgamesh sought the secret of immortality, he looked to the sea to find the flowers of immortality on the seabed. According to historical geographer Robin Donkin, the world's foremost authority on the history of pearls and pearl fishing, the plant might actually be a mythical rendering of either pearls or coral, both of which, apart from their uses for personal adornment, were also believed to have protective and medicinal properties in ancient times. Gilgamesh found the magic plant off the coast of the fabled land of Dilmun, which was for the Sumerians both a semi-mythical paradise – the Mesopotamian version of the Garden of Eden and original home of the Seven Sages – and an important trading state that controlled exchange between Mesopotamia, Africa, the Persian Gulf and India.[8]

Shell middens of pearl oysters and Mesopotamian Ubaid period (*c.* 6500–3800 BCE) pottery found in Bahrain provide evidence of pearl fishing and trading in the Persian Gulf dating back to the fifth millennium BCE.[9] The method that Gilgamesh used to recover the plant, by tying stones to his feet, was also employed by Bahraini pearls divers well into the historical period.[10] In addition to pearls, Dilmun was also a source of mother-of-pearl, which was made into inlays for high-status objects found in the ancient Sumerian cities of Uruk and Ur. The Red Sea and Persian Gulf pearl fisheries provided pearls and mother-of-pearl for a succession of ancient empires, including Egypt, Assyria and Persia. There were two other production areas for pearls in the Old World during antiquity: India and China. China had its own production of fresh- and saltwater pearls, dating back to 1100 BCE or earlier. The Han Dynasty (206 BCE–220 CE) exploited marine pearl fisheries in the Gulf of Tonkin. However, it is unlikely that pearls were traded to the West, even after the expansion of the overland Silk Road around 114 BCE, as local demand would have accounted for all East Asian production.[11] It is much more likely that the trade in pearls was from West to East, especially from India and Sri Lanka to China.[12]

Ancient India was connected to the Near East by trading links from the earliest times. The Indus Valley Civilization (3300–1300 BCE), which flourished in what is now northeast India and Pakistan, traded with Sumerian cities through the intermediary of Dilmun. Although no pearls have been found among the jewellery unearthed at Indus Valley sites, the presence of mother-of-pearl and coral means that pearls, too, must have been known. During the Vedic Period (1750–500 BCE), early texts, including the great Hindu epics *Ramayana* and *Mahabharata*, mention fresh- and saltwater pearls, but they become much more important both as commodities and as symbols in religious discourse during the Buddhist era. The *Arthashastra*, a manual of statecraft written in the third or fourth century BCE, lists ten areas that produced pearls: five in southern India, four in northern India and one in eastern India. After the conquests of Alexander the Great (356–323 BCE), Hellenistic geographers travelled east and reported on the high quality of pearls produced in India and Sri Lanka.[13]

The Erythraean Sea and Beyond

The trade in high-status luxury goods was not only dependent on the existence of elites with the economic resources to obtain them but also on those with the military clout to preserve the social and political stability that ensured that production and commercial networks were maintained. Between the first century BCE and the third century CE, stability at either end of the Silk Road was provided by the Han Dynasty in the East and the Roman Republic and Empire in the West. In terms of the trade in pearls, however, the production areas for the highest quality pearls – the Persian Gulf and India – were roughly halfway from the capitals of the two empires. In the West, when the Roman elite traded republican frugality for imperial excess, it vastly increased the Western demand for luxury goods from the East. After the Roman conquest of the Hellenistic kingdoms of the Near East and Egypt, Roman merchants established direct trading connections with the Gulf and India.

In terms of the history of the ancient pearl trade, one of the most extraordinary documents to come down to us from antiquity is the *Periplus Maris Erythraei* (Voyage around the Erythraean Sea), a first-century CE merchant's travelogue that describes the trading routes, tidal conditions and climates, ports, main exports and kingdoms of East Africa, Arabia, the Persian Gulf and India.[14] In the chapter dealing with the pearl fisheries of southern India, the *Periplus* explained that the fisheries there were worked by 'condemned criminals', indicating a change of status of the swimmers and free-divers who harvested the pearl oysters. In the areas where the exploitation of pearls became a lucrative government monopoly, the state employed what it considered disposable personnel: slave labour and condemned criminals.[15]

Although there remained some misunderstandings about the life cycle of the oyster during the Roman period, such as the fanciful notion that they swam in shoals and were caught in nets like fish, other ancient writers were much better informed and, like the anonymous author of the *Periplus*, had first-hand experience of what they were describing. In the first century CE, Isidorus, a native of Charax, a city at the head of the Persian Gulf, wrote of the island of Tylos (now Bahrain): 'The island is surrounded by bamboo rafts from which the natives dive twenty fathoms [36.5 m / 120 ft] of water and bring up bivalves.'[16]

Although the Western Roman Empire collapsed in 476 CE to be replaced by barbarian successor states, the Eastern Roman or Byzantine Empire, with its capital at Constantinople (now Istanbul), endured for another millennium. As long as the empire retained Egypt, it had access to the maritime Silk Road to India and its rich pearl fisheries. The mosaic portraits of Theodora and Justinian at Ravenna, where pearls of different shapes and sizes take pride of place on the diadems and other jewellery worn by the imperial couple, amply demonstrate the value placed on natural pearls by the Byzantine elite. Further evidence of their value is their use to decorate religious objects, including reliquaries, the covers of sacred books and icons.[17]

The Arab conquests of Persia, Egypt and the Near East during the seventh century CE not only transformed the geopolitical situation in the Mediterranean but effectively closed off the sources of supply of Eastern products, including pearls, to Christian Byzantium and Europe. The Red Sea and Persian Gulf fisheries that had once supplied the imperial courts of Rome and Constantinople were now monopolized by Arab merchants. At first, the austere Arabian warriors imbued with *jihad* would have had little use for pearls, but within a few centuries, gems of every kind were sought after in the Muslim courts of Damascus, Baghdad, Cordoba and Cairo.

We have several eyewitness accounts of pearl fishing in the Red Sea and Persian Gulf during the Islamic period. In 1183, when the geographer Ibn Jubayr visited the Red Sea pearl fisheries of Aydhab, he reported:

> The divers go to these islands in small boats and stay there some days and then return with what God has meted out to each according to his lot. The catch is not deep, and they bring it out in double sea-shells [whose flesh] is like a kind of fish resembling somewhat the sea-turtle. When they are split, the inside of the two valves show as silver shells. They are then opened and inside them is found the core of the pearl covered by the fleshy part of the sea-shell.[18]

In the Gulf, the Arabs had taken over both the trade in pearls and the harvesting of pearl oysters. According to the twelfth-century Islamic geographer Al-Idrisi, 'Collecting pearl-shells at depths of up to six fathoms [11 metres/36 ft] was a hazardous and physically demanding occupation.' He explained that the divers protected themselves from changes in pressure by plugging their ears and sometimes their nostrils with a combination of cotton wool, wax and sesame oil or wearing nose clips made of horn or tortoiseshell. The fourteenth-century world traveller Ibn Battuta referred to a kind of diving mask made from tortoiseshell, but otherwise collection methods had changed little since the days of Gilgamesh. He described how divers, each carrying a knife and a leather bag, descended to the sea bottom with ropes weighed down with stones.

He acknowledged the arduousness of the work: the men worked for two hours at a time, then ate and rested.[19]

On the other side of the Erythraean Sea, Marco Polo described the pearl fisheries of Sri Lanka as he made his way back to Europe in 1293. The pearl-fishing season in the Gulf of Mannar between Sri Lanka and India was short: 'The pearl-fishers take their vessels, great and small, and proceed into this gulf, where they stop from the beginning of April to the middle of May.'

Technically, like the pearl fishing in the Gulf, there was little changed since ancient times, according to Marco Polo:

> When the men have got into the small boats, they jump into the water and dive to the bottom, which may be a depth of four to twelve fathoms (7–22 metres/23–72 ft), and there remain as long as they are able. And there they find the shells that contain the pearls, and these they put into a net bag tied around the waist, and mount up to the surface and then dive down again.[20]

Marco Polo's erstwhile masters, the Chinese, continued to exploit freshwater pearls from local sources and obtained marine pearls from fisheries around Hainan Island and off the coast of Annam (now Vietnam), as well as from East Africa, the Persian Gulf and India. Pearls and beads of all kinds remained the most popular forms of adornment in China for millennia. The elaborate gem and pearl headdresses of Chinese empresses rivalled anything made for their Byzantine counterparts.[21]

In contrast, China's near neighbour, Japan, though it imported many aspects of Chinese culture, never acquired a taste for the wearing of pearls as personal adornment. Early Japanese art, design and fashion are famous for their sobriety and minimalist elegance. However, this was not always the case; during the short Azuchi-Momoyama period (1568–1600), known as Japan's 'Renaissance', Japanese craftsmen produced opulent *Nanban* wares for Japan's feudal elite and for export, which combined *raden* (mother-of-pearl inlay) with precious metals and lacquer.[22] Although historically

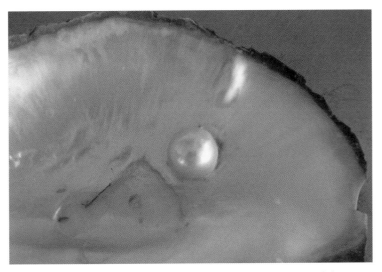

Cultured pearl from a Japanese akoya oyster. The Japanese patented the culturing process in the early twentieth century, revolutionizing the industry. At present 99 per cent of pearls sold are cultured.

Japan is not known for its appreciation of pearls, it is famous for its female pearl divers, the *ama*. The *ama*, however, dived for other types of marine products too, including lobster, abalone and seaweed, as well as pearl oysters, and their fame is perhaps more to do with their diving naked, clad only in a loincloth – a practice that they continued until the 1960s. It was the Japanese who perfected and patented the process of culturing pearls in the early twentieth century, replacing the haphazard collection of natural pearls through diving with industrial-scale production.

New World Riches

The European desire to access the riches of the East long pre-dates Christopher Columbus's first transatlantic crossing in 1492 and can be seen as one of the motivations behind the Crusades that began in the eleventh century. The failure of the Crusades to end the Islamic stranglehold on trade with China, India and Southeast Asia stimulated the Portuguese to find an eastern passage to the East around Africa and across the Indian Ocean, and spurred the Spanish to find a westward route. In the original *Capitulación* (agreement between Columbus and the Spanish Crown), King Ferdinand and Queen Isabella specified that finding pearls be listed among the navigator's primary objectives. He found nothing during his first and second voyages, but during his third, he found pearl mussels off the coast of Venezuela, triggering a 'pearl rush' to the area.

The instructions of Columbus's fourth and final voyage required him to 'Observe what gold, silver, pearls, [precious] stones, spices, and other products there might be'.[23] Although he sailed close to Isla Margarita and its rich oyster pearl beds, he left their exploration to others. His later disgrace was due as much to his failure to deliver sufficient quantities of gold and pearls as to the abuses of power he was accused of as governor of the Indies. The pearls found around the islands of Cubagua and Margarita, off Venezuela's Costa de las Perlas, were of such high quality that they were the single most valuable commodity exploited by the Spanish in the New World until the discovery of the silver mines in the province of Potosí (now a department of Bolivia).[24] According to Bishop Bartholomé de las Casas in the *Brevísima relación de la destrucción de las Indias* (A Brief Account of the Destruction of the Indies, 1522), pearl fishing was responsible for the death of countless Native Americans who were forced to dive all day on short rations and fell prey to exhaustion, mistreatment, hunger and shark attacks.[25]

The Two Pilgrims

Although those harvesting pearl oysters were slaves whose lives were of little account to their masters, the natural pearl as a commodity retained its enormous monetary and symbolic value in Europe, especially during the Age of Exploration and Discovery. Two of the world's largest and most expensive pearls share the same name but for one letter: La Peregrina and La Pelegrina (both meaning 'wanderer' or 'pilgrim' in Spanish). These much-travelled gems both have fantastical histories worthy of Robert Louis Stephenson or Alexandre Dumas. They were both discovered in the waters of the

Antonis Mor's portrait of Mary I of England from 1555 shows the queen wearing the La Peregrina pearl. Found by a black slave in the oyster beds around Isla Margarita off the coast of Venezuela, the pearl became a symbol of European monarchy, adorning the necks of monarchs and aristocrats for four centuries until it became the property of Hollywood royalty when Richard Burton bought it as a present for Elizabeth Taylor.

Costa de las Perlas, and they first made their way from the Indies to Spain, where they became possessions of the Spanish Crown.

La Peregrina, a teardrop-shaped pearl that originally weighed 223.8 grains, was presented by Philip II of Spain (1527–1598) to his wife, the Catholic queen Mary I of England, who unsuccessfully tried to bring Protestant England back into the Catholic fold. Returned to Spain upon Mary's death and the accession of Elizabeth I, the pearl was later stolen by the French during their occupation of Spain during the Napoleonic Wars. It remained in the possession of the Bonaparte family until the deposed French emperor Napoleon III went into exile in England in 1870. The emperor sold it to a British aristocrat, whose family in turn put it up for sale at Sotheby's in London in the 1960s. The buyer was the actor Richard Burton, who purchased it as a gift for Elizabeth Taylor. The actress admitted in an interview that the heavy pearl had once fallen off its chain, and she had had to rescue it from the mouth of one of her pet dogs – almost becoming the most expensive doggy chew in history.

The second pearl, La Pelegrina, a pear-shaped pearl weighing 133.16 grains, has had an even more eventful history, surviving not one but two revolutions. Philip IV of Spain (1605–1665) gave it to his daughter, the Infanta Maria Theresa, upon her marriage to Louis XIV of France, after which it became part of the French crown jewels. It disappeared – most probably stolen – during the French Revolution of 1789 but resurfaced in the possession of the noble Russian house of Yusupov. After the Russian Revolution of 1917, Prince Felix Yusupov (1887–1967) went into exile in France, where he was forced to sell the pearl to raise funds in the 1950s.

Fit for a Queen

For readers to appreciate the full significance given to natural pearls in the sixteenth and seventeenth centuries, I should like them to consider a portrait commissioned by Elizabeth I to commemorate her victory over the Spanish Armada of 1588. Every square inch of the 'Armada Portrait' carries personal, political or religious messages aimed at Elizabeth's Protestant subjects and Catholic enemies.[26] Since the painting commemorates a great naval victory, it is full of maritime imagery and symbolism. Most obviously, the Armada and its wrecking in a storm can be seen through the two windows behind the queen. The monarch sits on a throne-like chair with one hand resting on a globe showing the Americas, indicating her will to expand England's overseas empire at the expense of Spain, the colonial superpower of the day. To her left, a carved gilded mermaid speaks of the wealth of the sea and of its capricious feminine nature, which nevertheless, like Elizabeth's own femininity, was seen by many as the basis of England's stability, wealth and power.

The multi-layered allusions to the physical person of Elizabeth, the Crown and the sea in the portrait supplement and cross-reference one another, and the viewer does not need to be a citizen of sixteenth-century Europe to understand the clear messages they convey. The picture may be a coded allegory, but it is coded allegory writ in ten-foot-high neon letters. Most eye-catching of all is the queen's extraordinary outfit. In an age when rulers dressed to impress,

The 'Armada Portrait' of Elizabeth I, painted to commemorate the defeat of the Spanish invasion of 1588, is a triumph of royal propaganda. The person of Elizabeth as Gloriana, the Virgin Queen, adorned with countless pearls, symbolizes England's wealth, power and imperial ambitions.

Elizabeth's gown is monumental in scale and construction. It is definitely not something she would wear for a casual walkabout among her subjects, and it seems unlikely that the 55-year-old queen would have managed to get to her feet unaided, let alone have been able to walk any distance in the garment. The voluminous skirts and underskirts and outsized sleeves are covered in heavy silk brocade and set off by a contrasting black velvet bodice to which is attached a silk-lined cape. The brocade is further weighed down by hundreds of pearls sewn into medallions and bows and along the hems, hanging down to her waist in heavy coils around her neck and creating a tiara effect studded in her red wig. The finishing touch is an impossibly large lace ruff, fitted like a sunburst around the queen's livid, powdered face.

The person giving the portrait painter his instructions was most likely the queen herself. An accomplished politician, she had spent decades crafting and manipulating her own image, creating Gloriana, the incarnation of a triumphant, wealthy, Protestant England poised to replace Spain as the world's economic and military superpower. In the 'Armada Portrait', pearls symbolize not only royalty, wealth and power, but Elizabeth's much-vaunted virginity and chastity. In many ancient cultures, the iridescent pearl was associated with the moon – offsetting the queen's giant ruff and the golden suns embroidered on her dress, and thus elevating Gloriana to the status of a pagan goddess – a Tudor Artemis-Diana, the virgin hunter and goddess of the moon.

Beyond Price

Since the Second Industrial Revolution and the invention of chemical dyes and plastics, humans have been spoiled by the range of cheap manufactured goods, especially brightly coloured and patterned decorative objects, clothing and accessories. But think back to a time when most humans lived surrounded by various shades of mud, wood and stone, and you can begin to understand the attraction of natural products that stood out in the environment because of their vivid colours or patterns. Long before the age of metals and the discovery of how to polish gemstones, humanity's treasures came from the aquatic environment: brightly coloured shells and corals and what must have been the most spectacular discovery by foraging hunter-gatherers, the natural pearl.

The pearl, though it lost its rarity value after the discovery of the cultured pearl process in the late nineteenth century, retains its rich and varied symbolism in human culture: on the one hand, it represents the highest spiritual values – the 'pearls of wisdom' that Jesus enjoined his followers not to 'cast before swine' in the Sermon on the Mount or the pearls symbolizing wisdom and health in Buddhist and Taoist iconography; on the other, it is symbolic of great earthly wealth and power that often shades into the exact opposite of spiritual wisdom in religious discourse: vanity, luxury, corruption and evil, as symbolized by the pearls worn by the Whore of Babylon in the Book of Revelation.

The status of those harvesting the treasures of the sea changed over the millennia. In the earliest times, they were specialists honoured for their arcane knowledge and the favour of the gods who granted them such wonderful gifts. In myth they were represented as heroes and kings. With the development of complex social hierarchies, those who found pearls and other natural treasures were no longer their end users. In some cultures, the arduous task of collection was given to slaves or imposed as a punishment on condemned criminals. By rights, natural pearls should share the same dreadful associations as today's 'blood diamonds', especially those found in the sixteenth and seventeenth centuries in the Americas. But pearls were never tainted with the blood that had been spilled to acquire them. On the contrary, I would argue that pearls and other aquatic treasures reinforced the cultural and social value of swimming and free-diving. If prowess in the water had initially enabled our prehistoric ancestors to survive in a hostile environment, it later provided the products for the first international trading networks.

4
The Art of Swimming

Every young soldier, without exception, should in the
summer months be taught to swim; for it is sometimes
impossible to pass rivers on bridges, but the flying and
pursuing army both are often obliged to swim over them.
A sudden melting of snow or fall of rain often makes them
overflow their banks, and in such a situation, the danger is
as great from ignorance in swimming as from the enemy.

FLAVIUS VEGETIUS RENATUS, 'TO LEARN TO SWIM',
LATE 4TH CENTURY[1]

Our early ancestors, who by necessity lived by rivers and bodies
of fresh water to provide drinking water for themselves and
their animals and crops, or chose to live by the sea to exploit its
resources, would never have needed to learn to swim in any formal
sense of the word. As Elaine Morgan and others have claimed, we
seem to be much better adapted to aquatic life both physically and
physiologically than any other terrestrial mammal or primate, and
we also have an innate ability as newborns to hold our breath and
make sculling motions when immersed in water. Although today
we need to relearn how to swim and free-dive in childhood, our
ancestors – who might have been birthed in the water and who
would have accompanied their parents into the water on foraging
expeditions – would probably have been swimming before they
were walking.

At an early point in human history, however, the move inland
began. A combination of population pressure in coastal settlements
with the need to open up more land for agricultural production,
and the greater vulnerability of low-lying coastal sites to the weather
and to attacks from land and sea, might explain why humans
decided to move to less accessible sites. A prime example of an
early inland community is the Neolithic 'city' of Çatalhöyük in

southern Anatolia (Turkey), which was occupied from 7500 to 5300 BCE. Although the site is not fortified, over the centuries of building and rebuilding over the foundations of older dwellings, Çatalhöyük rose to be 20 m (65 ft) above the surrounding Konya Plain, an elevation that would have afforded the residents early warning of any approaching danger. From its architecture and city plan, Çatalhöyük is characterized as an egalitarian agricultural community with few distinctions based on gender or class. Its inhabitants grew cereals and other food crops and raised sheep and possibly cattle. Although Çatalhöyük is over 200 km (125 miles) from the sea, it maintained trading relations with the coast, as evidenced by the presence of Mediterranean seashells from Syria in the archaeological deposits.[2]

We do not know how many of the 5,000 to 10,000 residents of Çatalhöyük knew how to swim, but it would not have been high on their list of priorities considering their distance from the sea or from any other major body of water. This state of affairs would have been mirrored in other inland communities without easy access to water suitable for swimming. In later ages, when humans were crammed into ever larger inland cities, the problem of an inability to swim would only worsen. This, of course, would not have been a problem if humans never needed to swim, but there would always be circumstances that would make swimming a matter of survival: flood, shipwreck or an accidental ducking into the sea or a river. Even today, the news regularly features examples of people who drown after they have 'got into difficulty in the water', which may sometimes be shorthand for not knowing how to swim well enough to extricate oneself from difficulties.

The preservation of life might be sufficient motivation for many to learn to swim, but in ancient times there was another pressing need for young men to become competent swimmers: warfare. While an inability to swim might not have been of any significance for the isolated, self-sufficient inland communities of the Neolithic era, matters would change as humanity entered the Bronze Age, which was an epoch marked by the rapid development of metalworking technologies – in particular for the manufacture of weaponry and armour – and the emergence of large, centralized, socially stratified states. The inescapable corollary of these two developments was large-scale warfare and the appearance of the first empires. Swimming, which had played its part in the survival of humanity and the development of the first commercial networks, now took on a new role: as a skill required of the warriors of Bronze Age armies.

Swimmers at Arms

When British archaeologist Austen Layard (1817–1894) began to explore two vast sites raised around the surrounding plain, known to archaeologists as 'tells', near the northern Iraqi city of Mosul in the 1840s, he did not realize that he was excavating the ruins of the Assyrian cities of Nineveh and Kalhu,[3] capitals of Ashurnasirpal II (r. 883–859 BCE), Sennacherib (r. 705–681 BCE) and Ashurbanipal (r. 668–c. 627 BCE). He soon began to make extraordinary discoveries in their palaces, including bas-reliefs of their military campaigns. The Assyrians were not unique in decorating their walls with bas-reliefs of their triumphs, but while the Egyptian pharaohs commemorated their achievements in temples, where they could be seen by their subjects, Assyrian monarchs chose the more private

Mesopotamia – the Land between Rivers – presented major logistical headaches for campaigning armies. Without fords, bridges or the timber resources to build boats, the only way to cross the broad courses of the Tigris and Euphrates was by swimming. In this nineteenth-century reimagining, ancient Babylonians are shown using inflated goatskins as flotation devices to cross the River Tigris.

setting of their own palaces and thus were surrounded by graphic and sometimes gruesome scenes of sieges, battles and the torture and execution of prisoners.

Mesopotamia was defined by two things: being home to several of the world's earliest cities and the twin rivers Tigris and Euphrates that gave the region its ancient name, the 'Land between Rivers'. For ancient generals, rivers such as the Tigris and Euphrates, with their seasonal floods and unpredictable course changes, presented major logistical headaches. Without fords or bridges, the only way across was by boat or raft, but an invading army did not always have the leisure or materials to build boats for all its soldiers, horses, equipment and baggage train, so for many, the only way across would have been to swim. The difficulty and importance of such a crossing were underlined when Ashurnasirpal II chose it to be one of the subjects for the bas-relief panels in his throne room in the palace of his capital of Kalhu.

The ninth-century relief features the Assyrian army's crossing of the Euphrates before it controlled the riverbanks in the region. Hence, added to the dangers of the river itself were possible enemy attacks as the army crossed. While chariots are shown being ferried over in boats, the soldiers and their horses swim across. The larger figure wearing the headdress is a high-ranking soldier or official, and he and other soldiers are shown blowing into inflated goatskins – a kind of primitive flotation device – while a groom swims while holding on to the mane of a horse. Another palace relief show three high-ranking fugitives swimming for their lives as they flee from Assyrian archers. Two are shown blowing into goatskins to keep themselves afloat, while a third seems to be doing a version of front crawl despite his ankle-length robe.[4]

For three centuries, the armies of the Neo-Assyrian Empire (911–609 BCE) dominated the Near East. At its height, the empire stretched from Anatolia in the north to Egypt in the southwest and Elam (southwest Iran) in the southeast. We do not know whether Assyrian troops received formal swimming lessons but the skill was clearly required for campaigns in a region marked by so many great river systems. The soldiers who came from provinces of the empire that were near major rivers or the sea would have most likely known how to swim, but others might have come from inland Anatolian settlements such as Çatalhöyük and would have had to learn to swim. Unfortunately, the Assyrian kings, though they left us texts and relief carvings of their campaigns, did not include information about the training of their soldiers. Swimming remained a vital military skill through the Bronze Age and into the classical period, when the troops of the world-conquering Greeks, Macedonians and Romans demonstrated its value during their conquests.

The Cruel Sea

We know that the ancient Greeks were able swimmers who celebrated its importance through a pantheon of sea divinities and supernatural beings. Swimming also featured in the eighth-century Homeric epics, in particular the *Odyssey*, in which the much-shipwrecked Odysseus would never have made it home to Ithaca and to his faithful wife Penelope had he been unable to swim. Living on the coasts of the Balkan Peninsula or on the many scattered islands of the Aegean and Ionian seas, the ancient Greeks depended on exploiting the resources of the marine environment and engaging in maritime trade for their survival. Swimming was seen as such an important skill that during the classical period an ignorant person was proverbially someone who could neither read nor swim.[5]

In the fifth century BCE swimming played its part in the survival of the Greek city-states, whose destruction or conquest would have forever altered the course of Western European history. During the second invasion of Greece, launched by King Xerxes I of Persia in 480–79 BCE, a detachment of Greeks, led by King Leonidas of Sparta, famously held off the much larger Persian army at the Battle of Thermopylae. At around the same time, the Persian and Greek fleets fought a three-day engagement off Cape Artemisium. The Persians would be finally defeated on land at the battle of Platea and at sea at the battle of Salamis, but these victories would not have been as decisive without the valuable time gained and damage done to Persian forces and morale at Thermopylae and Artemisium.

According to the fifth-century BCE chronicler of the Persian Wars Herodotus, a man by the name of Scyllias (also given as Scyllus and Scyllis by other sources) played a crucial role in the outcome of the battle. A talented free-diver from the Greek city of Scione, he had been employed by the Persians to salvage ships lost in a storm as they sailed to engage the Greek fleet. Herodotus continued:

> He had for some time been wishing to go over to the Greeks; but no good opportunity had offered till now, when the Persians were making the muster of their ships. In what way he contrived to reach the Greeks I am not able to say for certain: I marvel much if the tale that is commonly told be true. It is said he dived into the sea at Aphetae, and did not once come to the surface till he reached Artemisium, a distance of nearly eighty furlongs.[6]

Although Herodotus dismissed the claim that Scyllias had swum 80 furlongs (16 km / 10 miles) underwater to join the Greek fleet, he confirmed that he had told the Greeks of the partial wreck of the Persian fleet and warned them that they had sent a detachment of 200 ships around the island of Euboea in an attempt to blockade the Greek fleet and capture it. The second-century CE travelogue writer Pausanias added to the story when he explained the origins of two statues that he had seen in the sanctuary of Delphi. According to Pausanias, Scyllias and his daughter Hydna had engaged in an early form of underwater warfare:

> When the fleet of Xerxes was attacked by a violent storm off Mount Pelion, father and daughter completed its destruction by dragging away under the sea the anchors and any other security the triremes had. In return for this deed the Amphictyons dedicated statues of Scyllias and his daughter.[7]

Less than a century after Athens had led the resistance against the Persian invasion, it was her turn to flex her imperial muscles. In 414 BCE, an Athenian fleet sailed west to Sicily in an attempt to

A miniature painted for the sixteenth-century Mughal emperor Akbar the Great, depicting Alexander's descent into the sea in a glass diving bell during the siege of Tyre. Although diving bells were in use during antiquity to salvage sunken ships, they could only be used in shallow water for short periods.

capture the wealthy port city of Syracuse, a former colony of Athens' great rival, the *polis* of Corinth. The Syracusans mounted a stout defence of their city, including building an underwater stockade of sharpened piles driven into the seabed to prevent the Athenians from sailing into the harbour and attacking their ships at anchor. The Athenians attacked the stockade, pulling out the piles by means of ropes fastened to their ships or by sending divers to saw them in half. Although the Athenians managed to destroy the parts of the stockade that were above the water, according to fifth-century BCE historian Thucydides, they now had to deal with a far more difficult problem:

> The most awkward part of the stockade was the part out of sight: some of the piles which had been driven in did not appear above water, so that it was dangerous to sail up, for fear of running the ships upon them, just as upon a reef, through not seeing them. However, divers went down and sawed off even these for reward; although the Syracusans drove in others.[8]

The Greeks were a highly inventive people, especially when it came to the application of scientific principles for military ends, but certain stories strain credulity beyond breaking point. According to one account, when Alexander the Great was besieging the Phoenician city of Tyre in 332 BCE, he was lowered into the Mediterranean in a glass diving bell, where he remained submerged for 24 hours without the aid of any kind of breathing apparatus or an independent air supply. Although primitive diving bell technology was in use during antiquity, unless Alexander's diving bell was huge – probably the size of a large building – he would have run out of breathable air very quickly, and if he hadn't suffocated for lack of oxygen, he would have been poisoned as the carbon dioxide produced through respiration built up to a lethal concentration. Either way, he would have been lucky to survive for 24 minutes, let alone 24 hours.

A more securely attested story about Alexander's tactical use of swimming is of an event during the Battle of Hydaspes in 326 BCE, which has been recognized by military historians as one of his most brilliant victories and a strategic masterpiece. The problem facing Alexander, who had reached the Indian subcontinent, was the army of King Porus, which lay on the other side of the river Hydaspes (now the Jhelum River in Pakistan). His enemy occupied the far bank in such strength that a crossing would have been suicidal. Leaving a decoy detachment that included an Alexander impersonator, and instructing it to move up and down the bank to give the impression that they were looking to force a crossing, Alexander went upriver with the main force of his army, where he swam his troops across under cover of a storm. By the time the Indians realized what Alexander was doing, he was already on the far bank. He defeated Porus, but it was to be one of the final victories of his world-conquering campaign, as his soldiers, exhausted after having conquered the Persian Empire, now refused to cross the Indus.[9]

Of Roman Matters

Rome's legions never got as far as India, but the empire long outlived Alexander's own and the kingdoms of his successors. Rome owed its longevity to many factors but primary among them was a superbly trained and organized military: the famous legions. The recruits, who came from the empire's diverse cultures and spoke different languages, were forged into a single fighting unit through what must have been extremely efficient, standardized training. Individually, they might not have been the greatest fighters in the world, but as fighting units, the legions were seldom bested, and even when they were, it was usually a case of losing a single battle and going on to win the war. We have the writings of great Roman commanders such as Julius Caesar, or their biographies, but these usually concentrate on their personal qualities and accounts of their lives and battles, and they give little information about the common soldiery who won their victories and how they were trained.

Only one Roman military manual, *Epitoma rei militaris* (The Military Institutions of the Romans), or more commonly *De re militari* (On Military Matters), survives from the fourth century CE.

The author, Flavius Vegetius Renatus, is an otherwise unidentified soldier who dedicated his book to the reigning emperor. Divided into three sections, it covers the training of recruits (I), military organization (II) and dispositions for action (III). Written in the closing years of the Western Roman Empire, *De re militari* was both a history lesson and a plea for military reform. Its significance for the present work is in the many references Vegetius makes to swimming. The first is a wistful evocation of the soldiers of the Republic, who had 'no pleasures, no luxuries to enervate them. The Tiber was then their only bath, and in it they refreshed themselves after their exercises and fatigues in the field by swimming.' There follows a section entitled 'To Learn to Swim' that summarizes its importance to ancient armies:

> Every young soldier, without exception, should in the summer months be taught to swim; for it is sometimes impossible to pass rivers on bridges, but the flying and pursuing army both are often obliged to swim over them. A sudden melting of snow or fall of rain often makes them overflow their banks, and in such a situation, the danger is as great from ignorance in swimming as from the enemy.

Several further references reinforce the message that swimming was not only a necessary activity in its own right for the passage of rivers (Book III), but was also a means to maintain physical fitness and discipline.[10] Vegetius did not use any historical incidents to illustrate his text, though he would have had plenty to choose from the preceding 900 years of the military history of the Roman Republic and Empire. He could have mined, for example, Plutarch's biography of Julius Caesar. One instance of the 'good will and zeal' of the men in Caesar's service that Plutarch cited was that of a legionary during one of Caesar's British campaigns who had swum across a river to rescue a comrade from the enemy. Another concerned the great man himself during his involvement in the internecine contest between Cleopatra VII and her siblings for the throne of Egypt. During one battle in Alexandria, Caesar found himself trapped, outnumbered and in danger of being captured or killed. According to Plutarch:

> He sprang from the mole into a small boat and tried to go to the aid of his men in their struggle, but the Egyptians sailed up against him from every side, so that he threw himself into the sea and with great difficulty escaped by swimming. At this time, too, it is said that he was holding many papers in his hand and would not let them go, though missiles were flying at him and he was immersed in the sea, but held them above water with one hand and swam with the other; his little boat had been sunk at the outset.[11]

Another account claimed that he also saved his commander's bright red cloak, not wishing to leave it behind as a trophy for his enemies. However, even by Caesar's day, many legionaries were unable to swim, and Roman writers, including Caesar himself, were surprised by the swimming abilities of their barbarian enemies, especially the Germanic and Gallic tribes. One reason for the change was a move away in Roman culture from swimming in rivers to bathing in the luxurious *thermae* that sprang up all over the empire.[12]

De re militari was one of the most popular ancient works known in the Middle Ages, when it was translated into many languages and circulated in manuscript form, until the invention of printing, when it was published in French, English, Italian and German editions. However, its impact on swimming in Western Europe was minimal.

The Swimming Renaissance

Humans did not stop swimming in medieval Europe, but for a number of reasons the skill was much less valued than it had been during antiquity, especially among the upper echelons of society. According to Nicholas Orme, the author of an exhaustive survey of swimming in the British Isles from antiquity to the eighteenth century, many peoples of late antiquity and the early Middle Ages, in particular the Welsh, Anglo-Saxons and Norse, were strong swimmers with a constructive relationship to the aquatic environment. Epic poems and prose stories such as the Welsh *Mabinogion*, the Anglo-Saxon *Beowulf* and the Norse sagas concern themselves with the deeds of heroes who performed extraordinary aquatic feats, such as Beowulf's killing of the underwater monster Grendel, or his swimming all the way from Frisia (now the Netherlands and Germany) back to Britain after he was defeated in battle. But Orme stressed the change in attitudes to swimming in post-Norman Conquest England that was probably mirrored all over Western Europe. This was due to changes in lifestyles and to the teachings of the Church.[13]

Christianity did not just eliminate the pantheons of pagan gods and supernatural beings and replace them with one omnipotent creator god, it simultaneously transformed attitudes to the body, which in turn brought an end to the Graeco-Roman artistic and athletic cultures that had glorified the naked male form. The gymnasia and bathhouses where Greeks and Romans of every social caste were unselfconsciously naked were closed because they were morally suspect. The Church discouraged swimming on moral grounds, but it went further, associating the practice with the dark arts of witchcraft. When a woman was accused of being a witch, she was put through an ordeal by water. Her hands and feet were bound and she was thrown into a nearby river or pond. If she sank, she was deemed 'normal' and was released (as long as she survived the ordeal), but if she floated, she was condemned and executed as a witch.

A related problem – at least in the medieval mind – were the health problems caused by waterborne diseases, such as malaria, which was spreading north during the period, as well as diseases spread by the pollution of urban waters by human, animal and industrial waste. As the causes of infectious diseases were not understood, illness was often blamed on supernatural agencies, such as witches. Such negative associations, compounding disease, immorality and witchcraft, served only to discourage the practice of swimming among the general population.[14]

'August', from *Les Très Riches Heures du Duc de Berry* (c. 1413–16), folio
8v, shows a group of peasants swimming naked in a river. They form
part of the background to the real subject of the illustration, which
is an aristocratic hawking party. The illustration underlines the social
differences between the naked peasants and the richly attired nobles,
and also classes swimming as a rural pastime practised only by the
lower orders.

Although Vegetius' treatise was one of the best-known ancient manuscripts during the Middle Ages, the section on swimming was sometimes omitted in medieval copies. And though swimming was listed as one of the seven knightly accomplishments, Orme points out that it would have been completely impractical and potentially fatal for a knight encased in heavy plate armour.[15] Not only were literary and artistic references to swimming far less frequent between the years 1000 and 1500 than during classical antiquity but they were also largely negative. The aquatic environment was an alien, dangerous place full of monstrous sea serpents and mermaids, from which men often had to be rescued through divine intervention.

There were, of course, exceptions. In *Les Très Riches Heures du Duc de Berry* (*c.* 1413–16), a lavishly illuminated book of days, folio 8v, 'August', shows naked men and women swimming in a river. However, the main subject of the illustration is an aristocratic hawking party, and the swimmers, who are peasants, merely form part of the background. During the Graeco-Roman period, emperors and kings had been portrayed naked, but in the Middle Ages clothing was an important marker of social status and identity. The contrast between the splendidly attired riders and the naked peasants only serves to reaffirm that swimming was a lowly pastime not suitable for the medieval elite, even at the height of the French summer, when both men and women wore long robes that would have been stifling in the warm weather.[16]

The Age of Rediscovery

The sixteenth century was not just the beginning of the Age of Discovery and Exploration in the wake of Columbus's first voyage to America in 1492 and the opening of the sea route to India by Vasco da Gama in 1498; it was also the Age of Rediscovery, with the revival of classical learning that had been gathering dust in monastic libraries for centuries. Not only had Western Europe's geographical horizons more than doubled in size, but her intellectual borders now extended far beyond the limits set by Christian orthodoxy, looking back to a glorious pagan past and forwards to a rational scientific future. Just as the invention of movable type had ended the Catholic Church's monopoly on the production and distribution of knowledge in the fifteenth century, the Protestant Reformation would end Catholicism's claim to be the guardian of true Christian revelation in the sixteenth.

The Renaissance, as this far-reaching revolution in human thought is rather understatedly known, transformed every aspect of life in Western Europe, including its medical and exercise cultures. While Italian physician Girolamo Mercuriale (1530–1606) pioneered the rediscovery of classical Greek athletics and its therapeutic applications in *De arte gymnastica* (1579),[17] it was an eccentric Cambridge don, Sir Everard Digby (*c.* 1548–1605), who wrote one of the earliest and most influential treatises on swimming, *De arte natandi* (1587). The difference between Mercuriale's and Digby's works is that the former based his on existing ancient Greek and Roman medical texts by Hippocrates (*c.* 460–*c.* 370 BCE) and Galen (129–*c.* 200 CE), which he was trying to marry with Catholic theology and the medical canon of his day, while the latter did not have any ancient authorities on which to base his explanation of the technical aspects of swimming.

Digby, however, was not writing in complete isolation but in an established tradition of British scholars who had an interest in the revival of swimming as a martial skill and for its health benefits. In *The Book of the Governor* (1531), a treatise on statesmanship and education dedicated to Henry VIII, the scholar and diplomat Sir Thomas Elyot listed three forms of exercise that would bring both 'recreation and profit': wrestling, running and swimming. But rather than a guide to swimming technique, Elyot merely recommended its practice, citing Vegetius and examples of military swimmers from classical history, including the aquatic exploits of Horatius Cocles, who with two comrades defended Rome against an Etruscan army, and Julius Caesar's involuntary ducking in Alexandria.[18]

A slightly more complete treatment of swimming can be found in educationalist and lexicographer Richard Mulcaster's *Positions* (1581). Mulcaster, who was headmaster of two of the leading schools of the period, Merchant Taylors' and, later, St Paul's, is best known for his advocacy of 'football'. He devoted one chapter in *Positions* to swimming, recommending its revival because of its martial applications but primarily for its health benefits. Like Elyot, he did not go into swimming technique but took a more practical, health-centred approach. He discussed the relative merits of swimming in cold and hot water and in fresh and salt water. Another book that Digby would have known was the printed editions of *De re militari*. In 1572, John Sadler published a new English translation complete with all the references to swimming.[19]

As with Mercuriale's work on athletics, there is no evidence that these books had any impact on the exercise habits of the Tudor elite. For example, we cannot be sure whether Henry VIII, England's most sporty monarch, who excelled in jousting, royal tennis, archery and hunting, was able to swim. And the response to several cases of drowning at Cambridge University was not, as might be expected, the institution of swimming lessons for scholars, but a complete ban on swimming or washing in the River Cam in 1571, with severe punishments for infringements: two public whippings, a fine of ten shillings (for BAS) and a day in the stocks for a first offence, and expulsion for the second.[20]

Digby's Illustrated How-to Book

The first book in Western Europe to feature practical advice on how to swim was Nicolas Wynman's *Colymbetes, sive de arte natandi dialogus* (1538). Wynman was public professor of languages at the University of Ingolstadt in Bavaria, and he wrote the book not to promote swimming as a martial skill or as a form of therapeutic exercise but to reduce the incidence of drowning – no doubt a common occurrence in a city built on the banks of the Danube. The book takes the form of a classical dialogue between Pampirus (the swimmer) and Erotes (the learner), who explains that he has been encouraged to swim by his mother, who wanted to stimulate his growth. Erotes, who may be based on the young Wynman, says: 'When I saw that boys were swimming everywhere in the water, I longed to imitate them and learn the art thoroughly.'

Rich in classical allusions, the book was more an essay in praise of swimming and a personal memoir than a teaching manual. However, it contained a methodical approach to the teaching of breaststroke. Wynman wrote at a time when swimming was not merely discouraged in German schools but banned. The prohibition was enforced with severe punishments, which were applied even to pupils who had died by drowning, whose lifeless corpses were whipped before interment. In writing *Colymbetes*, Wynman questioned both the religious prejudice against swimming and the civil ban. He also recommended swimming for health, basing his ideas on classical examples and early Germanic traditions.[21]

Five decades later, and with the same lifesaving aim as Wynman, Cambridge scholar Everard Digby wrote *De arte natandi*, one of the first illustrated how-to books published in England. Born the second son of a wealthy family in Elizabethan England, Digby was expected to make his own way in the world. He was a St John's 'sizar' – a poor scholar who received free board and tuition in exchange for serving the wealthier students. He matriculated in 1567, got his BA in 1571 and became a fellow of the college in 1573. In 1576 he took holy orders, as was expected of those pursuing an academic career at the time and which also provided him with an income from church benefices. From 1584, he began lecturing to scholars, and in 1587, he was elected a senior fellow of St John's.

Although he had a relatively successful academic career at the university, Digby was considered something of an eccentric, not just for his promotion of the suspect art of swimming, but, perhaps more understandably, because he was in the habit of running around the college loudly shouting 'Hallo!' at the fellows and scholars while blowing a trumpet. But it was his Catholic sympathies during the reign of Henry VIII's Protestant daughter, Elizabeth I, that were the real reason for his expulsion from the university. He was unpopular with the Puritan fellows at St John's, who engineered his dismissal on the grounds of unpaid debts, and despite a successful appeal to Lord Burleigh, one of the queen's most senior advisers, and to the Archbishop of Canterbury, he was forced to resign his fellowship in

1588. Although he lived in comfortable retirement on his benefices, he died an embittered man in 1605.[22]

De arte natandi is divided into two sections: Book I deals with theory and Book II, with practice. Digby defined swimming as a mechanical, as opposed to a liberal, art whose purpose was to prolong life by preventing drowning. To persuade his sceptical readers of the value of swimming, he made the claim that, as humans were superior to all other animals, they should be able to swim better than fishes. Book I concludes with practical advice on when and where to swim. According to student of Renaissance sport Arnd Krüger, the reason Digby's book was so influential is because it signals the beginning of modernity:

> In his method and reasoning we find all the later principles of modern science and that helps explain why his book has been such a success. It represents the modern way of thinking that has been with us ever since.[23]

As an occasional swimming teacher and coach, what interested me most was the second half of the book, which deals with swimming technique. *De arte natandi* covers all the basic skills you would expect to find in a modern swimming manual: safe entry into the water, propulsion, turning, floating, swimming underwater and diving. And – a first for any book on swimming – the forty chapters are illustrated, with 43 woodcuts gathered together in a central insert. The woodcuts all show men swimming in a river, indicating Digby's preferred location for swimming and swimming lessons. Of course, at the time, there were no swimming pools, but he did not seem to have considered the sea as an alternative, perhaps because of the even greater danger of drowning, or simply because he lived quite a distance from the sea in Cambridge.

The setting is an idyllic pastoral landscape with trees, shrubs and grazing animals, where men can disport themselves naked, reminiscent of Adam and Eve in the Garden of Eden and of naked Greek athletes training in a gymnasium. No women are shown, indicating that this is a men-only activity, and the swimmers undressing on

Woodcut from Digby's *De arte natandi* (1587) showing a man swimming on his back using a breaststroke kick, one of the four strokes described in Digby's treatise. Missing from the book is the front crawl, a stroke reintroduced to Europe in the nineteenth century. He described several forms of backstroke. In this illustration, the illustrator has tried to capture movement by using waves around the hands and feet, and indicates where the body is submerged with lines.

the riverbank are clearly gentlemen by their clothes. Krüger sees the illustrations as representing the beginning of a complete shift in attitudes towards swimming in the sixteenth century; he concludes:

> The fear of the unknown was transformed into a series of pictures and thus transferred into the known field. The first iconic turn helped in demystifying the element of water and man's relationship with a fearful part of nature.[24]

Digby described four strokes, but they are not the modern competition foursome of backstroke, breaststroke, butterfly and front crawl, but breaststroke, backstroke, sidestroke and doggy paddle.[25] Although we have evidence of a front-crawl-like stroke from antiquity, it seems to have fallen out of use in Europe during the Middle Ages. The dominant European stroke was the breaststroke, until the reintroduction of an overarm stroke in the first half

Woodcut from Digby's *De arte natandi* (1587) showing a swimmer performing a 'decorative feat': in this instance, holding two birds out of the water. In addition to teaching basic swimming technique, Digby recommended drills similar to those performed today for swimming, synchronized swimming and water polo, for the swimmer's own entertainment and to impress and amuse his friends.

of the nineteenth century. But perhaps most striking from a modern perspective are the 'decorative feats' that Digby enjoined swimmers to attempt to entertain themselves and to impress others. These included treading water, carrying articles out of the water, raising one leg out of the water and pretending to put on a boot and clip one's toenails, and floating on the back while 'dancing' with both legs, all of which are reminiscent of drills used in contemporary swimming, synchronized swimming and water polo.[26]

Despite the Latin text and theological arguments in the opening section, which will strike the modern reader as obscure, Digby managed something completely new and original as the first English author to produce an illustrated teaching method. While he recognized swimming's value as a means to improving health, his main aim was the preservation of life. In this he took a diametrically opposed view to the university establishment that responded to incidents of drowning with a ban on river bathing – an early example, to borrow from the modern British tabloid press, of a 'health-and-safety culture gone mad'. But perhaps most significant of all was that he fully appreciated the recreational aspect of swimming, as shown by his inclusion of 'decorative feats'. Previous writers, such as Elyot and Mulcaster, recognized the value of swimming but in an abstract way, and one does not get the feeling that they thought of it as a fun activity. From Digby, in contrast, we sense the kind of enthusiasm and expertise for his subject that can only have been gained from first-hand experience and genuine enjoyment.

In Digby's Wake

Christopher Middleton translated *De arte natandi* into English under the title *A Short Introduction for to Learne to Swimme* (1595). He simplified the text and added his own preface, in which he likens Digby to the Vegetius, Aristotle or Hippocrates of swimming – which is known in the publishing trade as 'buttering up your author' – no doubt vital to get the cooperation of the embittered, cantankerous old don. Middleton's translation, as he himself says, makes Digby's work more accessible to the reader who cannot read Latin.[27] Although the book remained the best work on the subject for 200 years, its author did not always get the credit he deserved. In 1658, William Percey, of whom little is known apart from the fact that he is described as 'a gentleman', published *The Complete Swimmer*. While he followed Digby's text closely, his one innovation was to recommend swimming to both men and women.[28]

A far worse case of inadvertent plagiarism occurred in 1699, when French scholar, traveller and diplomat Melchisédech Thévenot's (*c.* 1620–1692) *Art de nager démontré par figures, avec des avis pour se baigner utilement* (1696) was translated into English. Although Thévenot himself acknowledged his debt to Wynman and Digby in his preface, since he followed the latter's text, and the book's illustrations by Charles Moette are all based on Digby's originals, the frontispiece of the English edition made no mention of Digby. One of Thévenot's original contributions, which he sadly did not develop, was a remark on the aquatic skills of African and Asian peoples, whom he must have seen swimming during his extensive travels. Another innovation was his introduction of swimming aids and flotation devices for learners. In the English edition, the translator added a scientific appreciation of swimming in the light of the discoveries of seventeenth-century physics, as well as a discussion of stroke mechanics – the first time that the idea that swimming itself could be improved appears in English.[29]

We can see Digby's influence as late as the nineteenth century: for example, in Phokion Heinrich Clias (1782–1854), who had been hired by the British Army to provide a physical education curriculum for its recruits and was also a strong advocate of swimming. He wrote:

> Of all the exercises which should form part of our physical education, swimming is, without contradiction, one of the most useful; it contributes powerfully to the development of the body, to the increase in strength, and the preservation of health.

Clias, too, recommended swimming on grounds of hygiene and health, praising the benefits of cold baths, and for the preservation of life from drowning. Although he did claim that only a competent swimmer could get the most gratification from swimming, he did not discuss swimming as a form of recreation or a competitive sport. He describes different types of teaching aids and equipment, diving and lifesaving, and the three strokes covered by Digby – breaststroke, sidestroke and backstroke – but also adding 'the thrust', a very basic form of overarm stroke, which was just beginning to make its appearance in Europe in the early nineteenth century.[30]

The Enlightened Swimmer

Educational reforms had been proposed in the 1600s and 1700s – during the Age of Enlightenment – by writers such as John Locke and Jean-Jacques Rousseau to introduce physical education as part of a more balanced, child-centred curriculum. These were gradually put into practice during the Age of Revolutions, in particular in the states of the Holy Roman Empire.[31] Johann Guts Muths (1759–1839), a teacher of physical education at the Salzmannschule in Schnepfenthal near Gotha (now in Thuringia, Germany), wrote *Gymnastik für die Jugend* (1793), which was translated into English as *Gymnastics for Youth* (1800), with a chapter dedicated to swimming and bathing. In 1798, Muths produced a second book dedicated to the teaching of swimming, *Kleines Lehrbuch der Schwimmkunst zum Selbstunterricht* (Small Study Book of the Art of Swimming for Self-study). At a time when there was little or no provision for physical education of any kind, he wrote: 'For my part, I consider the cold bath as an essential object in good physical education; and a bathing place, as an indispensable appendage for a public school.'[32]

Guts Muths associates bathing and swimming; hence swimming is seen first as a means of keeping clean, second to preserve one's own life and those of others from drowning and third as a form of healthy exercise alongside gymnastic exercises revived from antiquity. Like Digby, he recommends swimming in a river rather than in stagnant water, but rather than swimming naked, he recommends 'linen drawers, reaching halfway down the thigh', possibly the first mention of swimwear in Europe and North America, where men continued to bathe naked until the end of the nineteenth century. Apart from this sartorial advice and a note that swimmers should not be over-concerned about their personal appearance – 'We are not afraid of disordering our hair, for it is merely combed in the simplest manner'[33] – he does not go much further than Digby in his conception of the functions of swimming or its techniques, describing aids for learners and the breast- and backstrokes and giving advice on safe entry into the water, lifesaving and how to deal with cramp.[34] Guts Muths drew his ideas on land-based physical education from Graeco-Roman models, but for swimming, which lacked ancient precedents, he turned to a near contemporary, the American polymath, statesman, diplomat and accomplished swimmer Benjamin Franklin (1706–1790).

According to his autobiography, Franklin taught himself to swim as a child and deepened his knowledge of the art by studying Thévenot's *Art de nager*, seemingly unaware of the Frenchman's debt to Digby. In 1724, the eighteen-year-old Franklin went to London, where he worked as a typesetter in a printing shop located in Smithfield. He taught one of his colleagues, a young man called Wygate, and another acquaintance to swim, with such success that he considered setting up a swimming school in the English capital, realizing that he could make his fortune in a city where so few people knew how to swim. Luckily for the history of the future United States of America, Franklin gave up this idea and returned to Philadelphia.

In 1726, before leaving London, Franklin was persuaded to demonstrate his aquatic skills to some of Wygate's acquaintances with whom he travelled by boat to Chelsea. Apparently needing little encouragement, Franklin

> stripped and leaped into the river, and swam from near Chelsea to Blackfryar's, performing on the way many feats of activity, both upon and under water, that surpris'd and pleas'd those to whom they were novelties.[35]

The story shows how few of the educated young men Franklin associated with in London knew how to swim, while at the same time revealing their interest in and enthusiasm for the activity.

Men like Franklin and Guts Muths were in the vanguard of the Enlightenment revival of physical education. But what popularized all forms of exercise across the European continent during the early nineteenth century was not the peaceful experimentation of men such as Guts Muths and Franklin but the advent of war in the wake of the French Revolution of 1789. When Emperor Napoleon I smashed the Prussian army at the Battle of Jena-Auerstedt in 1806, he shocked Europe by defeating the world's best professional army with an army of peasant conscripts. In response, a German nationalist, Friedrich Jahn (1778–1852), opened the first open-air *Turnplatz* (exercise field) in Hasenheide on the outskirts of Berlin in 1811, to strengthen the German race so that its own conscript armies could challenge French military dominance.[36] Although Jahn's *Turnen* (gymnastics) was land-based, it was part of a much wider movement that saw the redefinition of different forms of physical education, including swimming, as new weapons that could be used to win the major geopolitical conflicts of the day.

Interest in swimming as a military skill pre-dated the Napoleonic era. Around 1786, three years before the French Revolution, French swimming teacher Barthélemy Turquin opened his École de Natation on the River Seine in a floating pool near the Pont de la Tournelle in the 5th arrondissement. An eighteenth-century floating pool consisted of a converted barge or wooden tank enclosing a section of a river, with a planking bottom but with the sides open to allow the free flow of water through the swimming area. A mesh screen was fitted to filter out the larger pieces of refuse and other impurities floating in the water. Turquin's École was to become much more famous as the Bains Deligny, winning royal patronage after the restoration of the French monarchy in 1815. One of the stated aims of the Deligny, whose pool measured 106 × 30 m (348 × 98 ft), was to teach naval and marine corps cadets to swim. A peacetime sinking of a French naval ship had revealed that few cadets knew how to swim, as many had drowned in the tragedy.

After Napoleon had defeated the major European powers, similar military floating pools began to appear in Austria and the German states. In 1813, the Kaiserliche und Königliche Militär-schwimmschule (Imperial and Royal Military Swimming School) opened in Vienna, with similar establishments opening in 1817 in Berlin, Potsdam, Hamburg and Magdeburg. Military pools were sometimes open to women and were also used by horses, as these also had to be trained in aquatic warfare. The Netherlands, whose own tradition of swimming for humanitarian purposes dated back to the establishment of The Netherlands Society to Prevent Drowning in 1767, opened its first military floating pool on the German model in 1844. According to swimming pool historian Thomas A. P. van Leeuwen, we owe the rectangular shape of most of our pools to the military nature of these institutions, which were intended for swimming instruction and military-style swimming drills on the model of the parade ground.[37]

Harrow's 'Duck Puddle'

While Guts Muths was taking his charges for river swims, major English public schools, such as Harrow and Eton, were encouraging their students to learn to swim as a precaution against drowning, which was a particular concern for Eton College with its strong rowing tradition on the nearby Thames. The school had several officially designated bathing spots on the river as early as 1727, but clearly not all students learned to swim, as the first swimming test at the school was instituted in 1836 in response to the deaths of several students by drowning. In the 1780s and '90s, Harrow School (which is not near a river) taught its students to swim in the 'Duck Puddle' – a natural pond in the grounds of the school. In 1810 or 1811, this was superseded by a second, manmade 'Duck Puddle' – a large, in-ground but unlined pool that the students shared with fish, frogs and waterfowl and which was probably the first purpose-built swimming facility to be built at any English or probably European school. Again, the main aim of the pool was the preservation of life.[38]

Although Harrow, like other public schools, was an early exponent of competitive individual and team sports, swimming competitions did not begin at the school until 1857. The provision of swimming lessons in the British state education sector, established by the Elementary Education Act of 1870, came much later. Until 1890, state schools in London were forbidden to spend public money on the teaching of swimming, as it was not deemed to be part of the national curriculum established by the 1870 legislation. While state schools attempted to work around the ban by working with voluntary organizations, coverage remained patchy, and the situation was not rectified until 1893 in London, and later outside the capital.[39] The situation in the u.s. school system seems to have clear parallels with the UK during the nineteenth century, but in France, the situation was far worse, with provisions for swimming lessons in state schools being made only in the twentieth century.[40]

Although official provision of swimming lessons was slow to take off in the UK, there were several private attempts by charitable bodies to remedy the situation during the nineteenth century – something made all the more urgent by the incidence of accidental drowning, which between 1860 and 1900 numbered between 2,264 and 3,659 annually, rising to more than 4,000 if suicides by drowning were taken into consideration. The National Swimming Society (NSS), founded in 1837, promoted swimming as a humanitarian skill for the preservation of life. While the NSS provided lessons for boys who wished to learn to swim, little real progress in the mass teaching of swimming was made until the last decades of the century. In 1873 the Royal Humane Society instituted the Stanhope Medal, awarded to those who had saved someone from drowning. The first recipient was Captain Matthew Webb, famous for being the first man to swim the English Channel in 1875. In 1891, the Swimmer's Life Saving Society was founded, receiving royal patronage in 1904 as the Royal Life Saving Society.[41]

Another influential body that promoted swimming as a humanitarian skill was Robert Baden-Powell's (1857–1941) Scouting movement. Baden-Powell saw swimming and lifesaving as necessary accomplishments for the Scouts, and he established swimming badges for boys and later for girls, once the Girl Guides had been established. In his manual for the Scouting movement, *Scouting for Boys*, he wrote:

> It is very necessary for a scout to be able to swim, for he never knows when he may have to cross a river, to swim for his life, or to plunge to save someone from drowning, so those of you that cannot swim should make it your business to begin at once to learn.[42]

The quote is reminiscent of the brief excerpt from Vegetius used at the head of this chapter, though stripped of its military overtones. Until the first decades of the twentieth century, swimming retained an anomalous position in the world of sport and exercise, having the extra dimension of a humanitarian, lifesaving skill. Although this was not in itself negative, unlike any other form of exercise, it established a link between swimming and drowning fatalities.

Swimming Lost and Found

Swimming, which had played a central role in the development of urban culture, was eventually stifled by it, as populations moved away from the coasts and rivers and into ever larger, more crowded and polluted cities. At the same time the development of transport infrastructure such as bridges meant that there was less of a need for people to swim, especially among the military, who had once depended on the skill during their military campaigns. The medieval Church also played its part in the turn away from swimming, which it found morally suspect. Swimming, of course, was still practised by those connected through work to the aquatic environment during the Middle Ages, but it was no longer a pastime considered suitable for the educated elites. Indeed, the sixteenth-century response to an increase in the incidence of drowning among schoolboys and university students was a total ban on swimming.

Just as swimming seemed to be on the verge of disappearing altogether among the upper echelons of European society, it won the support of Renaissance scholars, who championed it on the grounds of health and for the preservation of human life, basing their case on the rediscovered writings of classical authors, which they used to fight the religious prejudice and civil bans against its practice. Although swimming regained intellectual respectability, it was seen primarily as a useful, functional skill rather than as a form of recreation or sport. Nevertheless, the renewed interest in swimming was evidence of a change in attitudes to the human body and its display, and to medieval Christian notions of the aquatic environment as an unknown, dangerous and quasi-demonic space inhabited by monsters and mermaids.

While the Renaissance initiated a change in attitudes to swimming, it did little to change the habits of the elites or of the population at large. The road back for swimming to regain its ancient popularity would be a long and arduous one. Educational reformers of the late eighteenth and early nineteenth centuries recommended swimming as a desirable skill and an enjoyable pastime alongside team sports and gymnastics, but because there was a limited infrastructure of swimming pools to match the gymnasia that were springing up all over Europe, swimming was only practicable for those with access to natural bodies of water or the few river baths and swimming schools that were set up in large cities. Of course, participation in swimming lessons was also limited to those who had the inclination to learn as well as the leisure time and resources to do so. As with the provision of land-based physical education, swimming lessons only became widely available to school students in Europe and North America at the end of the nineteenth century.

5
Pure, Clean and Healthy

Everywhere in many lands gush forth beneficent waters,
here cold, there hot, there both . . . promising relief to the
sick . . . To come now to the classes of water: some classes
of water. Waters are good for sinews or feet, or for sciatica;
others for dislocations or fractures; they purge the bowels;
heal wounds; are specific for head, or for ears.

PLINY THE ELDER, *NATURAL HISTORY*, AD 77–9[1]

I have described how the aquatic divinities and supernatural beings
of pagan myth are evidence of the intimate relationship between
swimming and the development of human civilization. As civilizations matured, however, the forms and functions of religion also
evolved. In Sumerian myth, the *abzu* / Abzu had several manifes-
tations over time: a physical place, the freshwater lagoon of the city
of Eridu; the mythical abode of the god Enki; and an abstract
representation of divinity that was reproduced in artificial pools in
Babylonian temple complexes. A similar transformation of a physical body of water, such as a holy river, lake or lagoon, into a site of
ritual involving water can be seen in many of the world's great
religions. For faiths as diverse as Hinduism, Christianity, Shinto
and Judaism, full immersion in a manmade pool or natural body
of water goes beyond the cleaning of dirt from the surface of the
body and becomes a means of cleansing the soul of sin and other
spiritual impurities.

One long-held view of purification rituals is that they were
primitive hygiene measures that preserved health by destroying the
vectors that carry diseases. But this would only make sense if our
ancestors had known about germ theory. Pre-scientific medical
systems, however, defined disease as imbalances of the 'humours' or
of internal energies such as *qi* or *prana*, or as a result of coming into
contact with bad air, or 'miasma', against which washing the external

surfaces of the body would have had no direct effect. In these medical traditions, bathing and swimming were seen as having an indirect effect on diseases by helping the body restore its own equilibrium.

Purity Preserved

The world's oldest purpose-built, in-ground, enclosed swimming pool is the 'Great Bath' of Mohenjo-daro (2,500–1,800 years BCE), one of the largest cities of the Indus Valley Civilization (IVC). The pool, which was part of a larger complex, measures 12 × 7 m (39 × 23 ft) and 2.4 m (8 ft) at its deepest. The superbly crafted structure, made from close-fitting bricks held together with gypsum plaster, was coated with a layer of natural tar to make it completely watertight. Bathers entered the water via two wide staircases at either end. Although the pool is just about long enough to do lengths, and deep enough to accommodate springboard divers, water polo and synchronized swimming, it is unlikely that it was ever used by the matrons of the city for lengths of 'old-lady breaststroke' or for any other kind of recreational swimming activity. Based on later Indian religious practice, one theory holds that the complex that housed the pool was a college for the city's priesthood and that the Great Bath was reserved for their purification rites.[2]

Uniquely among the most ancient urban cultures of Eurasia, the IVC did not leave behind a large corpus of written materials. The inscriptions found on Indus Valley seals are too short to allow their decipherment, and, thus far, no multilingual text like Egypt's Rosetta Stone has given linguists the leg-up they need to crack their code. As a result, we know little of the daily lives, social and political organization, customs and beliefs of the residents of IVC cities such as Mohenjo-daro, and much of what archaeologists think they know, such as how they imagine the Great Bath was used, is inferred from later Hindu practice. Because the pool was part of an important complex in the centre of the city, it is presumed that it was used by its elite – most likely its priestly class. But as Wendy Doniger reminds us in her alternative history of Hinduism, this inference might be completely mistaken. She suggests, a little tongue-in-cheek

The world's first in-ground enclosed swimming pool, the Great Bath at Mohenjo-daro, 3rd millennium BCE. Although not particularly long, the maximum depth of 2.4 m (8 ft) indicates that those using it would have needed to be competent swimmers. While we have no direct evidence of how or by whom the pool was used, later Indian religious practice suggests that it could have been used for purification rites by the city's priestly caste.

perhaps, that the building housing the pool, rather than a college of priests, might have been a dorm, a hotel or even a brothel.[3] The one thing that strikes me about the pool as a swimmer, apart from its rather modest length (as such it is not unlike many small hotel pools), is that it is quite deep. Whoever used it would have needed to have some competence in the water.

Purification rites in water continue to play an important role in Hinduism. At sunrise on the second day of my stay in the holy city of Varanasi (Benares), a city reputed to have 23,000 Hindu and Jain shrines and temples, I made my way to what must be the city's most extraordinary attraction, the ghats – the stone embankments that line the banks of the sacred River Ganges. The ghats are one of the most important funerary sites in India because to be cremated in the city and have one's ashes scattered in the Ganges is the Hindu

Ritual bathing in the Ganges at Varanasi, late nineteenth century. Pilgrims come to the ghats and wade out into the waters of the sacred river. Although polluted and posing a health risk, the waters of the Ganges are believed to give spiritual purification. This kind of ritual use of bathing stresses the difference between notions of physical hygiene and physical purification.

equivalent of being buried in Jerusalem in order to have a front-row seat for the Second Coming.

Walking down the stone steps that lead to the water's edge, I watched as a dead cow floated past, bloated and upside down, looking like a gruesome organic air mattress. This quickly put paid to any idea I had of joining the pilgrims and sadhus (Hindu holy men) who were already crowding the banks and venturing out into the water. Rather than swim, they walked out a few metres into the river where the water was deep enough so that they could fully immerse themselves. No one dived in to do a brisk 50-m dash. In hindsight, I wonder if any of them were able to swim. Although the reader might imagine that the practical function of the ritual is to clean off any dirt and sweat from the body, like an early morning shower, its real purpose is religious and by extension social: to cleanse bathers from ritual impurities that restrict their broader social interactions, for example, women who have menstruated or given birth and people who have been in contact with a corpse.

Similar rules apply in Orthodox Judaism, in particular for members of the Hasidic and Haredi communities, who are enjoined to bathe in natural bodies of water that are fed by springs or in the sea. Visitors to Tel Aviv will note the irony of the juxtaposition of three separate beaches on the seafront below the prime site of the Hilton Hotel in the city's Old North. The beach directly below the hotel is used by the city's large and thriving LGBT community, its neighbour, by the city's equally large dog-owning community and their faithful canine companions, and the third, now securely fenced in, by the ultra-Orthodox community, with segregated days for male and female bathers. Although, in theory, the bath ritual should consist in the full immersion of the body to purify it, the crowds that flock to the beach with inflatable rubber rings and rush into the water whooping excitedly, especially in the warmer months of

The *mikveh* in the Kahal Shalom Synagogue Museum on the Greek island of Rhodes. In order to have the right purifying properties, the *mikveh* must be fed by a natural spring, though this can be supplemented by rainwater, tap water or snowmelt.

the year, do not suggest sober religious practices but rather a group of people intent on having some beach-time fun. Those not lucky enough to live in Israel by the sea have to make do with a small spring-fed ritual bath, a *mikveh*, just large enough to accommodate a single person and deep enough to permit full immersion. The Christian traditions of baptism, especially those that favour the full immersion of the body in imitation of Christ's baptism by St John in the River Jordan, are based on these earlier Jewish practices. However, in Christianity, purification by water only occurs once. In early Christian practice, it was held that baptism absolved all sins and thus granted automatic admission to Heaven, so converts held off being baptized until the last possible moment – many on their deathbeds – so as not to risk sullying their souls again.

It does not take a huge leap of the imagination to understand the links between immersion in water and notions of bodily cleanliness, spiritual purity and physical health that were made by ancient peoples. In the realm of magic and religious ritual, as the anthropologist and student of religion James Frazer pointed out in *The Golden Bough* (1890), when humans formulate magico-religious rituals, they think metaphorically, transposing an action or idea from one context to another. For example, the idea of washing the skin clean of dirt and the concept of cleansing the spirit of sin. The great debate in anthropology when I was a student was between anthropological functionalism and structuralism. The former argued that all aspects of culture could be analysed in terms of their practical functions, and the latter held that myth and ritual were expressions of universal structures in the human psyche.

One of the most persuasive explanations for ritual purification practices was provided by anthropologist Mary Douglas (1921–2007) in her study of pollution and taboos in human culture, *Purity and Danger* (1966). For Douglas, rules about pollution and purity have nothing to do with hygiene or bodily cleanliness: they serve to define what is socially 'normal' in any given culture. Her theory is often summarized in the maxim, 'dirt is matter out of place.'[4] Thus full immersion of the body in water for the purpose of purification provides yet another link between human spirituality and the aquatic environment. While such rituals would not be so significant in societies with close, positive relationships to water, like the mermaid myth, they created a magico-religious link between terrestrial faiths such as Judaism and Christianity and the practice of swimming.

Beneficent Waters

Religious cults and thermal springs were closely associated during antiquity. Ancient cultures linked bathing and swimming in the waters of sacred springs with supernatural healing practices – hence forging the link between religious notions of spiritual purity and magico-religious rituals on the one hand and physical health and medical interventions on the other. The Roman Empire had the most sophisticated swimming and bathing infrastructure in the ancient world, consisting of *aquae* (spas) and *thermae* (public baths). By imperial times, the baths had become indispensable public spaces providing relaxation, recreation and social interaction between all classes of Roman society without the formality of the forum or the basilica.[5]

The quote by Pliny the Elder (23–79 CE) at the head of the chapter is evidence of the popularity of bathing practices in the first century CE, and of their close association with medicine.[6] Roman medical practices closely followed those of the ancient Greeks, whose foremost authority, Hippocrates (*c.* 460–*c.* 370 BCE), is credited with the pre-modern medical theory known as humorism, in which imbalances between the four humours or bodily fluids (blood, yellow bile, black bile and phlegm) were seen as the main causes of disease. He recommended baths for their curative properties because of their ability to regulate the humours: hot or cold baths could heat, cool or moisten the body, thus altering the humoral balance.

Although he misunderstood human anatomy and physiology and the causes of disease, Hippocrates is often described as the father of modern medicine because he rejected the idea that illness had supernatural causes, such as punishments sent by the gods or the work of sorcerers or evil spirits. The idea that the gods could intervene to effect miraculous cures did not disappear, but the magical rituals that were believed to achieve the cures were often accompanied by more pragmatic medical treatments. With a relatively minimal pharmacopoeia, Graeco-Roman physicians could only offer limited interventions, which were often restricted to advice about diet and exercise, and treatments such as bathing in natural springs. There were about 100 *aquae* (literally 'waters', but meaning spas) in the Roman world that were recommended for different ailments. Among the most famous were the spas of Baiae on the north side of the Bay of Naples, which attracted emperors and Rome's super-rich, who built their own luxurious villas near bath complexes that combined medical treatments with the social pastimes that are still found in today's seaside resorts.

The Romans developed spa complexes at mineral springs in all the provinces of the empire, such as Aquae Helveticae (Baden, Switzerland), Aquae Spadanae (Spa, Belgium), Aquae Granni (Aachen in Germany) and Aquae Calidae (Hammam Righa, Algeria), and in areas without natural thermal springs, they built equally luxurious *thermae*, where the water was heated artificially. The *aquae* often associated pre-existing cults connected to natural springs with a Roman deity. In ancient Britain, the Romans built Aquae Sulis (now the city of Bath) on the cult site of the Celtic goddess Sulis, whom they associated with the goddess Minerva. The complex built over the spring had a large indoor swimming pool, the 'Great Bath', measuring 24.5 × 11.5 m (80 × 38 ft) and 1.5 m (5 ft) deep.[7] Although the same size as a modern short-course pool (25 m / 82 ft), the pool was not used for recreational or competitive swimming.

Anyone wishing to experience what it was like to take the waters at Roman *aquae* or bathe in large urban *thermae* can visit the palatial Szechenyi or Gellert baths in Budapest. These large spa complexes, opened respectively in 1913 and 1918, are fed by natural springs and equipped with different types of indoor and outdoor pools, saunas, whirlpools and steam rooms, and offer a range of medical and spa treatments, as well as recreational facilities. Unlike conventional

The flooded Temple of Echo, part of one of the luxurious *aquae* complexes in the Roman resort of Baiae. The first-century BCE dome was the largest in the ancient world until the construction of Rome's Pantheon. Roman *aquae* offered medical treatments to their wealthy patrons, as well as providing many of the hedonistic pleasures that we associate with modern-day seaside resorts.

swimming pools, where swimmers do lengths, the order of the day here is relaxing and socializing.[8]

Paradoxically, and despite the provision of large pools, the Roman infrastructure of *aquae* and *thermae* had a negative impact on the swimming culture of the empire. Whereas, as Vegetius recalled with heartfelt nostalgia, for the soldiers of the Republic 'the Tiber was their only bath',[9] by imperial times, the *thermae* that had become the social hubs of Roman cities and were built in military installations and smaller towns and villages, made swimming unnecessary for anyone who could afford to go to the baths. In 33 BCE, Rome had 170 *thermae*, but their number had increased to 856 by the late fourth century CE. While Roman practices consolidated the link between bathing, swimming and medicine, their luxurious bathing facilities ultimately led to the decline and eventual disappearance of swimming as a popular pastime in Roman society. As we saw in the previous chapter, members of the elite, such as Julius Caesar, were able swimmers, because they could afford their own private pools and were regular visitors to Baiae. The less well-off

The outdoor pools of Budapest's neo-Baroque Szechenyi Baths recreate the Roman bathing experience. Although equipped with several large pools, the baths are designed not for fitness or competitive swimming but to provide a mix of spa and medical treatments and recreational activities.

went to the *thermae*, and though these could be vast buildings, such as the Baths of Caracalla (217 CE) and of Diocletian (306 CE) in Rome, which had *natatio* (swimming pools) that could accommodate 1,600 and 3,000 bathers respectively, these were shallow basins more suitable for sitting, soaking and socializing rather than for swimming.[10] Like so many other aspects of classical culture, swimming and bathing went into decline in late antiquity, heralding what, in 1862, French historian Jules Michelet called *mille ans sans bain* (one thousand years without a bath).[11]

Water Power

The Renaissance revived ancient notions of swimming and bathing not only for military use and the preservation of life but also as part of medical practice. However, considering the ideological and practical obstacles to swimming, it is unlikely that the encomiums and practical advice from scholars such as Wynman and Digby had any immediate effect on the habits of the social and intellectual elites or of the general population of their own day. The former, after all, had responded to incidents of drowning by imposing a total ban on swimming, and the latter, influenced by Church prejudice, continued to regard swimming both as dangerous and morally suspect. Nevertheless, the water, like the mermaids who were believed to dwell in it, held something of a fatal attraction for men and boys, who were drawn to it during the hot weather as a place where they could escape the heat and grime. As with all natural bodies of water, it could be treacherous, with unseen currents and riptides in the sea and obstructions, tidal currents, whirlpools, mud and shifting sandbanks in busy urban rivers.

The child of a French family who had been transplanted to England in infancy, I spent my early summers in old Orléans, home to my paternal and maternal grandparents. The city is built astride the River Loire, famous for its Renaissance chateaux and infamous for the number of victims it has claimed over the centuries. The river, which is quite broad when it flows through the city, creates large sandbanks that appear to be solid, permanent islands with

The sandbanks on the Loire can appear completely solid and stable, and may have vegetation growing on them, but they are constantly being undermined by the current. They can liquefy and collapse in seconds, dragging the unwary to their deaths by drowning or suffocation.

vegetation that can endure for months but which are also being constantly undermined by the fast-flowing current. The sudden liquefaction of the sandbanks has dragged even competent swimmers to their deaths. Rather than swim in the treacherous Loire, my father and uncle took their families to one of its smaller tributaries, the Loiret, whose shaded banks and slow, shallow course made it an idyllic spot for safe river fun.

Among my abiding memories of these summer outings is of a prank my father and uncle liked to play, first on us children, and after we had wised up to it, on any other unsuspecting bather in the vicinity. During a two-year stint in the colonial administration of Madagascar, my great-grandfather had acquired the hide of a crocodile, complete with head, limbs and tail, which had been preserved and stiffened so that it was waterproof and rigid, and if merely glanced at, quite lifelike. The underside of the beast was missing, so that one or two people could propel it on the surface of the water while being concealed underneath it. My father and uncle would surreptitiously unload *le crocodile* from the car's roof rack, where it had been concealed by a tarpaulin, and take it down the bank to a spot where they could enter the water unobserved.

Once hidden inside the hide and with their heads just above the waterline, they would wade out to the middle of the river, and then swim back down to the area where the families congregated. Crocodilians of any kind being rather sparse in northern France, the appearance of the lifelike reptile apparently swimming downstream caused quite a stir among the assembled picnickers and bathers. Suddenly making a beeline for the shore, the monster scattered shrieking children as parents looked on with a mix of concern and consternation. At this point, the pranksters would stand and lift the crocodile over their heads. I'm not sure how many times this actually took place, but it became the stuff of family legend, repeated at every family occasion.

Going Back to the Source

Balneotherapy, the medicinal use of natural springs, did not stop after the collapse of the Western Roman Empire in the late fifth century CE. During the Middle Ages new springs were discovered, and old springs continued in use or were rediscovered, offering cures that were mediated by saints rather than pagan gods. The cold, mineral-rich spring known to the Romans as Aquae Spadanae (Spa in modern-day Belgium) was rediscovered in the fourteenth century. Although the town did not offer bathing, its name was henceforth used to denote localities with hot or cold natural springs for both bathing and drinking cures, and in the modern period, for facilities offering a range of beauty and alternative health treatments. The fortunes of medieval spas waxed and waned, buffeted by the changing attitudes of the religious authorities and by the regular epidemics that swept through Europe, which were sometimes blamed on communal bathing.[12]

Along with all other aspects of medical practice, exercise and physical education, water cures and bathing were re-examined by Renaissance scholars and physicians. In 1571 natural philosopher and papal physician Andrea Bacci published the bestselling *De thermis* – one of several works by others that re-evaluated ancient Graeco-Roman bathing practices and water cures and recommended their use for a variety of ailments, while attempting to give them on a scientific basis and distancing them from earlier medieval magico-religious purification rituals. According to doctors A. van Tubergen and S. van der Linden of University Hospital, Maastricht, following these early Italian developments, the seventeenth century saw the development of two types of spa north of the Alps: hot springs for drinking and bathing and cold springs for drinking only. While in France taking the waters was seen a serious, sober activity in facilities devoted to medical treatments, in other European countries, such as Germany and England, spas quickly became fashionable resorts that offered diverse social and leisure activities.[13] The German spa town of Aachen (Aix-la-Chapelle), for example, was infamous as a place for high-class prostitution, while at the same time, its waters were recommended for the treatment of syphilis.

Another Continental development with hydrotherapeutic aims, but which had dubious medical value, were the *bains flottants* (floating baths) operated by Barthélemy Turquin, who would later

The spa at the German town of Aachen (Fr.: Aix-la-Chapelle) in 1682, showing communal bathing in the mineral-rich waters of the spring that was first used in Roman times. The spa was notorious for high-class prostitution and its water cures were recommended for the venereal diseases that its patrons contracted during their visits.

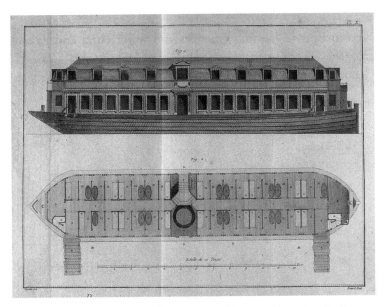

The Bains Poitevin were housed in a converted barge anchored to the Pont Royal in the heart of *Ancien Régime* Paris. The *bains* offered hot and cold baths and showers to the Parisian well-to-do. But as the water supply was drawn directly from the River Seine, bathers, far from improving their health, risked catching the many waterborne diseases transmitted by unfiltered and unpurified river water.

open the Bains Deligny, and by Doctor Poitevin in late eighteenth-century Paris. Poitevin converted a barge into a floating bathhouse that was anchored to the Pont Royal close to the Palais des Tuileries to provide hot and cold baths and showers for the Parisian well-to-do. As the cold baths consisted of barrels suspended in the Seine, and the patrons bathed in unfiltered river water, they must have emerged only marginally cleaner than when they went in, and ran the risk of contracting the many waterborne diseases and parasitic infections that abounded in what was Paris' main sewer. Nevertheless, Poitevin's and Turquin's *bains* were successes that inspired imitators in other European cities.[14]

The boom in English spas began in the 1620s when a Mrs Farrer or Farrow discovered a natural mineral spring at Scarborough. The North Yorkshire town is unique in having a mineral spring and being on the coast. In the 1660s, Dr Robert Wittie, author of

Scarbrough Spaw, recommended taking the waters for a wide range of ailments, and in the book's 1667 edition, he went on to make the revolutionary suggestion that gout sufferers should take sea baths to alleviate their condition. The town's website proudly boasts that it was also England's first seaside resort, with luxurious facilities for visitors who came to take the waters and bathe in the sea.[15] While there were fashionable spas such as Vichy, Aachen and Baden Baden on the Continent, according to medical historian Dr Roy Porter, it was in England – Europe's first 'consumer society' – where spas first became major commercial enterprises, with resorts such as Leamington Spa, Tunbridge Wells, Buxton, Scarborough and Cheltenham 'promising elegant healing rituals, social contacts and rich pickings for hoteliers and doctors'. But the jewel in this particular crown was the city of Bath (Roman Aquae Sulis), which first attracted royal patronage in 1702 when Queen Anne (1665–1714) went to the city to take the waters and bathe. Under the direction of unofficial 'master of ceremonies' and arbiter of good

The Grand Pump Room at Bath, opened in 1799, was built as a place to sample the waters of the spring that also feeds the neighbouring Roman Baths but mainly as a gathering place for the English upper classes who flocked to the city for its social season. The building, the scene for the elegant rituals of early nineteenth-century society, features in two novels by Jane Austen: *Northanger Abbey* and *Persuasion*.

taste Beau Nash (1674–1761), the city became the preeminent social centre of the late eighteenth and early nineteenth centuries, and by 1801, by 'mixing medicine and merriment', became England's seventh-largest city.[16]

Bath, notably, had the Great Bath built by the Romans, but the spa's seventeenth- and eighteenth-century patrons did not swim in its warm waters but simply immersed themselves. To preserve public decorum and ensure the modesty of seventeenth-century bathers, men and women were obliged to wear versions of the fashions of the day made of stiffened canvas, which would not mould itself to the body or become transparent when soaked; in the eighteenth century, they wore similar confections made of linen that served the same purpose. Anyone who remembers taking their school swimming certificate, for which they were required to swim a length of the pool in pyjamas, will appreciate the impossibility of swimming any distance at all in a canvas or linen floor-length dress with puff sleeves, topped with a wig and picture hat.[17] Weighed down, immobilized and suffocated by yards of heavy, waterlogged fabric, rather than enjoying the liberating experience of bathing and swimming in minimal swimwear, spa bathers must have considered immersion in the pool as a physical trial that could be justified only by its medical benefits.

Unlike its Continental counterpart, the English balneotherapy boom was not to last. Royal Leamington Spa, Warwickshire, illustrates the trajectory of England's spa towns during the nineteenth century. Major development began in the 1780s, when the medicinal qualities of the town's waters were recognized and widely advertised. The discovery of a new spring in 1811 prompted the construction of a grand neoclassical Royal Pump Rooms and Baths that rivalled the complex at Bath. Completed in 1813, and further expanded in 1816, the building contained seventeen hot and three cold baths. By the late 1840s, Leamington was suffering from competition from Continental spas and the new seaside resorts that were being developed in the wake of the railway boom. Attendance at the Pump Rooms went into steady decline, and in 1860, there was a plan to demolish the building in order to sell the land. Fortunately for later generations, in 1861, a consortium of local businessmen saved the Pump Rooms and refurbished them, adding a Turkish bath and a large swimming pool.[18]

According to van Tubergen and van der Linden, there were other reasons why balneotherapy continued to decline in England through the late nineteenth and early twentieth centuries. They claim that English spa resorts did not offer the same level of medical hydrology as those in other countries, and their overdependence on leisure activities made them vulnerable to competition from other types of resort. The *coup de grâce* came in 1948, when the newly founded NHS did not fund balneotherapy. This was not the case on the Continent, where post-war health and social care systems continued to fund and reimburse water cures.

In the second half of the twentieth century, the word 'spa' has been used for older resorts with hot or cold mineral springs, offering medical treatments, as well as for a new kind of 'day spa', which can be in an urban or rural setting and usually does not have access to natural springs. This modern reinvention of the traditional spa features facilities such as pools, saunas, steam baths, jacuzzis and solariums and offers a range of beauty treatments, alternative health procedures and health and fitness activities whose objective is age, weight and stress control rather than the treatment of specific medical conditions.

Steam and Ice

The Western world does not have a monopoly on medicinal and social bathing. The major difference between the Western and non-Western traditions, however, is in the provision of facilities suitable for swimming. The hammam steam baths found in many Islamic countries have architectural and social antecedents in *thermae*, and though they retain many features of Roman baths, they do not usually have large pools. On a visit to Istanbul, I went to the medieval Suleymaniye Hamami – an Ottoman-Islamic take on the Christian Romano-Byzantine bathhouses of Constantinople, where after having rinsed in warm water, you are enthusiastically

Sweat lodges were used across the pre-Columbian Americas as alternatives to immersion in water for cleansing the body, purification rituals and medical treatments. When using Native American sweat lodges, and their Old World analogues, Scandinavian saunas, Russian *banyas* and Ottoman hammams, participants are not required to immerse themselves in water or swim.

washed by the baths' attendants, who provide a skin-stripping lather massage that leaves you slightly dazed, completely relaxed and ready to lounge on the heated marble platform, looking up at its crowning Ottoman-Byzantine dome.[19]

The Finnish saunas and Russian *banya* are two closely related forms of steam bath, whose use does not necessitate full immersion in water. In a rural setting, if a suitable body of water is close by, the steam baths are interspersed with cooling dips, through holes in the ice in winter.[20] Similar in design to the sauna are the Native American sweat lodges and pre-Columbian Aztec *temazcal*, which were used for ritual purification and medical treatments. As with the sauna, the function of pre-Columbian steam baths was to cleanse and heal the body through sweating, and full immersion in water was not considered a necessary part of the activity.[21] The steam baths' invigorating and cleansing effect is not dependent on activating the body's musculature, as in swimming, but by regulating blood flow to the skin and promoting perspiration.

The non-Western tradition that comes closest to the Western idea of 'taking the waters' is the still-thriving *onsen* culture of Japan, though in Japan the water from the naturally heated springs is not drunk. *Onsen* resorts abound in the volcanically active Japanese archipelago. When I lived in Japan, I quickly adopted the local custom of staying at *onsen* resorts in the winter months. The most basic *onsen* I visited was in an isolated mountain temple and was free of charge. The unattended bath, housed in its own ornate wooden shed next to the temple proper, was about the size of a small plunge pool and was covered with a simple wooden cover. The most sophisticated and luxurious *onsen* are modern constructions equipped with several large indoor and outdoor pools, heated to different temperatures and offering a range of social activities to patrons.[22] Although many *onsen* have large basins, swimming plays no part in traditional Japanese spa culture.

This brief survey of non-Western medical and social bathing underlines the uniqueness of European spa cultures, because they included pools inherited from Roman *thermae* that were suitable for swimming, even if they were not initially used for that purpose. At the same time as inland spas were developing into fashionable resorts where the well-to-do could take the waters and bathe in mineral-rich springs, doctors began to recommend a new type of treatment for the diseases of eighteenth-century affluence, and one that would have a much greater impact on the practice of swimming: the seawater cure.

To the Sea Again

In her survey of exercise in eighteenth-century England, Julia Allen chose two leading figures of the day, lexicographer Samuel Johnson (1709–1784) and diarist Hester Thrale (1741–1821), as representative of prevailing attitudes to swimming. The study reveals just how much had changed in England between the publication of Digby's *De arte natandi* and the mid-eighteenth century. Although Johnson is now best known for his creation of *A Dictionary of the English Language* (1755), Allen reveals that during his lifetime he was also famed for his athleticism, and that 'He drew admiring comment when he plunged naked into the sea at Brighton.'[23] Johnson's definition of 'exercise' in the *Dictionary*, however, reveals that he still associated swimming with medical practices: 'E'XERCISE: Labour of the body; labour considered as conducive to the cure or prevention of diseases.'[24] Exercise and swimming were not limited to men and boys, as Mrs Thrale, who swam with Dr Johnson in Brighton, was also fearless in the water.[25] Thrale's aquatic exploits, though no doubt considered eccentric, did not arouse the moral outrage and censure that they would have done in earlier centuries. The scene of their watery adventures was Brighton, some 123 km (76 miles) south of London.

In the 1730s, Brighton was a town in serious decline, brought on by raids by the French, damage from major storms and the competition from other Sussex towns. Seeing Brighton today, with its elegant Georgian terraces, many large hotels, conference centre, Royal Pavilion and its two piers, it is difficult to imagine how easily the town could have sunk into total obscurity, becoming one of the many minor villages and hamlets strung along the English south coast. One reason that it did not was its relative closeness to London. But what drew the English elite down to the coast was more than its shingle beach and the picturesque Sussex views. In 1750, a doctor from the neighbouring town of Lewes, Richard Russell (1687–1759), published *De tabe glandulari, sive de usu aquae marinae in morbis glandularum dissertatio*, which was translated into English as *Glandular Diseases, or a Dissertation on the Use of Sea Water in the Affections of the Glands* in 1752, in which he recommended drinking seawater and sea bathing to treat certain glandular conditions, claiming that thalassotherapy, the medicinal use of sea bathing and drinking seawater, was far superior in the treatment of certain glandular conditions than the balneotherapy offered at inland spas such as Bath.

Russell's book, despite its rather unpromising title, was an eighteenth-century bestseller, going into its sixth edition in 1769. In 1753, Russell moved his practice to the Brighton seafront. His success brought patients and other physicians flocking to the town, followed by developers who began to construct new residential districts, hotels and thalassotherapy facilities. Johnson was advised to go swimming for his gout in 1775, and finally made it to the coast the following year, when – as mentioned above – he drew admiring

Dr Richard Russell, whose bestselling eighteenth-century book on the benefits of seawater to treat diseases of the glands began the transformation of Brighton into England's premier seaside resort. Although Scarborough can lay claim to being England's first seaside spa, it was eclipsed by Brighton because of its closeness to London, and the royal patronage of the Prince Regent.

glances as he dived into the waves naked. Mr and Mrs Thrale bought a house in Brighton and were regular visitors, with the formidable Hester Thrale swimming in the roughest of seas with Johnson.[26] Although I cannot confirm that Hester is the lady in question, an article in the September 1805 edition of the *Sporting Magazine* reported:

> A lady has lately made her appearance at one of our fashionable watering places, in the character of a Naiad. Her skill in the science of swimming has gained much admiration, and she has received the elegant appellation of the Diving Belle.[27]

For most, however, modesty was still the order of the day. Female bathers went into the sea in long flannel dresses that would have militated against any attempt to swim. While for a few, like Johnson and Thrale, sea swimming had become a diversion and sporting activity, for the majority, bathing remained a treatment or preventative measure for illness. In addition to the cumbersome clothing and segregation of the sexes, dips were often recommended in midwinter rather than in the balmier summer months. Bathing in the sea was again seen as a positive experience but not necessarily a pleasurable one. By the 1780s, Brighton's future as England's premier seaside resort was assured when the Prince Regent, the future George IV (1762–1830), gave the town his royal seal of approval when he began the construction of his fantastical Indo-Arabian residence in the town, the Royal Pavilion, in 1787. The Prince's father, George III (1738–1820), also favoured thalassotherapy, but he preferred to bathe in Weymouth, Dorset, when convalescing from his first attack of porphyria in 1788 – no doubt to be as far away as possible from the dissolute son he so cordially despised.

Similar developments were taking place across Western Europe. Nicolas Meynen's case study of nineteenth-century La Rochelle illuminates the relationship between thalassotherapy and the early development of seaside resorts. La Rochelle, a town on the French Atlantic coast, attempted to imitate the success of Dieppe, on France's Channel coast. In 1824, Caroline, Duchess of Berry, visited Dieppe with a large entourage, seeking an escape from the boredom of the court of her father-in-law, the elderly King Charles X (1757–1836). Much taken by the elegant neoclassical architecture, she stayed for six weeks and continued her attendance for the next five years. In her honour, the town renamed the Société anonyme des bains de mer de Dieppe as La Société des bains de Caroline.

In 1827, hoping to cash in on the new fashion for sea bathing, La Rochelle built the Bains Marie-Thérèse, which catered to the upper and middle classes and provided hot and cold seawater baths, social activities and games in a grand neoclassical building with separate men's and women's facilities, an assembly room and ballroom, and an artificial beach with screened-off sections for male and female bathers. Two further *bains* were opened later in the century: the Bains Jagueneaud, with two large concrete swimming pools, which was also aimed at the wealthier patrons of the resort, and the Bains Louise, with more modest facilities for the working classes. Unlike Brighton or Dieppe, however, La Rochelle never made the transition from thalassotherapy centre to recreational seaside resort. One important factor that Meynen cites was that the city did not have the beaches that people had come to expect by the later nineteenth century.[28]

The trajectory of what were to become the late nineteenth century's leading seaside resorts had been set. The most successful would combine thalassotherapy, sandy beaches, picturesque scenery and bracing sea air with fashionable spa and recreational facilities and luxurious accommodation, and like Brighton and Dieppe, they would be within easy reach of major population centres by road or rail.

A Marriage of Hygiene and Morality

Although Western European and North American elites reconnected with the aquatic environment through balneotherapy and thalassotherapy during the eighteenth century, swimming remained a minority pastime limited to certain locations and with very specific medical functions, out of reach of the vast bulk of the population, which was increasingly concentrated in the new industrial and mercantile cities. An unintended consequence of rapid industrialization and urbanization in the nineteenth century was a rapid decline in the physical health of the urban working classes because of unsanitary and overcrowded living conditions, long working hours and poor diets. High population densities also facilitated the spread of infectious diseases, and there were several devastating cholera epidemics in both Europe and the u.s. during the course of the nineteenth century. Lacking understanding of the microbial causes and epidemiology of diseases such as cholera, tuberculosis, typhus and typhoid fever, doctors in Europe and America could only promulgate public health responses that were at best haphazard, usually totally ineffective and sometimes unintentionally harmful.

While humorism and the theory that disease was spread by fetid miasmic air would be completely eclipsed in the nineteenth century by advances in scientific medicine, there remained an association in the minds of the middle- and upper-class elites in Europe and North America that the physical uncleanliness of the working classes was indicative of their degraded morality. In 1854, a Church of England bishop made a direct link between hygiene and morality: 'There is a natural analogy between the ablution of the body and the purification of the soul.'[29] This was a metaphorical leap no less fantastic than the magico-religious purification rituals that I examined at the beginning of the chapter – although here the concern was moral rather than spiritual. The truth, however, was that the poor were dirty because they did not have washing facilities and could not afford to go to private bathhouses. Prompted by their own experiences of medical balneotherapy and thalasso-therapy, the great and the good decided that one way to improve both the physical health and the moral well-being of the lower orders would be to provide them with facilities to wash themselves and their clothes.

This did not mean that working-class men and boys in Europe and America never bathed or swam. I refer the reader to Jeff Wiltse's excellent survey of American swimming pools and Christopher Love's equally informative social history of English swimming for descriptions of working-class swimming cultures before the pro-vision of swimming pools. Wiltse paints a particularly vivid picture of the wild, roughhousing swimming culture of eighteenth- and nineteenth-century America, which saw naked men and boys, and very occasionally women and girls, disport themselves in urban rivers and lakes, despite repeated bans and the imposition of fines. One factor that brought an end to this subculture was not the moral outrage of the middle classes or the heavy-handed policing of the authorities, but the increased levels of domestic and industrial pollution that turned many urban waterways into open sewers. A second was the provision of swimming pools in poor urban neighbourhoods.[30]

English 'Plunge Pools'

England, where the Industrial Revolution got under way in the eighteenth century, was at the forefront of socio-economic developments during the nineteenth. The novels of Charles Dickens illuminated the squalor and despair of urban life in Victorian England, while the theories of Karl Marx and Friedrich Engels attempted to explain its economic causes and socio-political consequences. What made the plight of the poor even worse from the point of view of the modern observer is that England and her empire were booming, and the middle and upper classes were wealthier than they ever had been. Social reformers argued the case for enlightened self-interest: epidemics knew no class boundaries and gradual reform was far preferable to bloody revolution. Charitable bodies lobbied for improvements to the living conditions of the poor, and ultimately persuaded the government to enact new labour legislation and improve health and sanitation in

The Lambeth Public Baths, first built in 1854 and extensively rebuilt or remodelled in 1897, boasted first- and second-class men's pools and a women's pool as well as individual baths and laundry facilities. The municipality justified the construction of large 'plunge baths' on the grounds that they could accommodate several hundred bathers at one time, leading to great savings in terms of water usage and in a reduction in the numbers of staff needed to supervise them when compared to individual bathing facilities.

inner-city slums. One area of particular interest to both charitable bodies and the municipal authorities was the provision of baths and washhouses in working-class areas.

The first indoor pool built with the intention of improving the sanitary conditions of the poor was a private initiative in the city of Liverpool: the St George's Baths, which opened in 1824. However, the water supply was pumped straight from the Mersey, so the pool was only marginally cleaner than the river. After a slow start, a construction boom in bathing and swimming facilities followed the passage of the Baths and Washhouses Act of 1846.[31] The Act was permissive legislation that allowed (but did not oblige) municipalities to spend ratepayers' money to provide subsidized bathing and laundry facilities, but it did not include any explicit provisions for the building of swimming pools. Those municipalities, such as Liverpool and several of the London boroughs, that wanted to purchase private swimming pools or build their own, got around this limitation in the Act by describing larger pools as 'plunge baths', justifying their use on the grounds of economy. In 1854, George A. Cape, secretary of London's Lambeth Baths and Wash-house Company, supported the construction of swimming baths in the following terms:

> As a matter of profit, the use of swimming baths should be encouraged; if a number of persons use them, the expense will be much less than if the same number of persons used private baths; the quantity of water used and wasted being much less, added to which, one attendant can look after a Swimming Bath, that will accommodate three or four hundred persons at once, while ten or twelve private baths are quite as much as one attendant can see to when in constant use.[32]

The bulk of English municipal facilities were built between the 1850s and 1870s. A survey of public and private swimming places in London conducted in 1861 listed six open-air locations (including the Serpentine Lake and the Thames) and nine covered pools. By 1870, this had increased to 22 pools, varying in size from large baths to pools around the same size as today's standard 25-m (82-ft) short-course pool. The Lambeth Public Baths, which opened in 1897, boasted three pools: two for men (a first-class pool measuring 40 × 12 m / 132 × 40 ft plus a cheaper second-class bath of 27 × 9 m / 90 × 30 ft) and one for women (17 × 7.5 m / 56 × 25 ft). However, the pools were closed during the winter to save money.

The 1878 Baths and Washhouses Act aimed to correct the deficiencies of the previous Act by setting out the ability of municipalities to build or purchase their own swimming pools. It also regulated maximum closing periods, alternative uses for the buildings and entrance charges. Similar developments took place in major urban centres outside London. Manchester, which had very little public provision for swimming and bathing, established a Baths and Washhouses Committee in 1876. The committee decided that Manchester needed four municipal baths, providing both plunge pools and individual baths. After a slow start, the city would have the most publicly funded pools outside London, purchasing or building fourteen facilities comprising 33 pools between 1878 and 1913. The problem with all these facilities, however, was the cleanliness of the water. Manchester introduced filtration systems for its pools in 1908, meaning that there were 'clean' and 'dirty' water days, as the pools were only emptied and refilled once a week. Chlorination of the water supply was introduced in England in 1920, decades after the microbial causes of disease had been understood.[33]

In this early stage of public pool provision in England, which was paralleled in many other European countries, the aim was not swimming for recreation, fitness or lifesaving, but primarily medical and moral – an attempt to inculcate middle-class values into the working classes. Until 1891, schoolchildren were refused admission for the purpose of swimming lessons, as this use was seen as contrary to the purposes of the baths as laid down by Parliament. But by the end of the century, the functions of municipal baths in England had changed completely, with the provision of swimming lessons for schoolchildren of both sexes and for adults, the encouragement of recreational swimming, experiments in mixed bathing and 'entertainments' put on by professional swimmers that attracted large crowds of spectators and promoted swimming as a leisure activity.[34]

Culture Conflicts

The same concern for the cleanliness and moral welfare of the working classes were being expressed in the U.S. from the mid-nineteenth century, but the construction of municipal pools was delayed by the outbreak of the American Civil War (1861–5), and then was made more urgent by the epidemics that swept through the country's post-war cities.[35] America is well known for its late twentieth- and twenty-first century 'culture wars' but historian Jeff Wiltse has uncovered several much earlier conflicts, centred on the use of America's nineteenth- and twentieth-century swimming pools, which highlight the class, gender and racial fault lines in the U.S. as it transitioned from an industrial to a modern society. What concerns us in this chapter is the early part of the story told by Wiltse, which deals with the construction of the first municipal pools in the northern U.S.

As in England several decades earlier, industrialization triggered the rapid growth of America's northern cities between 1830 and 1860, and the influx of immigrants from Ireland and southern Europe overwhelmed the social and health infrastructures and led to the creation of inner-city slums with all their associated problems: disease, deprivation, social exclusion and criminality. During the 1840s, social reformers produced reports focusing on the unsanitary conditions in the slums and how these gave rise to immorality, adding that the danger of epidemic diseases would quickly become a threat to all citizens, even those who sought to escape inner-city squalor by moving to the new residential suburbs. The private charitable and municipal responses were similar to those in England's great industrial conurbations during the first half of the century, with the emphasis on the provision of bathing and washing facilities as the main weapons in the war against disease and immorality.

Although Wiltse describes a vibrant masculine, working-class culture of swimming in natural waters that had flourished since the late eighteenth century, this was under threat because of ever more draconian bans on nude bathing in natural urban waters and increasing levels of pollution as the country industrialized. Boston, Massachusetts, was the first American city to make provision for free public baths for all its citizens. In 1866, it opened six pools, five of which were river baths on the Charles River and one a beach bath on Dorchester Bay. The city had ruled out in-ground pools on the grounds of cost; the river baths were enclosed structures with wooden tanks submerged in the river, measuring 7.5 × 4.5 m and 1.2 m deep (25 × 15 ft and 4 ft), but without any kind of filtration system, the water in the baths would not have been cleaner than the river they were suspended in. Nevertheless, the pools were extremely popular with Bostonians of every social class because they were free, though they were open only during the summer months. There were separate sessions for men and women, and a class division between different baths, with the middle and upper classes, especially women, preferring the sea bath, because this was outside the city with no tramline connection and therefore more difficult to access by working-class swimmers. In 1868 the city went on to open the first in-ground municipal pool in the U.S., the Cabot Street Bath. The bath was far from luxurious. The austere wooden structure housed two pools of 24 × 12 m (80 × 40 ft) that could accommodate thirty to forty bathers – one for men, the other for women.[36]

The city of Philadelphia was another prolific builder of municipal baths, with a total of nine pools in 1898, including river baths but also in-ground pools in neighbourhoods that did not have easy access to the river. The six in-ground pools – very basic covered asphalt tanks measuring 21 × 12 m (70 × 40 ft) – were located in residential slums and were conceived 'to aid citizens in maintaining cleanliness free of cost'. A report published in 1898 expressed shock at the murkiness of the water and commented that the pools were used by 'the lower classes or street gamins', both black and white.[37] The pools of the 1880s and '90s were built before the germ theory of disease was generally accepted. They had no showers because the pools themselves were the 'instrument of cleaning'.[38] Thus, the pools might have been instrumental in spreading waterborne diseases rather than controlling them. But Wiltse does not report that any major epidemic was started by these slum pools, and it is likely that other measures to improve sanitation and living conditions in America's cities at the turn of the century alleviated many of the most serious health problems.

In and Out of the Swim

Over five and a half millennia, humanity elaborated a complex web of relationships between physical cleanliness, spiritual purity, moral rectitude and physical health, involving immersion of the body in water and sometimes swimming. From the most ancient times, pools large enough to swim in were built for spiritual purification rituals – sometimes by terrestrial cultures that had few other links with the aquatic environment. The connection was strengthened and broadened by the Greeks, who prescribed bathing for certain medical conditions, and adopted by the Romans, who developed a large infrastructure of *aquae* and *thermae* across their empire. Ironically, it was the *thermae* that began to disconnect people from swimming in natural bodies of water and the sea, as they preferred the comfort and safety of the heated bathhouses.

The low point in the history of swimming in the Western world came during the medieval period. The Roman *thermae* had been destroyed or fallen into disuse, and the Church had strong moral objections against public bathing and swimming – a prejudice reinforced by fears that bathing spread epidemic diseases. During much of this period, religious practices such as baptism and ritual immersion in a *mikveh* maintained a positive link with full immersion in the water. The fourteenth century saw the beginning of the revival of spa culture in Europe – a movement that gathered pace during the Renaissance as scholars and doctors rediscovered the balneotherapies of the ancient world. By the eighteenth century, the European elites were flocking to spas that offered a mix of medical treatments and social activities. In the nineteenth century, balneotherapy and thalassotherapy declined in some countries and thrived in others, but in both cases they prepared the way for two major developments in recreational swimming: the appearance of seaside resorts and the development of swimming pools whose initial functions were to provide bathing and laundry facilities for the working classes of Europe's and America's great industrial cities.

6
Bathing Beauties

The sea became a refuge and a source of hope because it
inspired fear. The new strategy for seaside holidays was to
enjoy the sea and experience the terror it inspired, while
overcoming one's personal perils. Henceforth, the sea
was expected to soothe the elite's anxieties, re-establish
harmony between body and soul, and stem the loss of
vital energy of a social class that felt particularly vulnerable
through its sons, its daughters, its wives, and its thinkers.
The sea was expected to cure the evils of urban civilization
and correct the ill-effects of easy living, while respecting the
demands of privacy.

ALAIN CORBIN, *THE LURE OF THE SEA*[1]

Swimming as a recreational pastime is a relatively recent reintroduction to Western civilization. In the light of the centuries of
fear, religious censure and civil bans, and its association with fairly
unpleasant medical practices, what made Europeans decide that
swimming was not just permissible but an activity that they could
and should actively enjoy? The factors that made mass recreational
swimming possible go far beyond the existence of suitable bodies
of water where people could swim. Individuals needed the leisure
time and resources to devote to swimming, and, of course, the
ability to swim and remain safe in the water. This entailed a considerable expenditure of time, energy and money on the part of
individual swimmers, private bodies and the state in the provision
of education, safety measures and swimming infrastructure. But,
above all, what was required was the redefinition of swimming as
a positive, pleasurable activity that went well beyond eighteenth-
century medical and military ideas.

The elite had returned to bathing, though not necessarily swimming, at spas and seaside resorts, which, while remaining the gathering places of the upper classes, gradually became more socially

inclusive. In the two novels that Jane Austen set in Bath, *Northanger Abbey* and *Persuasion* (both published in 1817), the aristocratic patrons share the city's neoclassical Pump Room with people of more modest backgrounds – a Georgian foreshadowing of the much larger Victorian social phenomenon that gave the middle and working classes the leisure and income to engage in leisure pursuits. For many of those who identified themselves as belonging to the 'middling' classes, this meant abandoning the pastimes of their forebears and imitating their 'betters', which meant going to inland spas and seaside resorts.

The Alluring Sea

One of the first beach holidays that I can remember was spent in the resort of Dénia on Spain's Costa Blanca between Alicante and Valencia when I was about seven or eight years old. I know I had been to the seaside before, because I already knew how to swim, as well as dive underwater with a mask and snorkel, but I cannot remember those earlier occasions or how hard or scary it had been to learn. We were a large and boisterous party: my mother had rented an ancient rambling flat-roofed villa on the outskirts of the resort, and her younger siblings and their respective boy- and girlfriends, plus sundry friends, had tagged along for a cheap holiday of sun, sea, sex and sangria, away from their suspicious parents, but with their no less suspicious older sister.

Despite millions of years of weathering, the dark rocks of this stretch of the Spanish coast retained their sharp fissures and steep irregularities, but fortunately someone had had the foresight to build a concrete jetty that was wide and long enough for our whole party to lie out on, and if we got there first, to exclude anyone else, who would then have to perch precariously on the surrounding rocks. A broken, rusted metal ladder, whose use would now be banned on grounds of health and safety, allowed access to the water. After everything had been set up and out to my mother's satisfaction, and after the required interval to ensure that we had digested our breakfast of *pan dulce* dipped in hot chocolate had elapsed, we were finally allowed to take our first dip, with my uncle and aunt in attendance to make sure that we hadn't forgotten how to swim during the intervening twelve months since our last summer holiday.

The rocky sea bottom was a treasure trove of marine life: black and dark purple sea urchins, rocks corrugated with wear picked out by patches of bright orange lichen, translucent, gelatinous anemones in shocking reds and yellows, which I had been warned never to touch, and tiny iridescent fish that darted erratically around me as I swam. It did not have the riot of colours and the exotic life forms of the Great Barrier Reef, which I would visit twenty years later, but it was a magical place for an adventurous small boy with a mask and snorkel and a powerful imagination that led him to believe that he might come across the ruins of some sunken Atlantean temple or the fittings of a wrecked galleon that thousands of earlier holidaymakers had somehow failed to spot a few metres from the shore.

The quintessential summer holiday image: the crowded sand beach with adults and children standing, paddling and dipping in the water. In this traditional Mediterranean beach scene at Nice, Côte d'Azur, few people are actually swimming. Nevertheless, Europeans and North Americans are drawn to the sea in a way that would have baffled and shocked the vast majority of their forebears.

One afternoon early on during the holiday, I was in the water not far from the jetty when something made me panic. Instead of calmly swimming back to the safety of the ladder, I started to flail about madly and swallow water, doing my best impression of drowning boy cast adrift on the waves. Corinne, my nineteen-year-old uncle's girlfriend – a particularly striking, sporty Amazon – dived off the jetty to rescue me. Had I been on my own, out of sight of the shore, I might have been in real trouble, but I was so close to rescue that I was never in any real danger. This was the one and only time in a lifetime of swimming in natural and artificial waters that I have ever suffered a panic attack, which is maybe why I remember the event so vividly several decades on. No one took the incident very seriously; my mother scolded me for 'showing off'; my older brother teased me relentlessly for about ten minutes, and then forgot all about it; and my uncle joked that I had done it to attract his girlfriend's attention; but even after many years, I can recall something of the trauma of believing even for a few seconds that I was going to drown. I suppose that even in the most accomplished and confident open-water swimmer, there must remain, however deeply buried in his or her subconscious, a primeval fear of being swallowed up by the deep, dark abyssal waters through which they take so much delight in swimming.

My experience in Dénia was a salutary lesson to an overconfident child. Before it I had never felt the primal terror that my distant and more recent ancestors must have felt when venturing into the sea for the first time. I, like them, had good reason to be afraid or even terrified. While the Mediterranean is a relatively tame sea, there are still dangerous currents that can sweep the unwary away from land or pull him under, stinging jellyfish and hidden conger eels; even shark attacks are not unknown, though fortunately extremely rare. Yet counterbalancing the terror were several types of pleasure: first, the pleasure in overcoming one's own fear, although now chastened by my scare; but quickly taking over from this minor victory over the self was the physical pleasure of being in the water – swapping the overheated, sweaty, dusty Spanish air for the sudden coolness of the water. This was quickly followed by the experience, as the father of Utilitarianism Jeremy Bentham (1748–1832) expressed it, of:

> The pleasure of health, or, the internal pleasurable feel-
> ing or flow of spirits which accompanies a state of full
> health and vigour; especially at times of moderate
> bodily exertion.[2]

And this in turn became the gateway for different forms of pleasure: physical, aesthetic and imaginative, so that the act of swimming became its own reward, transforming an activity that was once unpleasant because it was so scary into a sensual pleasure that I longed for all year long, and later went to seek out at every possible opportunity. While our ancestors went into the water through necessity and later for medicinal reasons, mass participation in swimming was ensured by the conversion of fear into enjoyment that I experienced that day in Spain.

My attitude is in stark contrast with that of my eighteenth- and nineteenth-century forebears, who, as tenant farmers, market gardeners and shopkeepers, had few leisure opportunities, and with that of the vast majority of Europeans who lived before the eighteenth century. The last things they were likely to think of doing when they had a precious day off was to go to the seaside, let alone into the sea, unless they were forced to do so by some extremity, but during the intervening centuries, Western attitudes to the sea and coastline have been completely transformed, turning the beach into the twenty-first century's premier holiday destination – a preference that has now been exported to millions of consumers from the world's emerging economies.

But why is this the case? Quite apart from the expense, bother and, in recent years, the danger of travelling to overseas resorts during high season from overcrowded airports, we pale-skinned children of northern climes have to smear ourselves with factor 30–50 sunscreen lest we burn, exposing ourselves to skin cancer and premature ageing; many of us are far from confident in the water, a fact confirmed by the lamentably high number of deaths by drowning every summer – natural waters being considerably more treacherous than swimming pools, even for able swimmers. One could argue that seaside holidays have much more to offer than lying on the beach and cooling sea dips, in terms of social activities, diversions and sports; this is true, but the quintessential image of the summer vacation remains that of a crowded beach with children and adults dipping, paddling and splashing about in the surf.

Overcoming the Terrors of the Deep

In *The Lure of the Sea*, French historian Alain Corbin develops a complex, multi-layered thesis to explain when and how the seaside became the world's favourite summer holiday destination. He begins by reviewing the 'horror' and 'revulsion' that the sea and coastline inspired prior to the seventeenth century. Although I have explored the same territory and agree that, at certain points in human history and in certain locations, the sea did become an unknown, alien, monster-filled 'otherworld', this was by no means a universal view. Earlier, I argued that the mermaid myth might be taken as evidence of the survival of the close and positive ties humanity had established with the sea and swimming during prehistory and antiquity. And though during the medieval and early modern periods the sea was viewed with fear, Corbin may be exaggerating humanity's alienation from all things aquatic and marine, the better to make his case for the seventeenth- and eighteenth-century reversal in attitudes that he sees as markers for the beginnings of modernity.[3]

Having established that Europeans were not only terrified but also repulsed by the sea and coastline, Corbin reconstructs the process through which these negative attitudes were transmuted into something more positive. The very horror that the sea inspired became a source of catharsis that was able to 'cure the evils of urban civilization and correct the ill-effects of easy living'. He goes on to link the emergence of a new aesthetic of the sublime in the work of poets and artists with the doctrines of natural theology that sought to prove the existence of God through the scientific observation and classification of the natural world. Rather than something to be shut out and feared, nature became something to be studied and catalogued and, gradually, to be observed at first hand – a movement that would reach its zenith in the work of Karl Linnaeus, the eighteenth-century creator of binomial nomenclature and the father of modern taxonomy. Corbin cites two coastline districts at opposite ends of Europe where this took place: the small fishing village of Scheveningen in the Netherlands and the Bay of Naples in Italy.[4]

In the seventeenth century, the Low Countries (now the Netherlands) existed in spite of the sea and thrived because of it. With much of their country at or below sea level, the Dutch developed sophisticated water-management technologies to preserve and reclaim land, while their geographic position and expertise in ship-building gave them natural advantages in international long-distance trade. A great deal of early Dutch painting takes as its theme ships at sea and naval engagements, but during the Golden Age of Dutch painting in the mid-1600s, the subject was no longer confined to what Corbin terms the 'struggle of man and the elemental sea' but was extended to depictions of the peaceful seashore.[5] He cites the work of artists such as the seventeenth-century painter Jan van Goyen, whose pictorial exaltation of the coastline encouraged visitors to flock to the seaside to see it for themselves. In 1663, a paved road was built between The Hague and the then fishing village of Scheveningen so that

> For the growing number of visitors to Scheveningen, the proto-sublime experience of looking at the infinite sea went hand-in-hand with enjoying the picturesque qualities of the village's fishing activities.

Scheveningen would later become the country's leading seaside resort, with hotels and bathing establishments that attracted visitors from all over northern Europe, by 1904 completely eclipsing its role as a seaport and fishing village.[6]

For most historians, the roots of the contemporary mass travel and tourist industries are to be found in the Grand Tour of the

The Beach near Scheveningen (1648) by Jan van Goyen embodies the new aesthetic of the sea and coastline that began to emerge in the seventeenth century. The scene shows local fishermen and visitors on the beach at the small fishing village of Scheveningen, near The Hague. Although without amenities of any kind in the seventeenth century, the village was a favourite destination of the citizens of The Hague, who came to marvel at sublime vistas of the vast elemental sea and, at the same time, to enjoy the picturesque sights of a small fishing community.

late seventeenth and eighteenth centuries, when young English gentlemen visited Europe in search of the classical culture that had formed the basis of their school and university educations. The seas they crossed and coasts they passed by held little attraction until they reached the end of the typical itinerary at the Bay of Naples. Their admiration for this scenic gem was based on the appreciation of the area during classical times, when Baiae was the resort capital of Roman Italy. As with Scheveningen, the appreciation of the Neapolitan coastline was mediated by literary and artistic references.[7]

With the exception of young bloods, such as Lord Byron (1788–1824), who was a keen swimmer, it is unlikely that any of the burghers of The Hague who went to Scheveningen or many of the English gentlemen who marvelled at the view in Naples ever went into the sea to swim, partly because it was still associated with fairly unpleasant medical practices but mainly because they had never learned to swim. But the coast had become a place to be visited, experienced and appreciated – an appreciation that would grow and develop as neoclassicism gave way to Romanticism, when the natural world was seen as the mirror of the sublime and tortured soul of the poet and artist. To quote the title of historian of tourism John Urry, Westerners, though searching for the sublime, the elemental, the picturesque and the classical, discovered a much more prosaic 'tourist gaze', which spawned a million picture postcards and now countless billions of selfies.

Braving the Waves and the Dippers

The English elite began to swim for medical reasons, and the experience does not seem to have been a very pleasant one. Sea dips were often taken during the colder months of the year (which admittedly are not that different from the hotter months in England), and did not involve much swimming, because the aim was sea bathing and drinking salt water to cure a range of physical and mental ailments rather than recreation. While gentlemen (though not their male servants) continued to bathe naked until the late nineteenth century, women had to protect their modesty by ever more cumbersome means. The light materials of the day would become instantly transparent and figure-hugging when wet, so women wore voluminous garments made of coarser, dark-coloured materials that also made it impossible for them to swim. In order to change and enter the water unobserved, women used bathing machines, which first appeared in Scarborough in 1735 and were improved with the addition of a 'modesty hood', first seen in Margate a few years later.

The bathing machine was a small, horse-drawn, gabled-roofed hut on wheels with a door and steps at each end that was towed a little way into the sea. The inside of the machine would have been cramped, and increasingly smelly and sandy as the day wore on,

For Bathing in the SEA at Margate in the Isle of Thanet KENT.

The bathing machine – a horse-drawn hut on wheels – solved the problem of where eighteenth-century ladies could change out of their voluminous garments and enter the water, either naked or in their shifts, without being observed. The machine was taken a little way out to sea, and the swimmer, alone or assisted by a 'dipper', would descend the steps into the water out of sight of the shore. The addition of a modesty hood, first seen in Margate, ensured even greater privacy.

and would have been a space difficult to change in for women who wore full skirts and corsets and who were used to being dressed and undressed by maids. Once she had changed into appropriate swimwear, the bather would be led down into the water by a 'dipper', a female attendant and guide whom the landscape painter John Constable called 'hideous amphibious animals'.[8] They earned their name and fearsome reputation because they forcibly 'dipped' their reluctant charges into the sea. The tyranny of the dipper endured until the 1860s, but the profession had vanished by 1870, when bathing and swimming had been transformed from a trial to be endured for one's health to a pleasure in which to indulge.[9]

During the age of mass transit, which began with the development of the railways in the 1840s in England and quickly spread across the world, major cities, such as London, Manchester, Paris, New York and Los Angeles, were linked to coastal towns and resorts, some already well established such as Brighton in England, and some created from scratch such as Venice in California, founded as a resort in 1905. Labour reforms in the UK and U.S. granted many blue- and white-collar workers paid holidays for the first time, combined with a growing interest in sports and physical culture promoted in the UK by the German-born Eugen Sandow (1867–1925) and in the U.S. by Bernarr MacFadden (1868–1955) and by organizations such as the YMCA, whose brand of 'Muscular Christianity' equated fitness with godliness, created a demand for a new type of fitness and leisure infrastructure. Linked to major urban centres by the railways, coastal resorts were ideally placed to cater for that demand, and they attracted developers and entrepreneurs much as inland spas had done a century earlier.

'Venus's Bathing', *c.* 1800, one of several cartoons by Thomas Rowlandson that capture both the popularity and salaciousness of sea swimming at the beginning of the nineteenth century. Set in the resort of Margate, Kent, the print depicts a fashionable lady taking a sea dip in the nude. Although she uses a bathing machine fitted with a modesty hood, she can be seen by a crowd of onlookers on the cliff and beach, hence her headlong tumble from the steps of the bathing machine to escape prying eyes.

To escape the crowds of middle- and working-class holiday-makers and day-trippers that now thronged their former preserves, the English upper classes travelled to Continental resorts, starting fairly close at hand in Dieppe on the French Channel coast, which had already been made popular by the patronage of Princess Caroline in the earlier part of the nineteenth century. But after the French railways had caught up with the English, the influx of French tourists and day-trippers made them seek out further, less frequented resorts on the French and Italian Mediterranean coasts. However, it seems inevitable that where the rich and powerful lead, the crowds are sure to follow, so to retain their exclusivity, they had to go farther and farther afield, or retire behind the walls of private estates.

The Mediterranean was the world's first mass tourism destination and remains its most popular, witnessing an annual population shift from the colder, richer industrial north to the warmer, poorer agricultural south. In 2009, it accounted for £87 billion / $134 billion, almost one-third of the world's total tourism expenditure. Of course, this covers the whole Mediterranean basin, which now includes the Balkans, Turkey, the Middle East and North Africa alongside more established destinations such as Spain, Portugal, Italy and France. In North America, there are home-grown destinations such as the beach cities of southern California and Florida and resorts in Central America and the Caribbean. Undoubtedly, people do swim for pleasure at beachside resorts, but in my experience, for many, 'swimming' during a beach holiday is limited to cooling dips between sunbathing sessions or horsing around in the water with your friends or siblings.

Westerners reconnected with the sea in ever-growing numbers, but the existence and development of resorts was not synonymous with an increase in the number of people who engaged in recreational swimming in the sea. Photographs of pre-First World War resorts show crowded summer beaches, but visitors are covered head to toe in floor-length skirts for the ladies and suits for the men. For the vast majority, going to the seaside involved sitting on the beach fully clothed, and going into the sea meant literally a 'dip', as their swimwear, particularly the bulky, heavy women's swimsuits of the day, would have made it impossible to do anything more than wallow in the shallows. Late Victorian and Edwardian men were much more fortunate; they were allowed to get away with a one-piece garment that at least left the arms and lower legs uncovered. Although the fabric would have become waterlogged and heavy once wet, it allowed movement in the water. It is unclear how many men actually did do anything more than dip, because during this period, professional swimmers performing aquatic feats that would now appear commonplace were lauded as superhuman athletes and drew large admiring crowds to swimming 'entertainments'.

Beachwear to Swimwear

When I was doing the research for this chapter, I came across an entry in the British Library's online catalogue for a magazine article entitled 'Bathing Beauties: The Amazing History of Female Swimwear', published in 1976.[10] Having gone through the online ordering process, I was informed that I would need to consult the article in the BL's Rare Books and Music Reading Room. As the article in question had been published in 1976 and was neither 'ancient' nor 'rare', this meant that when it was acquired by the library, its contents were considered so risqué that they might corrupt the morals of even the high-minded researchers who used the BL reading rooms, so that it had to be read at special desks under the constant supervision of a librarian.

I also assumed correctly that the classification had not been reviewed since 1976, and it turned out that the article's only offence against public decency were two or three shots of topless models that would not elicit any comment if they appeared in a contemporary women's magazine or the pages of a British tabloid. The text was a measured, thoughtful and well-researched survey of the topic. Its antiquated BL classification illuminated the evolution in the public depiction of the naked human form in the media in the past four decades, as much as the seismic changes in what was considered appropriate beachwear for women in the past 200 years.

Beach fashions in the United States, *c.* 1870. Ladies wore bathing dresses over stockings, with slippers and a bathing hat or cap. The choice of materials that would not mould themselves to the figure or become transparent when wet probably made swimming impracticable even for strong female swimmers. Men, who had been allowed to swim naked for most of the century, were now expected to wear their underwear or a costume that covered the torso and thighs but left their arms and lower legs uncovered, giving them greater freedom in the water.

Looking at the illustration overleaf we can see how much women were expected to wear both on the beach and when going into the sea – outfits that made it impossible to swim any distance, if at all. Therefore, the evolution of swimwear is not just the story of evolving moral standards regarding what was considered appropriate in public, but also a measure of how much physical activity women were able and expected to take part in.

The first female swimwear, though in this case 'bathwear' might be a more suitable description, was the clothing worn by patrons of the English spa town of Bath. Celia Fiennes, a late seventeenth-century visitor, wrote:

> The ladyes go into the bath with garments made from fine yellow canvas, with great sleeves like a parson's gown, the water fills it up . . . so that your shape is not seen and it does not cling as close as other lining.

Tobias Smollett, writing a century later, described: 'The ladies wear jackets and petticoats of brown linen with chip hats, in which they fix their handkerchiefs.'[11] With the growing popularity of seaside resorts in eighteenth-century England and France, women, like men, swam naked at single-sex beaches or wore long, smock-like garments for dips in the sea. During the Victorian period this was no longer considered sufficiently modest, and women's bathing attire meant full coverage, with a full skirt over trousers, tights, slippers and a bonnet. In 1886, a British advertisement for the Zouvare Marine Swimming Costume boasted: 'A body and trousers cut in one which secures perfect liberty of action and does not expose the figure'.[12] In stark contrast, men in the UK continued to be allowed to bathe naked until the 1860s, when they were required to wear their underwear or a swimming costume that covered the torso, but left the limbs free.

Change came very slowly. By 1900, mixed bathing was becoming acceptable, but an English fashion magazine still recommended: 'Bathing gowns in red and navy serge, a short skirt reaching to the knee, some with knickers and very short skirts to the knee, others as combination garments'. Women were at least allowed to show their knees and ankles without outraging public morality. Conservative attitudes continued to prevail, even in the U.S. In 1907, Australian champion swimmer and diver Annette Kellerman (1887–1975), who would go on to star in Hollywood movies, was arrested for indecency when she wore her trademark one-piece diving suit on the public beach in Revere, Massachusetts. Although the suit covered her completely, it did show her rather curvaceous figure.[13] Her arrest was actually a well-planned and -executed publicity stunt, designed to promote her swimming and diving act at a local amusement park. She later used her fame to launch Annette Kellerman swimwear modelled on her own daring one-piece costume.

The revolution in female swimwear gathered pace during the interwar years, when it was part of a much wider movement of female emancipation that saw women get the vote in many Western democracies and go to work in growing numbers as the result of the labour shortages caused by the two world wars. New, more comfortable, lighter materials, such as satin and taffeta, were introduced, in brighter colours, while at the same time, the area of flesh covered shrank. In the 1930s, legs and backs were bared, and for the more daring, the midriff but not the navel, whose exposure seemed to have been as shocking as going topless. Jeff Wiltse comments that as swimwear became more revealing during the interwar years, the swimming pool and, by extension, the beach became eroticized public spaces where men and women could display their bodies and observe those of others without censure. He highlights the shrinking bathing suit as one of the causes of the pervasive culture of 'female nakedness and overt sexuality' that now reigns supreme in America and the rest of the developed world.[14]

As has often been the case, it was war that speeded up the process of social transformation in the area of suitable female dress, partly through necessity and partly because of a relaxation of codes of propriety during a national emergency. During the Second World War women finally felt empowered enough to 'wear the trousers', as they were doing jobs usually reserved for men in factories, the armed forces and on the land, but it was the cloth shortage in post-war France that was the pretext used to achieve the full relaxation of beachwear rules, at least in European resorts. In 1946, two designers – Jacques Heim (1899–1967) and Louis Réard (1897–1984) – competed to produce the smallest female bathing suit. What emerged was the 'bikini', named after the Pacific atoll where a nuclear test had just been held, because the new swimsuit, its manufacturer assured the public, would be just as 'devastating' as the A-bomb. The two-piece swimsuit, modelled by an exotic dancer because no professional fashion model would wear the garment in public, was first exhibited in 1946 at an outdoor swimming pool in Paris and was the first garment designed to show a woman's navel in public. The final technical development that has given us the contemporary swimsuit for both sexes was the invention of Lycra (also known as Spandex) in 1958 – a synthetic fibre that moulds to the contours of the body and that does not bag or go transparent when wet, making it ideal for swimwear and other sporting applications.

Australian swimmer and diver Annette Kellerman wearing the one-piece
bathing suit that led to her arrest and trial for indecency on an American
beach in 1907. Kellerman's outfit was considered shocking, not just because
it showed her arms and had a scoop neck, but because it revealed her figure.
Indicted but victorious, Kellerman went on to launch a range of swimwear
that transformed women's beach attire in Europe and the u.s.

For men, the journey was a much shorter one, as they had never been expected to cover up as much as women, and they quickly adopted the swimming-trunk style that has continued to become progressively skimpier until we now see such offences against fashion sense and good taste as the 'tanga' and the 'mankini'. In male swimwear, however, we also see a paradoxical 'covering up' in certain countries, where men and boys have abandoned trunks and briefs in favour of more modest jammers and board shorts. In my study of the gym, where a similar trend for more modest clothing is also apparent, I suggested that some heterosexual men are choosing styles of dress that provide much greater coverage of the body to differentiate themselves from increasingly out and proud gay men.[15]

Women and men visiting the seaside are now unencumbered and free to swim if they wish to, but it does not mean that they swim a great deal more than their Georgian and Victorian forebears. Contemporary swimwear has more to say about a relaxation of dress codes and the objectification of the human body and its sexualization in public than about any great turn to aquatic athleticism.

Wild at Heart

No survey of swimming in natural waters would be complete without a mention of wild and open-water swimming. The current popularity of the pastime, as evidenced by the success of works on the subject by British enthusiasts Kate Rew (b. 1970) and Roger Deakin (1943–2006), provides yet more evidence that a large constituency of swimmers in the developed world are turning their backs on supervised beaches and swimming pools to reconnect with the pleasures of unsupervised swimming in lakes, rivers, estuaries, seas and oceans.[16]

Wild swimming is subsumed within the broader category of 'open-water swimming', but since the inclusion of open-water swimming events in the World Aquatics Championships in 1991 and in the Summer Olympics in 2008, the umbrella term is more closely associated with the competitive and endurance aspects of

Wild swimming combines a rediscovery of the natural world at its most picturesque with a personal journey that rejects the repackaging of the aquatic environment as another sanitized product to be consumed.

swimming in natural waters. In contrast, wild swimming, as the choice of qualifying adjective suggests, refers to a non-competitive, unsupervised pastime dedicated to the pleasure of swimming in scenic spots – the aquatic equivalent of hiking in the countryside and mountain trekking – a form of the 'tourist gaze' applied to the aquatic environment.

Reading Roger Deakin's *Waterlog*, one immediately understands that for the wild swimmer, there is much more to the activity than a pleasant summer's day out or a way to keep fit. He writes:

> The more I thought about it, the more obsessed I became with the idea of a swimming journey. I started to dream ever more exclusively of water. Swimming and dreaming were becoming indistinguishable. I grew convinced that following water, flowing with it, would be a way of getting under the skin of things, of learning something new.[17]

His aquatic journey across the British Isles is as much a spiritual quest for himself and the real Britain as a physical journey to the country's prime wild swimming sites. He decries the way our experience of the world is being transformed into a virtual activity, not just because of the omnipresent Internet, but because of the official interpretation of the landscape and the landmarks within it through signposts, visitor centres and explanatory panels. He explains:

> It is the reason why walking, cycling and swimming will always be subversive activities. They allow us to regain a sense of what is old and wild in these islands, by getting off the beaten track and breaking free of the official version of things.[18]

The Noble Swimmer

Prior to the construction of artificial pools, all swimming was done in natural waters and was by definition wild or open-water swimming. In earlier chapters, I covered functional swimming for a variety of uses, including warfare, religious ritual, lifesaving and the exploitation of aquatic resources, and though pleasure might also have been involved, it would have been incidental to the main purpose of the activity. In certain cultures, however, functional and recreational swimming coexisted harmoniously. In his history of Polynesia, Douglas Oliver describes cultures where 'Children spent much time in the water – swimming, diving and playing tag – which culminated in their superlative aquatic skills.'[19]

European explorers such as Captain James Cook reached the Polynesian islands in the eighteenth century. Cook and his crew's reaction at seeing the inhabitants' aquatic skills in swimming and surfing was typical of other contemporary European visitors. According to Oliver:

> Many early accounts by Westerners expressed wonderment at Polynesians' – male and female, young and old

– capabilities, and endurance in swimming. Children acquired those abilities at a very early age, and in some societies spent much of their days in the water.[20]

This sense of wonder is evidence of how much Westerners had become alienated from basic human skills and the natural environment in their pursuit of a particular model of civilization.

Non-Western swimming practices made a significant contribution to swimming in Europe, not by providing models for the return to the water, but in the introduction of the sidestroke and front crawl. In 1844, two Native Americans of the Ojibwe Nation, Flying Gull (Wenish-ka-wen-bee) and Tobacco (Sah-ma), demonstrated an overarm stroke with an alternating flutter kick at a swimming exhibition in London. Although they easily outpaced British swimmers who used the breaststroke, the Native American stroke was considered 'ungentlemanly' and 'un-European'. Although it was not adopted, it did prompt the British to develop the faster sidestroke variant of the breaststroke.[21]

Three decades later, John Trudgen (1852–1902), who had learned an overarm stroke during a trip to Argentina, premiered what became known as the 'Trudgen stroke' at a local competition in 1875. The stroke employed the arm motion and side-to-side roll of the front crawl but favoured a scissor or breaststroke kick over the more streamlined alternating flutter kick that would become the standard leg kick for the front crawl in the twentieth century.[22]

The Ultimate Wild Swim

There is something in the Anglo-Saxon temperament that dictates that, as soon as a new pastime, sport or leisure activity is popularized, someone instantly turns it into an endurance test and tries to establish a record for the greatest distance travelled, the most people involved or the most mind-numbing number of repetitions performed. For example, as soon as the safety bicycle had been invented, enthusiasts were cycling the lengths and breadths of every country and continent, and in the case of Annie Kopchovsky, better known as Annie Londonderry, cycling around the world in 1895, a mere ten years after the first safety bicycle had left the workshop.

Often, as we shall see in Chapter Nine, in competitive swimming there was a financial motive in the form of a wager or prize money for these tests of swimming speed or endurance, but in other cases, the reason could be best explained by the old explorer's cliché of 'because it was there', and was probably more a test of the self than of the particular medium chosen. In this spirit, today thousands worldwide engage in a Christmas Day or New Year's Day swim, sometimes having to break the ice on their chosen stretch of water, though that is less likely in these days of global warming. The oldest of these is the Christmas Day swim organized by the Brighton Swimming Club, which attracted 450 swimmers and 4,000 spectators in 2004.[23]

The world's oldest endurance sea swim, which is also an English institution, is the Channel swim, which was first successfully completed by Captain Matthew Webb (1848–1883), who swam from England to France in 1875 in 21 hours, 45 minutes, battling exhaustion, jellyfish stings and unfavourable tides. Since Webb, another 811 swimmers have succeeded in this solo, unaided crossing, but the swim is no leisurely paddle in warm, subtropical waters. Even in the summer the water temperature in the Channel teeters in the teens Celsius (60s Fahrenheit), added to which there are the joys of starting the swim in the dark to catch the tides, the jellyfish, raw sewage and oil slicks, changeable weather and the host of tankers, ferries and pleasure craft that habitually crisscross the narrow stretch of water that separates England from continental Europe.[24]

The Born-again Swimmer

I have described the lengthy and convoluted process through which swimming in the sea and other natural waters became a mass-participation recreational activity in the twentieth century. The return to the sea had to overcome centuries of religious prejudice and civil bans, as well as the fear and revulsion inspired by the sea and coastline among those who were not familiar with it through their occupations or by virtue of their proximity to it. Although the medical uses of swimming created an infrastructure of seaside resorts, the association of thalassotherapy and swimming was not conducive to its perception as an enjoyable pastime. Hence, swimming had to be reinterpreted, initially through the arts and literature, which formed the basis for a new way of seeing the world: the tourist gaze.

In the seventeenth century, the seaside became a tourist destination, and by the eighteenth, the hardiest were experimenting with recreational dips. A century on, the day-trip to the seaside had become an institution, which in the twentieth century would develop into the mass-market package holiday. With the growing popularity of open water and wild swimming in the twenty-first century, we have come full circle to a more innocent, albeit dangerous, age of unsupervised swimming in the sea and other natural waters.

In the twenty-first century, we all have access to the seaside, at home and abroad. Our physical delight in the act of swimming, reinforced by its associations with summer holidays, plays a significant role in the contemporary popularity of swimming. But the association goes much deeper. At some point in our lives, before we can allow ourselves the pleasure of pushing off from the jetty or the beach's gentle sandy slope, we have to experience something akin to a religious conversion – a baptism both physical and psychological – first to overcome the terrors of the abyssal unknown, the improbable great white shark or the impossible Jurassic reptile, and second to curb the overconfidence that has taken the lives of many reckless swimmers. Most of us learn the mechanics of swimming in the comfort and safety of an indoor swimming pool, but it is only when we strike out, out of our depth in the sea, that we discover whether we have it in us to be swimmers.

7
Temples of Neptune

Trees enough remain to shade the visitor from the heat of
the sun on the brink. On a summer evening it is amusing
to survey the conduct of the bathers; some boldly dive,
others timorous stand and then descend step by step,
unwilling and slow; choice swimmers attract attention
by divings and somersets, and the whole sheet of water
sometimes rings with merriment.

WILLIAM HONE, DESCRIBING THE PEERLESS POOL, LONDON,
1826[1]

Swimming in the sea and natural waters provides only half the
story of recreational swimming. Access to natural waters is
limited to the warmer months of the year, and often they are located
far away from the major inland centres of population. As a consequence, until the eighteenth century, year-round swimming was
practicable only for those who lived next to a suitable body of water
in an area with a warm climate, or who had the leisure time and
financial resources to travel to one. But in order for swimming to
become a year-round mass-participation activity, water would have
to be brought to the swimmer, as had been done during the Roman
period through the provision, at vast expense on the part of the
state, of large subsidized bathhouses in the major cities of the
empire.

The swimming pools that formed part of the Roman infrastructure of *aquae* and *thermae* that had long fallen into disuse in Western
Europe were recreated in sixteenth- and seventeenth-century spas,
preparing the ground for the appearance of the first purpose-built
recreational swimming pools in Europe in the eighteenth century.
In the nineteenth century, a new programme of pool building in the
great industrial cities of Europe and North America was intended
to teach the urban poor the Victorian virtues of physical cleanliness

and moral probity, but from the very beginning, urban waters were also used for recreation. A parallel culture of far more luxurious private pools in private athletics clubs always included a recreational element, though this was a highly structured one subsumed within the sporting and health and fitness ethos of these institutions.

Once little more than a muddy hole in the ground or a tank suspended in a river, filled with water of dubious cleanliness, the recreational pool has evolved in two directions: the small, private domestic backyard pool and the giant 'aquapark', featuring pools for lane swimming, shallow pools for infants, and artificial lagoons with water slides, waterfalls and wave machines. Of course, in much contemporary practice, especially swimming that takes place in in-ground pools, there is a blurring between swimming for recreation and swimming for health and fitness. However, for the purposes of this book I have established an artificial division between them: having covered the medical aspects of bathing in the previous chapter and competition in Chapter Nine, this chapter will examine pool swimming purely from the perspective of recreation.

Classical Waters

Among the ancient Greeks, swimming was considered a necessary accomplishment for all educated men, and it was said that a dull-ard was a man who could neither read nor swim. Depictions of swimming or diving, however, are extremely rare in Graeco-Roman art, especially when compared to the many examples of painted ceramics depicting terrestrial athletics and sports, and the many statues of land-based athletes. Unlike running, discus, long jump and wrestling, swimming and diving, while no doubt commonplace skills and leisure pursuits in ancient Greece, were not competitive sports; thus, there was no reason to depict or glorify them in public or domestic art. A rare exception is to be found in a tomb in the Greek colony of Paestum in southern Italy. In the fifth-century BCE Tomb of the Diver, a mural shows a naked young man diving from a high platform into what is probably a natural body of water but could also be a manmade pool. The scene is not a military one,

Mural from the Tomb of the Diver, *c.* 470 BCE, in the Greek colony of Paestum, southern Italy. The scene has no military or commercial connotations and shows a young man caught in the act of diving into a lake, river or manmade pool from a high diving platform.

like those of the Assyrian palace bas-reliefs of swimming soldiers, and though it may be symbolic of the deceased's entry into the Underworld, it also represents a real leisure activity of the period. The high diving platform, with its ladder-shaped struts, is clearly constructed, and not just some handy rocky outcrop, and though a swimming teacher would fault the position of his head, the diver is otherwise shown in a proper diving attitude.

Four centuries later, we have a reference in the works of Roman historian Cassius Dio (155–235 CE) to the wealthy patron of the arts and adviser to Emperor Augustus, Maecenas (68–8 BCE), whom he claims was the first to build a heated swimming pool in Rome.[2] This covered, in-ground pool, no doubt intended for Maecenas' private use, was followed by many heated public pools in the empire's luxurious *thermae*, but these large, shallow basins were designed for bathing and socializing rather than for swimming. The super-rich, such as Julius Caesar and many later emperors, built swimming pools for their own use; until swimming became a skill practised solely by the elite. With the end of Roman bathing culture in

Western Europe, it took another 1,000 years before the first new in-ground pools were built, for medical purposes, often at the site of ancient Roman spa resorts.

Post-classical Waters

It would be difficult to state categorically when and where the first purpose-built in-ground outdoor recreational pool was built in the early modern period, but in England, this distinction probably goes to the Fellows' Pool, Emmanuel College, Cambridge, which was first used around 1690 and remains in use by the fellows and students of the college.[3] The first reference I could find to an indoor pool in England dates back to Restoration London (1660s), when they were a feature of *bagnios*, an English take on the Turkish bath, or hammam, some of which had plunge pools. An advertisement for the Leman Street Bagnio in Whitechapel, London, for example, boasted of a swimming pool 13 m (43 ft) long. Although they survived into the nineteenth century, *bagnios* doubled as brothels, so doing forty lengths in the pool was definitely not high on the list of their patrons' priorities, nor would they become the basis for an infrastructure of urban indoor pools.[4] Nevertheless, the presence of pools in London's *bagnios* provides an early link with the physical sensuality and bodily pleasure that countered and completely overcame swimming's associations with lifesaving, military training, hygiene and medical practices.

Customizing Nature

In his illuminating study of the swimming pool as cultural space, *The Springboard in the Pond*, architectural historian Thomas van Leeuwen traces the history of contemporary swimming pool design back to the Renaissance. In discussing the rectangular shape of most pools, he points to their origins in eighteenth-century Europe, when they were built as military training facilities. They were the aquatic equivalent of the barrack square – all right angles and straight lines – for the aquatic equivalent of marching drills. This model would be adopted for pools intended for non-military health and fitness training and, by extension, for competition pools, which had to have standardized dimensions like the pitches, grounds and courses of other competitive sports. In this respect the pool's function determines its form, which in turn defines the type of swimming that can be practised there.

The origins of another quite separate tradition of recreational pool design can be traced back to the grotto, a decorative garden feature first built in Roman times as places to escape the summer heat and, when they included a water feature, to swim. They were revived during the Renaissance and have since remained an integral part of garden design. Early grottoes were fantastical recreations of the natural world – artificial caverns studded with rocks and stalagmites and populated with statues of nymphs and fauns peeking out of the shrubbery or caught in the act of undressing in preparation for a swim. But rather than being slavish imitations of nature, they were designed 'to improve on the savage state and so establish a customized *belle nature*'. The fantasy found in grotto architecture reappears in contemporary pool design; van Leeuwen cites the examples of aquaparks, with their artificial waterfalls, water chutes, meandering rivers and wave machines.[5] Even the highly functional competition pools of the Aquatic Centre for the 2012 London Olympics are sheltered under architect Zaha Hadid's extraordinary undulating roof – a solidified wave or sand dune – whose stark modernity nevertheless harks back to the Baroque grotto.[6]

Peerless Pools

The first purpose-built outdoor in-ground pool in London was the Peerless Pool, in Baldwin Street, off the City Road, London, just north of London's financial district. But rather than just a single swimming pool, the Peerless was the capital's first multi-use urban resort, equipped with a large outdoor swimming pool, the Pleasure Bath, measuring 52 × 33 × 1.4 m (170 × 108 × 4.6 ft), accessed by stone steps and with a fine gravel bottom; a smaller indoor pool (11 × 5.5 m / 36 × 18 ft); a large pond, used for fishing and sailing model boats and skating when it froze over in winter; a bowling green; and a changing area and library housed in a neoclassical marble vestibule. The Peerless Pool was part natural and part manmade, as it was dug on the site of a spring whose overflow had created a pond known as the Perilous Pond because it had taken the lives of several unwary swimmers. Rather than a municipal enterprise, the complex was a philanthropic project funded by jeweller William Kemp, who had been cured of a 'violent pain in the head' by a dip in the waters of the pond.

Screened and shaded by trees, the pool opened in 1743 and continued in operation until the area was redeveloped in 1850. A one-year subscription cost one guinea (one pound and one shilling), with an additional charge of nine shillings for access to the indoor pool or alternatively a one-shilling charge per single swim. Converted into modern-day prices, this would be equivalent to the cost of a membership or the daily admission charge of the city's more expensive athletics clubs and swimming pools, so clearly the pool was used exclusively by the wealthier citizens of the city.[7] The fishing pond was filled in to make way for Baldwin Street in 1805, but William Hone's description, written in 1826 and quoted in part at the head of this chapter, shows that the pool had lost none of its attractions, especially for the pupils of the nearby Bluecoat School:

> Every fine Thursday and Saturday afternoon in the summer columns of Bluecoat boys, more than a score in each, headed by their respective beadles, arrive and some half strip themselves ere they reach their destination. The rapid plunges they make into the Pool and their hilarity in the bath testify their enjoyment of the tepid fluid.[8]

There were similar private facilities outside London in Bristol, Birmingham and Liverpool. The largest outside London was the Ladywell Baths, Birmingham, which had individual baths, a *mikveh* (ritual bath) for local Jewish women and an outdoor swimming pool measuring 33.5 × 16 m (110 × 52 ft). In 1831, the charge for a single swim was sixpence (equivalent to approximately £2.50 in 2016).[9] The existence of these pools is evidence of a culture of recreational swimming in mid-eighteenth-century England, alongside therapeutic bathing at spas and seaside resorts and swimming for military training and lifesaving. Prior to the opening of the Peerless Pool, Londoners wishing to cool off in the summer could swim in the Thames – a dangerous proposition because of currents, boat traffic and increasing levels of pollution – and in various natural or man-made lakes and ponds in and around the capital that again had safety and health issues and lacked any amenities. The longevity of these pools underlines that such facilities were clearly popular with city-dwellers until the mid-nineteenth century, when they were made redundant by the opening of new private and public heated indoor swimming pools.

Floating Palaces

Paris' Bains Deligny were originally conceived as a swimming school for the military, but quickly developed into one of the French capital's leading attractions and the summer meeting place of the rich, powerful and famous. Suspended in the waters of the Seine, but anchored to the river bottom by piles rather than moored to a quay or bridge, the pool's swimming basin and deck combined were a generous 106 × 30 m (348 × 90 ft). While the pool itself was rectangular, true to its original military functions, it also boasted the facilities of a luxury hotel: four pontoons accommodated 340 changing cabins on two floors, six private salons, seven common rooms, a private royal suite, a café, a restaurant and an amphitheatre. The royal suite hosted Charles x (1757–1836) and his successor Louis-Philippe (1773–1850). In 1937, the basin was sealed off from the surrounding river, and pumping and filtration systems were installed to improve the water quality. The *bains* became the Piscine Deligny, which was completely remodelled after a fire in 1953, with a pool 50 × 15 m (164 × 49 ft) surrounded by a large sun deck. During the post-war period, it continued to attract a celebrity crowd and was also known as a meeting place for Parisians of all sexual proclivities.

Its reputation as a meeting place for Paris' LBGT community might explain the night-time bomb that sent the Deligny to the bottom of the river in 1993.[10]

The Deligny was one of several floating pools that served the population of Paris during the nineteenth century. There were similar facilities in London, including a covered pool with a cast-iron and glass roof in the same style as the Crystal Palace that was anchored by Waterloo Bridge in the 1870s. The Germans and Austrians built military training floating pools after their defeat by Napoleon, and these gradually morphed into public swimming facilities. In 1881, the Dutch, who were famous for their hydrological engineering and whose country has no shortage of water resources, opened the largest floating pool complex of its day, the Bad-en Zweminrichting van Th. Van Heemstede Obelt in Amsterdam harbour (now near the site of Amsterdam's Central Station). It comprised three swimming pools, for men, women and children; 250 cabins for men and 60 for women; service rooms, showers, hot baths and a restaurant. The bottoms and sides of the pools were made of planks and metal mesh to keep out the larger impurities. The wooden bottom, whose depth inclined from 0.6 to 3.5 m (2 to 11.5 ft), was covered with white sand to give the impression of an unspoiled tropical beach.

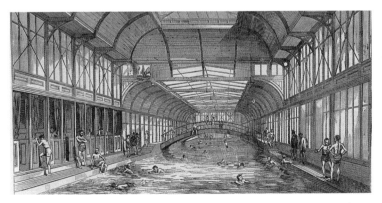

The floating baths anchored near Waterloo Bridge, London, *c.* 1870. Built in the grand wrought-iron and glass style that was used for the Crystal Palace and many of the capital's railway termini, floating baths were nevertheless much cheaper to build and maintain than in-ground pools. Without effective water purification, however, they presented a serious health risk to users.

Zurich's Frauenbad (Ladies Bath), which opened in 1888, is a rare survival of a nineteenth-century floating pool in an urban location. While floating pools could be built on any suitable body of water, they could not compete against in-ground heated pools that could be used all year and could control their water quality.

Floating baths were not only built in urban river waters. Concerns about water quality and pollution prompted the building of similar facilities in coastal waters, such as the Bagno Maria in the Bay of Trieste, opened in 1858 when the city was part of the Austro-Hungarian Empire. The Bagno Maria boasted a colossal pool and deck area measuring 190 × 100 m (623 × 328 ft).

Apart from the Deligny, most of Europe's floating pools closed before the end of the nineteenth century, with one other exception, the Frauenbad (Ladies Bath) in central Zurich, which had been in continuous operation since 1888.[11] Floating pools were cheap to build and had low running costs, but when compared to the in-ground pools of the period, which required a constant supply of mains water and expensive heating and water purification plants, they had many drawbacks: in colder northern latitudes, they could only be used for part of the year and they were vulnerable to damage from storms and collisions with river traffic.

The main problem, however, was the increasing pollution of urban waterways during the nineteenth century that turned rivers such as the Thames and Seine into foul-smelling sewers. But even without this problem, floating pools would have succumbed to the competition from heated in-ground pools that could be used in the colder months, and in the warmer months from the beaches of the seaside resorts that were springing up all over Europe and were now within easy reach of major cities, thanks to the railways. Floating pools were private institutions with subscriptions and entrance charges that excluded the working classes, who would have to make do with swimming in natural waters, if they swam at all. But by the nineteenth century, swimming was a well-established leisure pursuit among sections of the middle and upper classes, and one that they increasingly expected to be able to enjoy, not just in spa towns and at seaside resorts, but in the cities where they lived and worked.

Going to Ground

With increasingly polluted natural waters and growing demands for facilities for year-round bathing and swimming, the only way to go in northern Europe's major cities was to build in-ground, heated indoor pools. I have covered the development of English municipal baths in Chapter Five, and there was a certain amount of overlap between the functions of the pools built under the provisions of the Baths and Washhouses Acts of 1846 and 1878 and recreational swimming. In addition, private pools continued to be built and operated, though these were often purchased by municipalities as a cheaper alternative to building their own pools.

The first English city to involve itself in the provision of public bathing since the Roman era was the port of Liverpool in 1794, when it purchased a riverside bathhouse that had operated in the city since 1756. When the original building was demolished in 1817 to make way for Prince's Dock, the city built the St George's Baths – a large building in the Greek Revival style – with a men's pool of 14 × 8 m (45 × 27 ft) and a ladies' pool of 12 × 8 m (39 × 27 ft). Water was pumped from the river into a reservoir by a steam engine, which was then filtered, heated and pumped into the baths. Like the Peerless Pool and the Ladywell Baths, the St George's Baths charged a hefty sum of one guinea for a six-month subscription (in

1829), which would have excluded the working-class population of the city, who, if they wished to swim, would have had to have used the increasingly polluted and crowded waters of the Mersey.

Even before the provisions of the 1846 Act had come into force, there had been several private initiatives to provide swimming facilities in London. In 1842, the Metropolitan Baths opened in Hoxton, east London, featuring two large pools for first- and second-class users. The Tepid Bath was 33.5 × 14.5 × 0.9–1.5 m (110 × 48 × 3–5 ft), and the Wenlock Bath, at 55 × 21 m (180 × 70 ft), remained the largest covered pool in the city until 1934. The following year the National Baths opened in Little Queen St, High Holborn, also boasting two pools for first- and second-class bathers. The T-shaped Tepid Pool was 41 × 21 m (135 × 70 ft) at its widest. The water supply was obtained from an underground spring, pumped by a steam engine, filtered and heated to 26.6°C (79.8°F), slightly chilly when compared to today's average of 29°C (84.2°F).[12]

The restored London Fields Lido, a heated 50-m (165-ft) outdoor pool. Originally opened in 1932 as a leisure facility for the residents of the East End, the lido closed down in 1988. Saved from demolition by community action, it reopened in 2006.

London has so many municipal and private pools, covered pools and open-air pools and lidos that it would be impossible to cover them all; hence, I have chosen two that are fairly representative of the city's leisure pools: Oasis Sports Centre and London Fields Lido, pools where I have been privileged both to swim and coach. Covent Garden's Oasis Sports Centre encapsulates the history of in-ground bathing and swimming in London since the eighteenth century. The presence of a natural spring on the site in an era long before mains water prompted the opening of a bagnio in around 1728, which operated until 1840, when the spring that fed it was cut off. Next to occupy the site were the St Giles and St George Bloomsbury Baths and Wash Houses, which opened in 1852, providing residents of the parish with 73 individual baths, 56 wash tubs and first- and second-class plunge pools measuring 12 × 7 m (40 × 24 ft) and 11 × 7 m (36 × 24 ft) respectively.

The baths, renamed the Holborn Baths, were extensively re-modelled in the 1890s and the original pools merged to form a single larger basin suitable for swimming, while another pool was also added. Redevelopment of the site and the construction of an ambitious 'Swimstad' scheme that included two large indoor pools began in 1937 but was interrupted by the outbreak of the Second World War. In 1946, the centre finally reopened with a single outdoor pool measuring 27.4 × 10 m (90 × 33 ft) – the odd dimensions explained by the fact that it was part of the pre-war scheme and had been converted into a water tank during the war. In 1960 the 25 × 9 m (82 × 29.5 ft) indoor pool was added, and its roof opened as a sun deck.[13]

My second choice, London Fields Lido, is representative of the interwar era of British swimming pool design. The lido opened in 1932 and was designed specifically as a leisure facility catering to both genders and all classes and ages. Any notion of bathing for personal hygiene or to acquire middle-class Victorian values had long been forgotten in an era that saw the take-off of mass tourism, though at this time limited to travel within the country rather than overseas as it would be in the post-war period. The pool at London Fields is 50 × 20 m (165 × 66 ft), with a maximum depth of 2.3 m

(7½ ft); it is surrounded by a concrete sunbathing deck, lockers and changing cabins. The lido was modernized in 1951 and operated until 1988, when it was forced to close, unable to compete with other leisure facilities, such as gymnasia, and newer heated indoor pools. Almost demolished during the 1980s, the lido was saved by community action that included several volunteer-led clean-ups. It reopened in 2006 as one of London's few heated outdoor long-course swimming pools, quickly becoming one of the capital's premier summertime venues for city-dwellers keen to escape the heat or sunbathe.

Going to Ground on the Continent

Despite its head start with floating pools, Paris was a relative late-comer to the construction of in-ground facilities, building its first pool, the Piscine Château-Landon, in the 10th arrondissement in 1884 and the second, the Piscine Rouvet, in the 19th arrondissement in 1889. Both these establishments provided *bains-douches* (baths and showers) and served the same function as the earlier English baths and washhouses. According to van Leeuwen, the first indoor purpose-built recreational pool in continental Europe was not a French innovation but an Austrian one. Vienna's Dianabad opened on the banks of the Donaukanal in 1843, on the site of an earlier bathhouse. At 36 × 13 m (118 × 42.5 ft), the Dianabad was the largest covered swimming pool of its day, housed in a hall 53 × 20 m (173 × 65 ft) that doubled as a concert hall and ballroom in winter when the pool was closed.

In 1900, the Dianabad became part of a luxury hotel. This second incarnation featured two swimming pools: a lap pool for men and a pool for women equipped with a wave machine. The complex also included steam rooms, a sun deck, a sanatorium, boutiques, a hairdressing salon and beautician, a restaurant, a dry-cleaner and a veterinary office and dog grooming salon. The description of the pools and its ancillary facilities suggests a private establishment reserved for the use of hotel guests and of the wealthier citizens of the city. The hotel was seriously damaged during the

Paris' Piscine Keller, which opened in 1967 – one of the French capital's 39 municipal pools. Comprising a 50-m (165-ft) pool and a 15-m (49-ft) paddling pool and spa, the Keller is equipped with a retractable roof for the summer. After a slow start, Paris now has some of the best public provision of pools in the Western world.

Second World War but the pool reopened in 1946 and remained in use until the site was redeveloped in 1974, with the construction of a modern office block that included a third Dianabad. The area was redeveloped again in 1996, and the municipality opened the current and fourth Dianabad in 2000.[14]

The Dianabad had a wave machine as early as 1900, and another pool of the period, the Undosa Wellenbad in the lakeside resort of Starnberg, Upper Bavaria, Germany, had a wave machine that was one of the town's major attractions from 1905 until 1921, when the machine was decommissioned. According to van Leeuwen, 'Including waves and simulating rainfall belonged to the Renaissance tradition of recreating nature under artificial circumstances.'[15] But it also served another important function: once the germ theory of disease became widely accepted in Europe, pool managers and owners used these recreated natural features to reassure users of the wholesomeness of the water they were swimming in.

Paris, having begun the century with what must have been Western Europe's worst provision of in-ground municipal pools, now boasts what must be among the best urban swimming provision with 39 facilities, many of which have 50-m (165-ft) Olympic-size pools. The first wave of construction of *piscines* and *bains-douches* in the late nineteenth century was followed by a second wave during the interwar years, with pools such as the Piscine de la Butte-aux-Cailles in the 13th arrondissement, which opened in 1924 – the first pool to make a clear distinction between bathing for hygiene and swimming for recreation. There followed a third wave of building in the late 1960s and '70s, including the Piscine Keller, a 50-m (165-ft) pool with a retractable roof. Recent pools include the Piscine Joséphine Baker – a floating pool on the Seine moored at the Port de la Gare in the 13th arrondissement – which was opened as part of the 'Paris Plages' project in 2006.[16]

Europeans reconnected to the joys of recreational swimming in pools in a process that followed a similar pattern across the Continent. The process had begun in England, the first country to experience major industrialization and urbanization, and therefore to provide bathing and basic swimming facilities for its working classes as they could not afford their own bathrooms or to pay to go to private bathhouses. As the century wore on, bathhouse pools in mainland Europe were gradually converted into leisure and sporting facilities. The first half of the twentieth century, in particular the interwar years, witnessed the building of larger and larger pools whose sole purpose was recreation. Post-war municipal pools attempt to merge very different functions – leisure and socializing, swimming lessons for adults and schoolchildren, fitness swimming, swimming clubs and competitions – which they try to achieve with varying success by setting aside whole pools or one or more lanes for different activities throughout the day. Despite their high building and maintenance costs, pools, like gyms, are leisure facilities that are bucking the trend for retrenchment and austerity in public finances. In the UK, many pools that had formerly closed and were scheduled for demolition and redevelopment have been restored and reopened, such as the many formerly derelict city and coastal lidos, and new pools continue to be built. Swimming, it seems, has been transformed from the pastime of the eccentric, wealthy few into a 'human right' that a city of any size or prominence is expected to provide to all its citizens.

Aquatic Americana

I am treating recreational pools in the U.S. separately because its swimming culture exhibits some striking differences from those of England and continental Europe.[17] Just as in Europe, the city fathers of many American cities built public baths in inner-city slums, as instruments to inculcate the middle-class values of cleanliness, hard work and self-discipline into the working classes. However, what happened in America was unique, because of what had come before the introduction of municipal baths and the way they developed after the First World War.

Wiltse describes what came before the provision of public pools in late nineteenth-century America as a vibrant working-class swimming subculture – a culture of roughhousing and recreation that was completely at odds with the aims of the city fathers and taxpayers who had paid for the pools:

> Swimming had been a popular activity among working-class boys and men throughout the nineteenth century. They swam in the lakes, rivers, and bays that surrounded most American cities and created a plebeian and masculine swimming culture that violated Victorian norms. They swam in the nude, they swore, they fought, and they evaded authority.[18]

Although we know that working-class men and boys swam and bathed in natural waters in England – usually from the records of drowning incidents in the Thames, the Serpentine in London's Hyde Park and the Perilous Pond (Peerless Pool) – I could find no record of an American-style male swimming culture being imported into the plunge pools of nineteenth-century baths and washhouses.

According to Wiltse, America's working-class swimming culture dates back to the end of the eighteenth century, to the early years of the young republic. He has reconstructed this early swimming culture from newspaper articles complaining about the antics of men and boys in urban waters, and from the civic ordinances that the cities enacted to control them. In 1786, Boston passed a law banning swimming on the Christian Sabbath. Because swimming was associated with pleasure, rebelliousness and immorality, the last thing the puritanical authorities of nineteenth-century Boston were willing to tolerate was that anyone should be having fun on

Photographic study for a later painting entitled *Boys at the Swimming Hole* (1884–5) by American photographer, painter and sculptor Thomas Eakins. A vibrant masculine swimming culture in urban natural waters had existed in the u.s. since the late eighteenth century. When cities began to open municipal pools, working-class boys and men thought it natural to import their culture of fun and roughhousing into establishments with much loftier moral aims, leading to protracted conflicts over use and ownership of these 'contested waters'.

the Lord's Day, and worse that they should be doing so naked. In 1808, New York imposed a ban on swimming in the East River, this time not on religious grounds but because of the offence caused to middle-class passers-by by the sight of naked boys and young men swearing as they roughhoused in the water.

Although many northern cities imposed total bans on swimming within their city limits, these were never systematically enforced. Labourers, who had no washing facilities at home, flouted the bans in summer, claiming that they had a natural right to bathe in urban waters. When Boston and Philadelphia opened the first municipal pools, the boys who had controlled the local rivers and lakes expected that these new artificial waters would be their new playgrounds. Despite strict rules forbidding smoking, profanity, roughhousing and noisy conversations, sometimes enforced by the presence of police officers, the boys continued to see the pools as places to have fun rather than institutions where they were expected to become hardworking, sober citizens. In both Boston and Philadelphia, the new pools attracted an overwhelming majority of boys and young men, who took them over, imposing their own standards of riotous behaviour.

The city of Milwaukee, Wisconsin, was the second most prolific builder of municipal in-ground pools in the nineteenth century, opening three natatoriums between 1889 and 1903. The first pool opened in 1889 with a ceremony during which the city fathers were supposed to make the inaugural swim. At the last minute, however, the good burghers of Milwaukee demurred, unwilling to strip off the clothes that were the visible expression of their social status and power, thus sparing themselves the merciless ridicule that their youthful onlookers would have immediately subjected them to. As soon as the natatorium opened, the boys immediately made it their own, turning it into their playground on days when there was no charge for using it and importing the adolescent rituals they had practised in the natural waters of the Milwaukee River and Lake Michigan. No matter what they tried, the authorities never managed to gain full control of these contested artificial waters. The only thing they could do was to exclude poorer swimmers by ending free swimming days, but while the pools were now used for what the city fathers considered to be more constructive and respectable purposes, it also ended their original function of aiding 'citizens in maintaining cleanliness free of cost', and turned them into middle-class leisure facilities.[19]

The Great Water Divide

The first municipal pools in America were segregated according to gender and class but not along racial lines. In Chapter Five, I quoted a report on Philadelphia's pools published in 1898 that remarked matter-of-factly that they were used predominantly by street gamins, both black and white. What the writer was highlighting was not the mixing of different races and ethnicities, which he did not think was noteworthy, but the lowly social origins and physical dirtiness of the majority of swimmers. During America's Progressive Era (1890s–1920s), the general acceptance of the germ theory of disease prompted a reconsideration of the form and function of municipal bathing facilities. As pools could no longer be used as 'instruments of cleaning', several northern cities stopped building them altogether. New York and Boston opted for bathhouses with laundries, individual baths and showers, but other cities, most notably Chicago, continued to build pools, but with a more recreational remit. Swimming provision retained some of its earlier moral overtones, however, in that they were conceived as public spaces where new immigrants could be socialized into American life and values, that would improve the lot of the urban working classes and that would also serve to keep boys and young men, who might otherwise engage in anti-social or criminal activities, gainfully occupied during the warmer months of the year.[20]

Wiltse calls the two decades between 1920 and 1940 'The Swimming Pool Age', when cities built resort pools in prominent public locations such as fairgrounds and parks. These were no longer the cramped, austere, indoor rectangular basins of the Victorian era but large open-air pools that could accommodate thousands of bathers in and out of the water, built in a variety of shapes and with artificial beaches, lawns and concrete decks for sunbathing and socializing, with changing facilities, showers, restaurants and cafés. Resort pools such as the Astoria Pool in Queens, New York City, the Cameron Pool in West Virginia and the Fleishhacker Pool in San Francisco democratized swimming, attracting many new swimmers, especially families, because they were no longer segregated by class or gender.[21]

The Swimming Pool Age, however, while introducing many more people to swimming, also witnessed the exclusion of African Americans from municipal pools. In the southern states, racial segregation was enforced by law but in the north it was imposed by violent means, with racist white swimmers attacking any African American who tried to access what they believed to be white-only spaces. An early example of the onset of racism in swimming pools was the exclusion of African Americans at the St Louis open-air resort pool that opened in Fairground Park in 1913, although blacks and whites had swum together in the city's earlier municipal pools. Wiltse explains that the change was brought about by increasing levels of integration of European immigrants and by the gradual replacement of working-class solidarity – which had allowed blacks and whites to swim together – with racial prejudice, because white men did not want African American men to interact with white women in the intimate setting of public swimming pools.[22] These unofficial exclusions led to early civil rights protests to integrate pools in the north, but these failed because the authorities and police colluded with the racists and failed to protect African American protesters, who were often attacked and injured and sometimes murdered.[23]

The Privatization of American Swimming

In the early 1990s, when I was travelling regularly to the United States for work, to visit friends and family and for holidays, I went to stay with a school friend who had married her American boyfriend and moved to Fort Lauderdale, Florida. They lived in one of the city's leafy, canal-ringed suburbs, but because they were just starting out, they had rented a house that did not have its own backyard pool. As soon as I'd been installed in the guest bedroom and unpacked the Florida-issue shorts and flip-flops, my hostess announced that we would be going to swim at 'the club' – a ubiquitous institution in American suburbia, with its tennis courts, gyms and large outdoor swimming pools surrounded by lawns and decks where members could enjoy a leisurely lunch or drink al-fresco or in the air-conditioned clubhouse. Although this was decades after desegregation, I did notice that the membership was overwhelmingly white, and the only African and Hispanic Americans to be seen were employees.

The private athletic and social club has a long history in the United States and created a parallel swimming culture to that of municipal pools. The model for many later institutions was the now venerable and still very exclusive New York Athletic Club (NYAC), founded in 1868, which opened its first City House on 55th Street and Sixth Avenue, Manhattan, with a glittering gala attended by the city's nineteenth-century elite families, 'The Four Hundred'. The club's marble and tile pool, lit by chandeliers, could not have been more different from the spartan wood and asphalt municipal tanks of the same period. Members-only clubs such as the NYAC and the Chicago Athletic Association (CAA), founded in 1890, were overwhelmingly masculine institutions. They had a strong health and fitness and amateur competitive ethos, hosting the country's first swim meets and water polo competitions and providing the nucleus of the U.S.'s Olympic teams. Quite a few rungs down the social ladder from the NYAC and CAA, the Brooklyn YMCA was the first to build a swimming pool, in 1885, though of modest dimensions at 14 × 4.5 m (45 × 15 ft), making swimming affordable for respectable, middle-class Christian young men. By 1895, seventeen YMCAs had pools dedicated to health or fitness and sporting competition, catering to the craze for physical exercise that gripped the nation at the turn of the century.[24]

Although the desegregation of municipal swimming pools in America's northern states probably ranks quite low on the lists of achievements of the civil rights movement, it turned out to be a bitter-sweet victory that had a profound effect on the provision of public swimming in the U.S. Desegregation did not lead to the integration of African, Hispanic and white Americans but to whites abandoning municipal pools for private clubs and their own back-yard pools. The large public resort pools of the Swimming Pool Age closed and no new facilities were built, and as a result many poorer Americans no longer had access to swimming or public spaces where they could exercise, relax and forge community bonds. In the 1960s a new programme of pool building was prompted as one response to the race riots that were setting many American cities ablaze. But these were not the large, well-appointed pools of the interwar years; they were small, austere facilities that Wiltse describes as 'recreation asylums, not leisure resorts'.

Just as many public pools were closing, the number of private domestic pools was skyrocketing. In 1950 there were 2,500 back-yard pools in the U.S., but by 1999, there were 4 million, a startling increase that Wiltse cites as a symptom of civic disengagement by many white, middle-class Americans, who had withdrawn into suburban enclaves. Those who did not have their own pools joined their local sports and social club, which, though no longer officially segregated, was in practice – by virtue of its location, membership structure and pricing, which together ensured the exclusion of poorer African and Hispanic Americans.[25]

The Triumph of Artificial Waters

Swimming pools have a long history in the Western world. We can trace their origins to two Roman innovations: the water features and grottos found in elegant villa gardens and the pools of spas and bathhouses. With the revival of all things classical in early modern Europe, the grotto and spa and their associated pools were revived, reshaped and reinterpreted. Hence, the West owes its well-developed infrastructure of urban pools to a historical accident that was not reproduced in other parts of the world where full immersion of the body in water was not considered to be an integral part of their bathing culture.

The first pools to be associated with swimming as a recreational pastime were amenities of England's eighteenth-century *bagnios*. But these disreputable establishments that doubled as brothels had a very limited impact on Britain's swimming culture. We owe the development of recreational swimming to the much worthier civic amenities that were built in English cities during the nineteenth century. When indoor pools were no longer seen as a means of providing basic hygiene and promoting middle-class morality, their main functions were swimming instruction, fitness training and recreation. The wrought-iron-clad and tiled bathhouses of Victorian England evolved into the lidos (in the UK) and the resort pools (in the U.S.) of the early twentieth century, which produced today's multi-pool aquaparks and eternity pools suspended eighty storeys above the urban landscape.

Pools are among the most highly prized public amenities that municipalities continue to provide, despite their high building and maintenance costs. When neighbourhood pool closures are mooted, they are violently opposed by their local communities, even though many residents may only use their local pool in the summer months. Why are public pools valued so highly that they seem immune from the programmes of spending cuts that affect every other aspect of post-recession urban life comparative to other facilities provided by local authorities. The pool benefits from the layering of multiple social and personal meanings: its associations with childhood leisure time and seaside holidays; nostalgia, as it is in a public or school pool that most of us learned to swim (though, in my case, I do not remember school swimming lessons as being particularly carefree or enjoyable); and the sensuality of swimming, to which we can add the positive feelings born of 'overcoming one's personal perils', to quote Alain Corbin on the rediscovery of the alluring sea, as well as the sense of personal achievement gained from completing a brisk thirty laps in the pool. We should never discount sex as a factor in the popularity of swimming – both in the contemplation of the desirable other and our own exposure to the other's gaze – in an urban setting where, uniquely, we are allowed to cavort among our fellows as near naked as public decency will allow. If we overcome our primal fears by swimming in the sea, what comparable function does swimming in a pool provide? Perhaps they are the one public place where we can strip off the constricting corsetry of status, wealth and power, momentarily freeing ourselves from all the things that bind and define us.

8
The Silent World

> We found an assembly of three moderate-sized cylinders
> of compressed air, linked to an air regulator the size of an
> alarm clock. From the regulator there extended two tubes,
> joining on a mouthpiece. With this equipment harnessed
> to the back, a watertight glass mask over the eyes and nose,
> and rubber foot fins, we intended to make unencumbered
> flights in the depths of the sea.
>
> JACQUES COUSTEAU, *THE SILENT WORLD* (1988)[1]

In the early modern period, many Westerners were alienated from
the sea while at the same time they were attracted by its wonders
and riches, both real and imagined. Even for mariners, fishermen and
divers, what lay beyond the relatively shallow waters of the immediate
coastline was a complete mystery – *mare incognita*. For the makers
of medieval *mappa mundi*, the seas and oceans were almost invisible,
compressed into insignificant rivulets or relegated to the outer limits
as a thin blue ribbon around the central landmasses.

The journeys of the Age of Exploration and Discovery restored
the oceans to their rightful size but did little to unlock their secrets.
On the contrary, mariners came back with stories of giant sea serpents and mermaids, leading an ever more imaginative infill of the
unknown with sunken continents and undersea kingdoms of scaly
merfolk kings, knights and commoners, a distorted mirror – either
a more perfect or a monstrous one – of the surface world. Humans
could dream of visiting these other worlds and acquiring their
treasures by magical means, but in reality, how deep humans could
go was limited by the capacity of their lungs and the solidity of
their eardrums.

Until the eighteenth century, the technology for harvesting
aquatic resources had advanced little since early humans had learned
to free-dive and to use stones to transit to the sea bottom more

quickly and efficiently; what had changed was the scale of the operations needed to meet the ever-growing worldwide demand for food, sponges, dyestuffs and luxury goods such as pearls and corals. In order to reach and exploit additional resources, humans needed to develop new technologies that would allow them to reach greater depths and remain there for much longer. Like flight, it was a dream that was imagined centuries earlier than it was realized.

In an era of expanding maritime trade, there was another pressing reason to be able to be able to find a means of diving deeper and for longer periods: the salvage of wrecks carrying valuable cargo. The inability of free-divers to reach many wrecks has been a boon to modern underwater archaeology and treasure hunting. One of the world's most spectacular finds, at least from the financial point of view, was the discovery of the *Nuestra Señora de Atocha*, part of the 27-strong Spanish treasure fleet that had set sail from Havana in the autumn of 1622, departing late and, fatally, at the height of the hurricane season.

The *Atocha*'s cargo included several tons of silver and gold bullion and a cache of Colombian emeralds. On 4 September, the fleet was caught in a storm near the Florida Keys, and the galleon sank in 17 m (55 ft) of water, coming to rest on a sandbank that made the ocean there shallow enough for the ship's mizzenmast to be above the waterline. Although five members of the crew, clinging to the mast, were rescued and the location of the wreck was known, nothing could be salvaged from it because it was too deep for free-divers. A second storm tore off the mast, and the wreck was lost until it was rediscovered in 1985 by salvage expert Mel Fisher. His $450 million treasure trove is thought to represent half of the *Atocha*'s precious cargo.[2] Fisher owed his success to one invention: scuba (self-contained underwater breathing apparatus), an invention perfected just four decades earlier by one of the great names of undersea exploration, conservation and cinematography, Jacques Cousteau (1910–1997).

Like Columbus's three transatlantic journeys, Cousteau's underwater documentaries opened up the hitherto unknown 'Silent World' of the oceans to a host of disciples and imitators. Since the

1950s, the development of the first commercial Aqualung has spawned a vast recreational diving industry on reefs and wrecks worldwide. Growing in parallel, but largely unknown to the general public, are a host of commercial, engineering, military, archaeological and scientific applications of diving that have made the continental fringes of the silent world a little less silent and deserted.

Aristotle's Kettle

As we saw in Chapter Four, the ancient Greeks often had a pressing need for swimmers and divers, to attack the ships or destroy the naval defences of their enemies. Additionally, the waters of the ancient Greek world – around the Balkan Peninsula, southern Italy and Asia Minor – are notorious for their hidden rocks and reefs. A common trope in many Greek epics is the shipwreck – in the case of Homer's *Odyssey*, multiple shipwrecks on strange shores get Odysseus and his crew into many extraordinary scrapes. In his last adventure, when he finally makes it back to Ithaca, Odysseus disguises himself as a shipwrecked mariner so that he can enter his palace unrecognized by either his family or the many suitors that are sexually harassing the faithful Penelope.

Without navigation aids or charts, the wooden-hulled ships of the classical world had to keep within sight of the shore, and without engines to get them out of harm's way in bad weather, they were often driven onto reefs, holed and sunk. Salvaging cargo from sunken ships was a recognized profession during antiquity. We have a scale of payment set out for salvaging cargo from sunken ships from third-century Rhodes, which specified what percentage of the salvage the diver earned depending on the depth of the wreck and difficulty of the salvage. The statutes of the *Lex Rhodia* were incorporated into Roman law and, centuries later, they became the basis for modern salvage legislation.[3]

No matter how skilled a free-diver, however, there were wrecks and underwater resources that were known about but remained out of reach. No less a figure than Aristotle (384–322 BCE), more usually associated with philosophy, rhetoric and the dramatic arts, applied himself to the problems faced by sponge divers. In 'Problems Pertaining to Ears' in Book VI of the *Problems*, he speculated about why divers' eardrums sometimes burst underwater. Having no concept of the difference between air and water pressure as the diver goes deeper, he speculated that this phenomenon was due to the 'hardness' of water when compared to that of the air. He also described a primitive diving bell that could supply divers with a supply of air while underwater:

> In order that these fishers for sponges may be supplied with a facility for respiration, kettles are let down to them in the water so that they may not be filled with water, but with air.

Aristotle does not specify the size of the kettles but classicists have speculated that he might have meant large upturned metal cooking cauldrons into which a diver could surface to replenish his air supply.[4]

Although Aristotle's kettle idea was feasible, the difficulties of keeping receptacles filled with air the right way up meant that it was far from practical, especially in rough seas or in areas with strong currents. Ancient tales of diving bells large enough to accommodate a man, such as the story of Alexander the Great's undersea adventure during the siege of Tyre, did not take into account that, without a constant air supply, the oxygen in a sealed vessel would quickly be exhausted and replaced by poisonous carbon dioxide. Aristotle's idea was revived centuries later by the father of scientific empiricism, Sir Francis Bacon (1561–1626). In *Novum organum*, he described a more sophisticated take on the kettle idea:

> A hollow tub of metal was formed, and sunk so as to have its bottom parallel with the surface of the water; it thus carried down with it to the bottom of the sea all the air contained in the tub. It stood upon three feet (like a tripod), being of rather less height than a man, so that, when the diver was in want of breath,

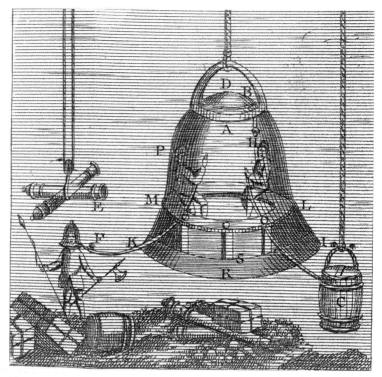

Illustration of Edmund Halley's diving bell (patented 1691), showing the various components of the system used for the salvage of wrecks and underwater construction. The air within the sealed diving bell was replenished by barrels lowered from the surface; and divers were able to work on the sea bottom by wearing helmets supplied with air by hoses attached to the diving bell.

he could put his head into the hollow of the tub, breathe, and then continue his work.[5]

In 1691, Edmund Halley (1656–1742) patented a diving bell that was supplied with air from weighted barrels lowered down from the surface. He recorded dives of 20 m (65 ft) lasting ninety minutes, demonstrating that the system was practical, though not always safe. Halley suffered from one of the earliest recorded cases of middle-ear barotrauma – damage to the inner ear caused by pressure during a dive. Halley's diving bell was used to salvage wrecks and for underwater construction, for example of harbours and bridges. In a further refinement, divers could also be supplied with air from hoses connected to the bell; however, the divers' range was limited by the length of the hose and their safety assured by its watertightness, long before the invention of rubber and waterproof plastics.[6]

A greater understanding about the composition of the air, the respective roles of oxygen and carbon dioxide in respiration and of the pressure differentials that cause decompression sickness and barotrauma were accompanied by technical improvements in diving bell technology. In 1837, Augustus Siebe (1788–1872) perfected what became known as standard diving dress (SDD). Although a one-man suit, SDD could best be described as an individual diving bell. With its large spherical metal helmet with glass portholes attached to a waterproof suit, the suit gave the diver unprecedented range, but the heavy helmet and metal boots only allowed him to walk across the ocean floor. Like a diving bell, SDD was not self-contained but linked to the surface by a fragile air hose that was subject to snagging and whose rupture often led to serious injury and death. Cousteau, the inventor of the Aqualung, the first successful commercial scuba set, had experience of SDD, which he described in the following terms:

> I thought of the helmet diver arriving in his ponder-
> ous boots at such a depth as this and struggling to
> walk a few yards, obsessed with his umbilici and his
> head imprisoned in copper . . . a cripple in an alien
> land.[7]

Leonardo's Frogman

The diving bell and SDD gave humans limited access to the under-water world but the ideal (or until the mid-twentieth century, the dream) was of a man as free in the water as he was on land; that is, carrying his own air supply and unencumbered by a heavy suit or restricted by an umbilical to the surface. Foremost among the dreamers who imagined a humanity equally at home on dry land, underwater and in the air was Leonardo da Vinci (1452–1519). In the *Codex Atlanticus* (1478–1519), the great man sketched two underwater suits, the first supplied by a hose attached to a surface float, and the second with its own self-contained air supply. Although both these suits have since been constructed and look somewhat modern, neither would have worked in practice. The air-hose-float model would not have worked beyond a metre in depth as water pressure would have made breathing impossible, and Leonardo's primitive scuba did not have a means of removing toxic carbon

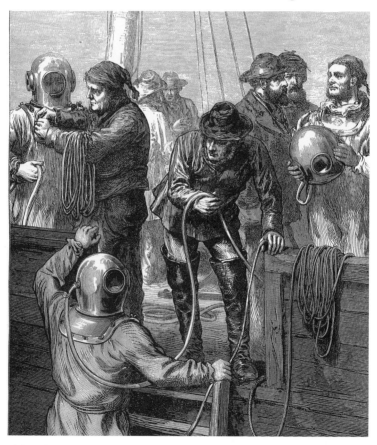

Although not 'self-contained', standard diving dress (SDD) gave the diver unprecedented range underwater for an extended duration. The design and weight of the suit made swimming impossible, but the diver was able to float to the sea floor and ascend to the surface by altering the buoyancy of his suit.

Leonardo da Vinci's design for a diving suit used a reinforced breathing tube connected to a float to keep the air hole above the waterline. The suit would not have worked at any significant depth as the water pressure would have been too great to allow the diver to breathe. A second more advanced design that featured a self-contained air reservoir would have failed because without a functioning purification system the diver would have quickly succumbed to carbon dioxide poisoning.

dioxide, condemning a diver to death in a matter of minutes had his air supply lasted even that long.

Almost two centuries later, in *De motu animalium* (1680), Giovanni Borelli (1608–1679) published his own scuba design, consisting of an outsized helmet acting as a portable air tank, a piston to help the diver's descent and ascent, and a pair of clawed fins – the first ever attempt at swimming fins – which suggested that the diver might be expected to swim as well as walk underwater. The helmet was meant to supply the diver with air for up to thirty minutes and was equipped with a purification system that, if it had ever been built and used, would not have worked, leading to the diver's almost certain death.[8]

By the beginning of the mid-nineteenth century, SDD and diving bell technologies had allowed humans to go deeper and stay longer underwater than had ever been possible for free-divers, but they were trapped inside cumbersome suits and tied to the surface by the umbilical hose that provided their air supply. Although the problem of a dependable air supply that would not poison the diver had been resolved, diving remained a dangerous activity, causing many fatalities and injuries. Equipped with SDD, humans had taken their first hesitant steps underwater, but visionary French novelist Jules Verne (1828–1905) had his characters living and working deep underwater in *Twenty Thousand Leagues under the Sea* (1870), something far beyond the technologies of his own time.

Gradually, advances in physics, physiology and engineering combined to improve the safety of divers and give them greater freedom of movement. An 1865 SDD featured a compressed air reservoir on the diver's back, which allowed him to breathe at will and exhale spent air into the water, but the reservoir was resupplied by a hose from the surface. At the turn of the twentieth century, French marine zoologist and pioneer of underwater photography Louis Boutan (1859–1934) took an important step in the development of scuba when he devised the *Scaphandre autonome à respiration normale*, essentially SDD with a compressed air cylinder that gave him a completely independent air supply for up to three hours.[9] Although Boutan had severed the connection with the surface, he was still walking, and not swimming, underwater.

Open and Closed Circuits

The development of scuba, like that of many other inventions of the Second Industrial Revolution, was a process of trial and error conducted by gifted amateurs like Boutan, for whom it solved the practical problem of how to stay underwater long enough and with enough freedom of movement to carry out his photographic experiments; by engineers, who were faced with specific commercial or industrial needs; and by the military, who quickly realized the value of stealth attacks on enemy port installations and ships by military frogmen using the cover of the seas.

Just as with the development of sound recording, radio and electrical power transmission, enthusiasts, inventors and engineers explored different technologies to achieve the same ends. This led to the development of two main types of scuba: open and closed circuit. The latter is also known as a 'rebreather' because the used air is recycled rather than vented into the water. Late eighteenth-century models used the same principles as Leonardo's and Borelli's designs, but with the significant difference that the chemical substance that scrubbed the carbon dioxide from the recycled air actually worked. The first models of close-circuit rebreathers were not designed for marine use but for mines and tunnels, which could become flooded with water or filled with toxic fumes, and were later adapted for marine use.

In 1879, British engineer Henry Fleuss (1851–1932) perfected a self-contained rebreather set that used a tank of compressed oxygen. The design proved itself during construction projects and was later adapted to be used as an escape suit for submariners. The reader might wonder why the open-circuit scuba, perfected in the mid-twentieth century, is now the most common, as rebreather technology is much older and more economical in terms of the amount of gas needed to be carried by the diver. However, closed-circuit sets had several drawbacks over their open-circuit rivals: early models were limited to around 12 m (40 ft) in depth and because of their greater complexity, they were more likely to fail than simpler open-circuit scuba.[10] The rebreather, however, had a particular attraction for the military, as it did not leave a tell-tale trail of exhaled bubbles, making it admirably suited to stealth attacks.

War under the Sea

We left underwater warfare in the West with tales of Greek divers attacking Persian ships and sunken Sicilian fortifications, and of the aquatic prowess of Julius Caesar when fleeing from the vengeful Egyptians in Alexandria. While Vegetius' fourth-century CE *De re militari* lamented that swimming had become a lost art among the military in the late Roman world, the situation only worsened during the medieval and early modern periods, when many sailors and naval and marine cadets were unable to swim. Although swimming was one of the skills medieval knights were expected to master, there was no provision or infrastructure for teaching it until the eighteenth century.

The idea of underwater warfare conducted by submarine dates back to the seventeenth century and produced several designs, including one by Borelli; but without the means of carrying large amounts of air or the means of purifying it, these 'submersibles' were little more than fantasies, or partially submerged surface vessels. The first true submarines began to appear in the mid-nineteenth century, and with them the necessity for means for the crew to escape back to the surface when these early *Nautilus*es came to grief – a need met by the compact rebreather, already proven in construction and mining.

By the time Jules Verne imagined the armed divers of *Twenty Thousand Leagues under the Sea*, real submarines were in service in the world's navies, though they were much smaller and less powerful than the *Nautilus*. Submarines were in use during the first mechanized war, the First World War, but there was no significant use of scuba because the SDD of the time was far too restrictive and vulnerable to be used in combat. In 1918, two Italian divers attacked and sank an Austro-Hungarian warship riding on a human-guided torpedo with detachable warhead into the Istrian harbour of Pola (now in Croatia), but they were not using scuba gear, and the sinking took place after the Austro-Hungarian surrender, when the warship was no longer a threat.[11] Between the wars, the Italians continued to develop human-guided torpedoes and midget subs to attack enemy shipping.

Leading the Italian effort was maverick naval officer Angelo Belloni (1882–1957), who, just before the outbreak of the First World War, stole a newly built Italian submarine destined for the Imperial Russian Navy, with which he planned to attack Austro-Hungarian shipping in order to force Italy to join the war on the side of the Triple Entente (Russia, France and Britain). Although facing charges of piracy, Belloni was quickly pardoned when Italy entered the war

A member of the elite u.s. Navy Seals equipped with the latest in computerized rebreather technology and waterproof equipment, making him as formidable an opponent as a land-based commando, with the added advantage that he is completely undetectable from the surface.

against Germany and Austro-Hungary. He played a significant role in the development of underwater warfare with submarines, human torpedoes and divers equipped with the 'vestito Belloni', a rebreather suit used by Italian divers to attack British shipping in Gibraltar and Alexandria harbours during the Second World War.[12]

The success of Italy's underwater campaign, which sank sixteen British ships in Gibraltar alone between 1941 and 1943, led to an arms race between British and Italian divers and submariners, who sometimes engaged in pitched undersea battles.[13] In the u.s., Christian Lambertsen (1917–2011) developed the LARU (Lambertsen Amphibious Respiratory Unit or 'Lambertsen Lung'), a semi-closed-circuit steady-flow oxygen rebreather that was adopted by the Office of Strategic Services (oss) in the autumn of 1940, a few months before America's entry into the Second World War. By 1942, the oss was training combat divers, the u.s. Navy's future 'frogmen' who would see action in the Pacific, European, North

African and Indian Ocean theatres alongside the skin-divers of the Underwater Demolition Teams who were already used by the U.S. Navy for reconnaissance, mine clearance and sabotage missions.[14]

The OSS disbanded its combat diver units at the end of the Pacific War, though the divers themselves were transferred to the U.S. Navy. But as post-war euphoria was replaced by Cold War panic, the major powers created special forces units that included submarine and diving specialists. In 1949, because of a shortage of Lambertsen Lung rebreathers, the U.S. Navy acquired its first Cousteau Aqualungs. Units such as the British Royal Marines Special Boat Services (SBS) and the U.S. Navy Seals are typical of special operations forces that have been deployed in every major conflict since the Second World War. Wearing the latest computerized rebreathers that do not leave the tell-tale trail of bubbles, and equipped with the most sophisticated underwater weaponry and equipment, the SBS and Seals are trained to pilot mini subs and enter and exit from special compartments built into the hulls of warships and submarines.

The military use of scuba is probably the field that has made the greatest progress since the 1950s, but the secrecy that surrounds all military matters allows us only a glimpse into what might be going on beneath the surface. An intriguing window on the U.S.'s capabilities is sketched out in *Naval Forces under the Sea: A Look Back, A Look Ahead* – the proceedings of a historical symposium at the United States Naval Academy in 2000, with contributions by the leading naval experts on all aspects of undersea warfare, surveillance and salvage.[15]

The Underwater Club

Open-circuit scuba saw significant developments in France during the interwar years with the collaboration of inventor Maurice Fernez (1885–1952) and naval officer Yves Le Prieur (1885–1963). As a child, Fernez almost drowned, suffering from barotrauma and injuring his foot, which left him with a lifelong limp; as an adult he was determined to design an inexpensive, lightweight underwater breathing apparatus that could be used for lifesaving and that would not require thirty minutes to put on like SDD.

Patented in 1912, the 'Fernez1' supplied air through a rubber hose fitted with a mouthpiece kept afloat on the surface of the water, but it suffered from the same drawback as Leonardo's earlier floating snorkel design: the compression of the lungs any deeper than around 1.5 m (5 ft) made breathing through the tube impossible. He solved this problem by adding a one-man manual Michelin air pump used to inflate tyres to supply air to the diver. Instead of the massive SDD helmet, the diver wore a pair of Fernez goggles and a nose clip to prevent him from inhaling water. In the summer of 1912, Fernez tested his design, staying almost an hour at a depth of 5 m (18 ft) in the river Seine, surfacing only because of the cold. In 1920, he improved his design: the 'Fernez2' has a 46-m (150-ft) hose, a more powerful two-man pump and a full face mask instead

Maurice Fernez testing his lifesaving apparatus in the Seine in 1912. Designed to be lightweight and to be deployed rapidly in cases of drowning, the equipment was revolutionary when compared to the heavy standard diving dress that took thirty minutes to put on. With air supplied from the surface from a pump through a rubber hose, Fernez was able to stay underwater for almost an hour at a depth of 5 m (18 ft).

of goggles and nose clip. The Fernez2 attracted international attention when it was purchased by the Greek government for use by its sponge divers.

The advantages of the Fernez1 and 2 were the speed with which they could be deployed in a lifesaving situation, and also the unrivalled freedom they gave the diver once in the water. When diving enthusiast Captain Yves Le Prieur saw the Fernez2 at an industrial exhibition, he realized the design's full potential for recreational and military diving. He was searching for a way to combine the advantages of a self-contained air supply with the freedom of skin-diving with goggles or a face mask and snorkel. In 1926, the two men collaborated on the Fernez-Le Prieur scuba. It used Fernez's air hose, mouthpiece, goggles and nose clip but replaced the surface air pump with a 3-litre (¾-gallon) cylinder of compressed air worn on the diver's back that gave him about ten minutes underwater.

In 1933, Le Prieur designed a second scuba, without Fernez. 'L'Appareil Le Prieur' replaced Fernez's nose clip, goggles and mouthpiece with a full face mask supplied with air from a 6.5-litre (around 1½-gallon) compressed air cylinder, which gave the diver thirty minutes underwater but just ten minutes at 12 m (40 ft). The *appareil* had a primitive user-operated regulator, but it supplied air into the mask as a continuous flow rather than on demand and was therefore extremely wasteful. However, it was good enough to be adopted by the French Navy in 1935 and the French fire brigade the following year. In 1935, with fellow diving enthusiast and filmmaker Jean Painlevé (1902–1989), Le Prieur established the world's first diving club, the Club des sous-l'eau (the Underwater Club), which would be renamed the Club des scaphandres et de la vie sous l'eau (the Divers and Underwater Life Club). Among its members was French Navy Commander Louis de Corlieu (1888–1967), the man credited with the invention of the first rubber swimming fins in around 1930. The club was short-lived however, as a row between the two founders led to its dissolution in 1936.[16]

Just before the outbreak of the Second World War, all the elements of modern open-circuit scuba were in place: the compressed air tank, rubber hose and mouth piece, the depth and pressure gauges and a primitive on-demand regulator, swimming fins and face mask. In 1939, Le Prieur made the acquaintance of one of the men who would perfect his invention and whose name would become synonymous with scuba diving, Jacques-Yves Cousteau.

One Small Splash for Man

My parents' generation were amazed by Cousteau's books and feature-length movies, while mine was treated to a weekly hour-long adventure – most memorably, the American-made *The Undersea World of Jacques Cousteau* (1973–6), which had a native English narrator but many contributions by Cousteau himself, speaking in his fluent but heavily accented English and sounding like a Charles Aznavour of the deep. The world watched entranced as the divers on board the research ship *Calypso*, in their ever more sophisticated scuba gear and their saucer-shaped two-man sub, became 'aquanauts', who, like the Apollo astronauts who were taking humanity's first hesitant steps on the Moon, were entering the hitherto unknown and uncharted deeper realms of the aquatic world. Each episode seemed to feature another first: first scuba dive in a submerged cave system, first scuba dive in Lake Titicaca, first scuba dive under the polar ice, and first scuba dive in the Amazon River system.

Anyone who has been on the most basic diving course will be aware of the amount of time and preparation needed for even the shortest and shallowest of dives. Not only does the diver himself need his certification but there is also getting to the diving site and the care, maintenance and donning of the equipment – the second skin of the wetsuit, the air tanks and their network of gauges, hoses and mouthpiece, the mask and, worst of all for the neophyte, the flippers that are not only hell to put on, but then require you to walk like a circus clown with comedic oversized shoes to the side of the tender. For all the freedom the scuba gives you underwater, it turns you half-blind, half-deaf and almost paralysed on land. And, once in the water, your troubles have only just begun, because there is also the natural buoyancy of the human body, wetsuit and air tanks, which has to be corrected with weights, lest you spend your dive time bobbing on the surface like some discarded rubber bath toy.

Scuba requires that you master all the procedures that would save your life, such as taking off and putting on your Aqualung underwater, emptying a flooded mask and sharing your mouthpiece with a stricken buddy – of course, only the most experienced and foolhardy would ever dive alone, as all the technical wizardry that is keeping you alive underwater is also very fragile, and like all manmade equipment, prone to failure. Once you have got to your dive spot, you need to stay with your buddy, despite a field of view restricted pretty much to the front and a near total absence of external sound, which, though not absent from the undersea world, is drowned out by the rasping sounds of your breathing or the crackle of your radio if your mask is fitted with one.

Keeping one eye on your depth gauge, the other on the air tanks, a third on your diving buddy, and a fourth on what you came to see, you run out of time and have to consider how long you need to return to the surface safely without risking barotraumas or decompression sickness. The reader may have got the impression that though I love swimming, skin-diving and snorkelling, I am less than completely enamoured with scuba diving. Granted, I never progressed beyond the early stages of the sport, but when I compare the ease of walking, cycling or, worst-case scenario, driving to a likely rocky cove, in a swimsuit and carrying only a mask, snorkel and flippers in a bag slung over your shoulder, to the scale and complexity of a diving expedition, the comparison that springs to mind is between the mountain hiker going for a weekend hike and the high-altitude mountaineer making an attempt on a Himalayan peak. The views may be breathtaking from a mountain summit, but I'm quite happy to make do with a stunning hilltop view.

Even though in his documentary films and TV series Cousteau endeavoured to show the preparations for dives and the divers at work when filming, he still made it look far too easy. Behind the scenes there was the huge complex machinery of the research vessel and its associated land-based administration, support and funding, and the crews of technicians and cameramen, and unless the whole episode had been devoted to the many hundreds of hours of preparation and filming, and to the dangers involved, the viewers could never appreciate how difficult and complex a project it was to bring them their weekly unforgettable dose of coral reefs teeming with multicoloured life, barnacle-encrusted wrecks and cathedral-like polar ice caves. Although contemporary audiences have become jaded by decades of outstanding nature films, at the time, Cousteau amazed viewers as he discovered worlds never before seen by human eyes. Just as humanity was discovering outer space with NASA's Moon shots and probes, Cousteau was revealing the equally alien seascapes of inner space.

Cousteau, like Le Prieur, was a true diving enthusiast who yearned for the freedom to explore what he called *le monde du silence*, the silent underwater world. A French naval officer before the outbreak of the Second World War, he was familiar with pre-war diving equipment: the tried and tested but restrictive SDD; the rebreathers with their technical drawbacks and complexity that made them prone to failure and only allowed relatively shallow dives; and the early open-circuit scuba such as the Le Prieur apparatus, with its wasteful continuous-flow air supply and hand-controlled regulator. Cousteau did not let such a small thing as the Fall of France in 1940, the occupation of half its territory by the hereditary enemy, the Germans under the murderous Nazi dictator Adolf Hitler, and the collaboration of Marshal Philippe Pétain's Vichy regime get in the way of what was really important: the development of the first commercial scuba set – *scaphandre autonome* in French.

Les Mousquemers

Cousteau's accomplishments during his fifty-year career were extraordinary, because, to misquote another famous TV explorer, 'He boldly swam where no man had swum before.' But Cousteau was the fortunate heir of a generation of French inventors and diving enthusiasts, which included de Corlieu, Fernez and Le Prieur, and he himself was part of a team of three – with fellow divers Philippe Tailliez (1905–2002) and Frédéric Dumas (1913–1991),

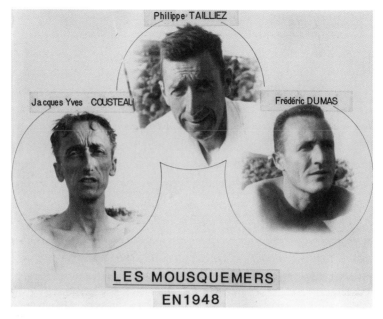

Philippe TAILLIEZ

Jacques Yves COUSTEAU

Frédéric DUMAS

LES MOUSQUEMERS
EN 1948

The three *Mousquemers,* Philippe Tailliez, Frédéric Dumas and Jacques-Yves Cousteau, skin-diving enthusiasts and spear fishermen who met before the Second World War on France's Mediterranean coast. They would remain together until 1949, when Cousteau left the French Navy. Interestingly, in this picture of the daredevil trio, Cousteau is only given second billing to Tailliez, possibly because the latter was the senior naval officer.

nicknamed *Les Mousquemers* in honour of Alexandre Dumas' three *mousquetaires* (musketeers) who each contributed to the development of scuba. The Three Musketeers had their d'Artganan, and the *Mousquemers* would not have been able to have their adventures without the fourth member of the crew – no daredevil diver he, but lab-bound gas engineering specialist Émile Gagnan (1900–1979), who worked on the Aqualung and persuaded his employer, Air Liquide, to finance the development of the prototype.

The account that Cousteau gives of his early diving career could be straight out of *Boy's Own* adventure fiction, but it is not romanticized, exaggerated or invented; his recollections in the autobiographical *The Silent World* are confirmed by Axel Masden's unauthorized but still very sympathetic biography.[17] Before the war, the young Cousteau had decided to join the French Air Force as a pilot but a car accident forced him to abandon his plans. This unhappy personal tragedy had the happiest of consequences for the worlds of diving and oceanography, because he opted instead to enlist in the French Navy. It was as a young naval officer stationed on France's Mediterranean coast that Cousteau first met his diving companions, fellow naval officer Philippe Tailliez and civilian diving enthusiast Frédéric Dumas, who were both avid skin-divers and spear fishermen. The trio free-dived with Fernez goggles, swam with mask and *tuba* (snorkel) and propelled themselves with de Corlieu fins. They saw Le Prieur's scuba and experimented with the earlier surface-supplied Fernez designs. On one dive, when Cousteau was on the surface and Dumas was using a Fernez apparatus, the air hose ruptured and Dumas was forced to return to the surface much faster than was safe. It was only his experience as a free-diver that allowed him to escape serious injury.[18]

The outbreak of the Second World War in September 1939 temporarily split up the *Mousquemers*, but France's lightning defeat in the spring of 1940 quickly reunited them. A naval officer without a navy, Cousteau concentrated on keeping his family safe and fed during the Axis occupation of the French Côte d'Azur, which fortunately for the *Mousquemers* was by the Italians and not by the much more hard-line Germans, who were to become notorious for their savage reprisals on the civilian population after attacks by the French Resistance. From their base in Bandol, halfway between Marseilles and Toulon, the three men resumed diving and were constantly on the lookout for ways to improve scuba technology and the diving experience. In December 1942, Cousteau visited Émile Gagnan in Paris to ask him to collaborate on what would be patented as the CG (Cousteau-Gagnan scuba set) and more imaginatively christened as the Aqualung – a shrewd marketing move by the Anglophile Cousteau. When Cousteau explained his ideas for a new *scaphandre autonome*, Gagnan showed him an automatic shut-off valve that he was working on to regulate the flow of natural gas to motorcar engines – an adaptation made necessary by the shortages of petrol in occupied France. The valve would become the basis for the on-demand regulator that was one of the key elements that gave humans both the necessary range and freedom of movement to explore the sea.

Gagnan and Cousteau tested the new valve in the Marne river, and Cousteau immediately realized that the regulator only worked properly if he was horizontal in the water, rather than vertical like an old-style diver wearing SDD. It seems obvious to us, with sixty years of hindsight, that the natural way for man to travel underwater would be swimming like a fish, but at the time free-divers and snorkellers swam and surface-supplied divers walked. Cousteau had to make the leap that would forever free humans underwater from being 'cripples in an alien land'. A second test in a pool in Paris persuaded Air Liquide to manufacture the first prototype Aqualung, which was delivered to an impatient Cousteau in 1943.[19]

There was still the small matter of the war. While the rest of France experienced an ever more brutal occupation by the German forces, now pressed on several fronts by the Allies and harassed by the French Resistance, Cousteau and his friends and family lived in a bubble in their villa hideaway. They were not quite isolated from the hardships of the occupation, however. Food was rationed, and because divers expend many more calories than workers engaged in terrestrial work, the team stocked up on beans to make up the calorific shortfall caused by meat being so strictly rationed. The sea is a natural larder stocked with all kinds of high-protein edibles, but the calorific expenditure used up in an undersea hunt with a harpoon or spear gun would have exceeded the resulting calorific gains.

On his first Aqualung dive in the Mediterranean, Cousteau temporarily resolved the food-supply problem when he stumbled onto a calorific treasure trove. Shadowed by Tailliez and Dumas in a boat, the latter ready to free-dive to Cousteau's rescue should the Aqualung fail, while his wife Simone followed him on the surface with fins, mask and snorkel, Cousteau recalled the elation he felt on his first outing:

> I swam across the rocks and compared myself favour-
> ably with the sea bream. To swim fishlike, horizontally,
> was the logical method in a medium eight hundred

times denser than air. To halt and hang attached to nothing, no lines or air pipe to the surface, was a dream . . . Now I flew without wings.[20]

The Aqualung performed faultlessly, and Cousteau gave in to his curiosity and investigated an underwater cave. The cave mouth was a tight fit, and the air cylinders scraped the rocky sides. He realized that he was risking the rupture of the fragile rubber hoses that kept him alive, but ignoring the danger, he swam and scraped his way into the cave. He was rewarded by a sight that, though only a short distance from the shore and below the waves, and one that had no doubt been swum, rowed and sailed over ever since humans first entered the Mediterranean, was, by virtue of its depth, one that no other human had ever seen: the ceiling of the cave was covered with lobsters – among the first sea creatures to succumb to this human invader in what had until then been a secure refuge from lobster pots, fishermen and skin-divers.

All danger forgotten, Cousteau collected a couple of lobsters and swam up to Simone, instructing her to stash them somewhere on shore. She swam back to shore and asked a fisherman to keep an eye on her catch. The man was amazed as Simone went back and forth bringing up more lobsters, completely unaware of the unseen Cousteau beneath the waves. Dining on a lobster feast that evening, the *Mousquemers* discussed the colonization of the sea, dreaming of making its vast spaces and untold riches available to humanity – hoping, no doubt, to put an end once and for all to the wars caused by humanity's petty squabbles over land and natural resources.

Filming the Silent World

Cousteau's subsequent fifty-year career is recorded in a total output of twelve short films, four full-length feature films, and sixty television shows, including 36 episodes of *The Undersea World of Jacques Cousteau* (made for ABC) and twelve episodes of *Oasis in Space* and *Cousteau Odyssey* (made for PBS and TBS).[21] After the war, Cousteau remained in the French Navy, where he and the other two *Mousquemers* continued to hone their diving and cinematographic skills and to improve the design of the Aqualung. It is difficult to say who benefited most from the arrangement: Cousteau, from access to the resources of the state during a time of rationing and reconstruction, or the French Navy, from his scuba expertise. Their association ended in 1949, when Cousteau won the assistance of influential and wealthy sponsors, including British politician, businessman and philanthropist Loel Guinness, who financed the purchase and conversion of *Calypso*, a decommissioned British minesweeper that became Cousteau's research vessel and diving tender until his death in 1997.

In 1957, Cousteau was appointed director of the Oceanographic Museum and Institute of the tiny Mediterranean principality of Monaco. Again the arrangement that brought Cousteau to Monaco was one of mutual benefit: he gained a permanent base of operations independent of any major European country, with a Mediterranean coastline, which would become significant in 1960 when he opposed the French Nuclear Agency's plan to dump radioactive waste in the Mediterranean; the ruler of Monaco, Prince Rainier III (1923–2005), was able to capitalize on Cousteau's international fame to revive the principality's flagging fortunes after the war. Sailing out of her Monégasque anchorage, *Calypso* would circumnavigate the world numerous times, visit its polar oceans and navigate its great river systems. A pioneer of marine conservation, Cousteau understood, long before most scientists and politicians, the fragility of the aquatic ecosphere that for millennia had been humanity's highway, larder and dumping ground.

Cousteau's true genius, however, was in his ability to share his adventures, discoveries and concerns with a worldwide audience through the medium of film. His entire diving career is recorded in feature-length films and shorts and several made-for-TV documentary series, which, though they are no longer shown, are available free of charge on archive sites such as YouTube, Google and Vimeo. Cousteau's cinematographic career pre-dates the Cousteau-Gagnan scuba set. In 1942, he, with companions Tailliez and Dumas, shot the first French underwater short, *Par dix-huit mètres de fond* (Eighteen Metres Deep), which won him the first of many awards. His next film, *Épaves* (Wrecks), shot in 1943, again with Tailliez and Dumas, was the first to make use of the full potential of scuba as the *Mousquemers* visited a series of shipwrecks off the French coast. Because of the shortage of cine film, the team had to splice together rolls of black-and-white still film stock. The result, however, was masterly, and the film won an award at the first post-war Cannes Film Festival in 1946.[22]

The movie that turned Cousteau from the diver's diver, explorer and oceanographer into an international celebrity was *Le Monde du silence* (The Silent World), made with the collaboration of French filmmaker Louis Malle, which was shot on board *Calypso* during two diving seasons in 1954–5 and released in France in 1956. According to Axel Masden, the film stunned its audiences because it was shot in full colour at a time when much film and TV output was still in black and white. His lyrical description of the impact that the film had on its audiences made me think that he was talking of his own reaction:

> From the introduction of divers with phosphorous torches moving through the blue-grey depths, to images of never-before-seen life forms on the deep magenta of coral carpets, scenes of the businesslike deck of the research vessel, of thundering along white-caps with racing Dolphins, and gazing into the purple coils of a sea anemone, the movie was one hour and twenty-seven minutes of marvels and thrills.[23]

The year of its release, *Le Monde du silence* won the Palme d'Or at Cannes and the Academy Award for Best Documentary Feature – at the time, a rare accomplishment for a foreign-language documentary.

Cousteau's Living Legacy

The Aqualung was the right invention at the right time, give or take a few years to wrap up the Second World War and to get French post-war reconstruction going. But Cousteau used the remaining wartime years and his time with the French Navy to lay the foundations for the huge commercial success of the Aqualung – not consciously, because making money from his invention was never his aim, but by exploring the full potential of scuba and making his adventures available through the medium of books and films. Quickly adopted by the Western world's navies and special forces in the late 1940s, the Aqualung next found a ready market in the expanding post-war leisure industry.

The huge popularity of open-circuit scuba for leisure led to the early creation of sub-aqua clubs – such as the Club alpin sous-marin, founded in Cannes in 1946 by Frédéric Dumas, and the Brighton Bottom Scratchers, founded in 1954 as an affiliate of one of the oldest swimming clubs in the UK, the Brighton Swimming Club[24] – and also of recreational diving and diver training organizations. The world's two earliest scuba diving organizations appeared in France in 1948, merging to form the Fédération française d'études et de sports sous-marins in 1955. In Britain, the British Sub-aqua

One of Cousteau's many firsts included the first use of scuba to excavate an underwater marine site – the wreck of a Roman galley found off the Tunisian coast that had been partially excavated by divers using SDD earlier in the twentieth century. Pictured here is a marine archaeologist examining the cargo of amphorae from an ancient shipwreck in the Mediterranean.

Jacques Cousteau giving a lecture after he had given up the idea of colonizing and developing the oceans to pioneer the conservation of all aquatic environments and their protection from dumping, pollution and over-exploitation. One of his early victories was preventing the dumping of nuclear waste by the French government in the Mediterranean in 1960.

Club was founded in 1953 and was recognized as the governing body of the sport in 1954. The three largest organizations that now assure the training and certification for recreational diving are CMAS (Confédération mondiale des activités subaquatiques), founded in Monaco in 1959; NAUI (National Association of Underwater Instructors), founded in 1960 in Florida; and PADI (Professional Association of Diving Instructors), founded in California in 1966.[25]

In addition to inspiring generations of recreational divers and underwater cinematographers to visit reefs, wrecks, lakes, rivers and cave systems, Cousteau had a hand in the development of every field of scuba diving, including marine archaeology, when he was involved in the excavation of a sunken Roman ship off the Tunisian coast; underwater habitats, with the Conshelf experiments; submersibles, with his design for the diving saucer; salvage and underwater rescue; as well as saturation diving experiments for underwater engineering, construction and oil exploration and exploitation, which I shall cover in greater detail in Chapter Eleven.

Although Cousteau was no master submariner, archaeologist or engineer, he led the way in all these fields, demonstrating the extraordinary potential of open-circuit scuba to specialists who then took his work forward. One area, however, where he was not only a trailblazer but also became a leading expert and campaigner, was marine conservation. Having begun his diving career with dreams of colonizing the ocean bottom with cities, farms, mines and industrial installations, Cousteau quickly realized the fragility of the aquatic ecosphere and its vulnerability to damage from pollution, dumping and the over-exploitation of biological and mineral resources. Having prevented the French Nuclear Agency from dumping radioactive waste in the Mediterranean, he devoted much of his career to protecting the oceans from further depredations.

Although our seas and oceans are under serious threat from climate-change-generated acidification and the scourge of dumped plastics entering the marine food chain, their plight would have been far worse without Cousteau's sustained conservation initiatives over four decades. These have allowed us the great pleasure and privilege of visiting the underwater world in a way that our ancestors could only dream of, while at the same time, his work ensured that there would something worth seeing when we got there.

9
This Sporting Life

Tuesday afternoon three men, for a wager of eight guineas,
swam from Westminster to London Bridge. The victor
was carried on shoulders of porters to a public house in
Borough, where he drank such a quantity of gin, that he
expired in about half an hour after his victory.

JOHN GOULSTONE, *A CHRONOLOGY OF BRITISH SWIMMING,
1766–1837* (1999)[1]

Two of the activities that sustain the modern love affair with
swimming are leisure and fitness. When I started researching
this book, I took it for granted that the third would be competition
in four of the five regulated aquatic sports: short- and long-course
swimming, open-water swimming, water polo and synchronized
swimming.[2] After writing this chapter, however, I do not think that
competition plays such an important role in the current popularity
of swimming, though historically it did play a significant role in
making swimming such a conspicuous and ubiquitous feature of
modern life in the Western world. Although swimming is a hominid
skill that pre-dates the appearance of our species, and the history
of organized competitive sport is 2,800 years old, competitive swimming as an amateur sport is less than 200 years old. In order to
explain this discrepancy, this chapter must explore the origins and
development of sport over the past three millennia, covering lengthy
periods during which swimming was not practised as a sport (or
sometimes at all by the majority of the population). Nevertheless,
it would be impossible to understand contemporary aquatic sports
without understanding earlier conceptions of sporting competition
that excluded the aquatic disciplines.

Organized sport traces its origins back to ancient Greece in the
eighth century BCE, but the sports-mad Hellenes did not consider
swimming or any other aquatic discipline worthy of consideration

An iconic image of modern competitive swimming from the 2016 Rio
Olympics. In the early twenty-first century, competitive swimming is once
again what it had been in the early nineteenth: a grand popular spectacle,
in which the athletes not only win kudos but are able to earn state
government funding and commercial sponsorship.

as a competitive sport. Thus, the first question this chapter needs
to answer is why a seafaring people like the ancient Greeks, who
routinely exploited the commercial and military aspects of swimming and free-diving, did not value aquatic skills in the same way
as they did the athletic and equestrian events that formed the basis
for competitions in the ancient world for approximately twelve
centuries. By late antiquity, a combination of Roman prudishness,
barbarian incursions and Christian intolerance had led to the abolition of all sporting festivals in Greece. Without the structure of
organized sport that sustained it, the culture of male athleticism
that had been fostered in the Greek world's gymnasia since the sixth
century BCE withered and died.

Despite the Church's fears about displays of the body, combined
with the belief that people should be on their knees praying rather
than having a good time, games, contests of skill, physical pastimes
and entertainments did not disappear: children continued to play,
and adults to divert themselves either as participants or spectators,
but the concept of playing sport for its own sake, national and

international competitions, as well as the status of the professional athlete, disappeared for almost 1,500 years. During the European Renaissance, the rediscovery of texts outlining the ideals and practices of classical athletics, vividly illustrated by ancient artworks depicting athletes engaged in sporting activities, did not lead to the immediate revival of ancient practices and institutions, but it did set in motion the lengthy process that would lead to the emergence of new types of organized sport in the eighteenth century.

Swimming provides a case study of how a physical activity that had not been a sport in the ancient world became a trial of skill and endurance practised by a handful of gifted individuals for monetary gain in the eighteenth century and then gradually morphed into a form of mass entertainment and a nascent competitive sport in the first half of the nineteenth century. During the second half of the nineteenth century, swimming became firmly established in the industrialized world, with a growing infrastructure of regulated open-water venues and indoor and outdoor pools, swimming clubs, governing bodies and competitions, but its subsequent trajectory was not dictated by considerations specific to the sport of swimming but by the position its organizers and participants took in the much wider debate about whether sport should be an amateur pastime pursued for its own sake, or a professional activity from which participants could earn a living.

The amateur–professional divide continued to influence the development and practice of competitive swimming at all levels until the closing decades of the twentieth century, when changes in the ways sport was funded made the distinction redundant. Today, the five aquatic disciplines take pride of place at the great sporting jamboree that is the modern Summer Olympics, with extraordinary sums lavished on providing state-of-the-art facilities to ensure the maximum coverage of all events, turning them from the Cinderellas of the sporting world into true spectacles that rival anything tennis, athletics and team sports have to offer. However, though swimming is undoubtedly a mass-participation leisure and fitness activity, and the competitive aquatic disciplines have a large number of participants at local, national and international levels, organized swimming is not a mass-participation spectacle on a par with sports such as football, rugby, cricket and baseball.

There is a strange disconnect between elite competition and the leisure and fitness swimming that the bulk of the population practise and enjoy. To express it in terms of recent sporting personalities, though many aspiring sportsmen seek to emulate the financial and sporting successes of David Beckham and Cristiano Ronaldo, how many want to follow in Ian Thorpe's and Michael Phelps's wake?

The Greek Legacy

Competitive sport is now such an integral part of contemporary Western culture that it is easy to forget that, in historical terms, it is a relatively recent revival. The archaic Greeks (eighth to sixth centuries BCE) incorporated athletic events into their religious festivals, turning several of these into national and international contests that completely eclipsed the original religious celebration. During the classical periods (fifth to fourth centuries BCE), Greek athletes commonly competed in six athletic disciplines: running, long jump, discus, javelin, wrestling and *pankration*,[3] as well as in equestrian events, including horse and chariot races at the four major Panhellenic sporting festivals: the Isthmian Games held on the Isthmus of Corinth, the Nemean Games held at Nemea, the Pythian Games held at Delphi and, the most famous, the Olympic Games, held at the sanctuary of Zeus at Olympia from 776 BCE until their abolition in 394 CE.

In addition, individual cities held their own sporting contests in which athletes competed in the Olympic sports, as well as events with a more local flavour.[4] What is absent from the historical record, and needs to be accounted for, is any mention of swimming events, although the classical Greeks celebrated many festivals dedicated to the divinities of the sea to whom they owed their survival, livelihoods and defence against their main foes, the Persians. Although one of the Panhellenic contests, the Isthmian Games, were dedicated to the sea god Poseidon, they featured the same athletic and equestrian events as the other Panhellenic games. The events the

The ancient Greeks were a maritime people who exploited the resources of the sea for survival and trade; yet, they did not consider swimming a suitable activity for sporting competition. The sports they practised at the local and Panhellenic games were athletic and equestrian events, and one of the highlights of the ancient Olympic Games was the *stadion* foot race, the equivalent of today's 100-m men's final. Painter of Oxford, storage jar, *c.* 500 BCE.

sea god was most closely associated with were the equestrian events, because, in addition to his duties as the ruler of the seas and oceans, Poseidon was known as the 'father of horses', whose origins were probably among the land-based horse-riding nomads of the Pontic steppes who had migrated south with their gods.

Participation in competitive sport was a privilege accorded to all freeborn male Greeks, though once Greece had been incorporated into the Roman Empire in the second century BCE, all freeborn Roman citizens were allowed to compete in the Panhellenic games. For the classical Greeks, participation in sport had a variety of inter-related meanings: a religious obligation, service to one's city-state, for the glory of sport itself, as a form of military training, a means of attaining one's *arete* – one's full potential as a citizen and human being – and, for the gifted few, a full-time and very lucrative career as professional athletes. The Greeks, however, made no formal distinction between what would later be called amateur athletes and professional sportsmen.[5]

Ancient Greece's sporting events had a distinct martial flavour, and they had their origins in military training. What were conspicuous by their absence in ancient competitions were any aquatic events. Although swimming and free-diving were valued skills and had their own military applications, they were taught formally like other martial and athletic skills, as discussed earlier. Indeed, being able to swim, like literacy, was taken for granted – a skill that was expected of all freeborn male citizens even if they did not take part in other types of sporting competitions. The question remains as to why the ancient Greeks, whose lives were governed by a deeply ingrained spirit of competitiveness, did not consider swimming a suitable activity for competition.

Several possible answers present themselves, the first being purely practical. Unlike the Romans, who built both private and public swimming pools and baths, the Greeks did not equip their cities with lavish *thermae* until the Roman period. Greece also lacks deep rivers and large bodies of fresh water where open-water swimming races could be held. However, it is a peninsula, and many ancient sites are on the coast or within easy reach of it, so there was no reason for swimming events not to be staged in the sea. During the first modern Olympiad, held in Athens in 1896, funds could not be found to build the planned swimming pool in the Olympic complex, so the swimming races took place in one the bays of the nearby port of Piraeus.

A second reason could be to do with the nature of the festivals with which the games were associated. Ancient Greek festivals were 'spectacular' in both senses of the word: they were on a very grand scale and involved the participation of the entire population of the city or province, or in the case of the four Panhellenic games, of representatives and spectators from all over the Greek world. Until the era of underwater cameras, aquatic events suffered when compared to terrestrial sports in terms of their visual impact. However, as we shall see later, long before the advent of film and

TV, swimming races and entertainments drew large crowds of appreciative spectators.

Reason number three could be that swimming was not seen as a specialized skill, such as wrestling or a prowess with the discus or javelin, but more like a universal ability such as walking. Running, however, is no more specialized than swimming, yet the foot races were among the highlights of the ancient games. A related explanation is that rather than a martial skill, swimming was too closely associated with manual labour, which in classical Greek society was performed by slaves and never by freeborn citizens. However, in the story of Scyllias, the diver who sabotaged the Persian fleet and whom I discussed in Chapter Four, we find a respected professional free-diver performing a valued military service for the Greek cause.

One final possible explanation might lie in the origins of the peoples who migrated into the Balkan Peninsula. Although there is no general agreement as to their exact origins, it seems likely that several of the migrating groups that settled in Greece came from the Central Asian steppes – an area distant from the sea and with few major rivers. Evidence of their terrestrial origins, I suggested in Chapter Two, can be seen in the attributes of the sea god Poseidon, who was also the god of earthquakes and horses. If the Proto-Hellenes were nomadic pastoralists with little or no experience of the aquatic world, it could explain the terrestrial and equestrian bias of the athletic events with which they chose to honour their gods.

Although the ancient Greeks never competed in swimming, it is important to understand their attitudes to competitive sport because Greek practices and sports festivals were revived in the modern period, and Greek ideals, or rather their reinterpretation by nineteenth-century educators and sporting enthusiasts, were used to shape the development and practice of many sports and define who could and could not compete for much of the twentieth century. What the Greeks would not have understood was the distinction between amateur and professional athletes – the term athlete is derived from the Greek verb *athlein* meaning to compete for a prize – therefore being financially rewarded for victory was always part of Greek sporting culture. Although the Panhellenic games did not award cash prizes, victorious athletes were richly rewarded by their cities, and local games provided lavish prizes in kind that could be converted into ready cash. One of the most successful ancient athletes was the professional wrestler Milo of Croton (*fl.* sixth century BCE) who, while winning a record number of titles at all Panhellenic games, acquired a vast fortune that would rival or exceed the earnings of the most handsomely sponsored Olympian or richly paid professional football or baseball star today.[6]

The Games People Played

The Church is usually given the blame for eliminating any aspect of classical culture that had survived into late antiquity. And while it is true that it was the late fourth-century Christian emperor Theodosius the Great who abolished all pagan cults and their associated festivals, including the Olympic Games in 394 CE, he merely completed a process that had begun centuries earlier. The Romans played their part with their disapproval of athletic nudity and their demilitarization of the Greek city-states, which removed one of the main reasons for athletic training and competition. More significant, however, was the damage caused to the sporting infrastructure by the mass migrations of Germanic and Slavic peoples into Europe that took place between the third and fifth centuries CE.

Organized sport re-emerged some 1,500 years later in England, a country that lay on the northern fringes of the Roman world. Roman Britain, though wealthy and civilized by Roman standards, was also the most distant province from the Greek-speaking eastern half of the empire and its capital, Constantinople (now Istanbul). Romano-British sporting culture consisted of the gladiatorial combats favoured by the Romans rather than the athletic displays favoured by the Greeks. While in the east, the empire endured for another millennium and the Christian Orthodox Church was central in eliminating the last remnants of pagan culture, in Britain, Christian Romano-British culture succumbed to the pagan Anglo-Saxon invaders in the fifth century.

Between the fifth and eleventh centuries, England was transformed by successive waves of migrants and invaders, starting with the Anglo-Saxons. Once they had been Christianized in the seventh century, they themselves succumbed to new pagan intruders, the Norse, between the eighth and tenth centuries, before both Anglo-Saxons and Norse were themselves conquered by the Normans in the eleventh century. Many of the sports played in England during the Middle Ages had their origins in Germanic and Norse lands that had never been part of the Roman Empire. Individual sports included archery and wrestling and team sports, primitive versions of golf, cricket, football and hockey.[7] One of the major motivations for participating in sport was military training. As historian of medieval sport John Carter explained: 'The peasant's sport and games, like those of the warrior class, were often directly and sometimes indirectly influenced by the endemic warfare of the feudal epoch.' He added that even the sedate game of chess could get out of hand, with the players resorting to violence.[8] But he pointed out that sport had other functions for commoners:

> These sports serve as an index of the age. Sports in England and Normandy were inseparably linked with man's occupation and with man's physical and spiritual survival. Such sports as falconry and hunting tended to be monopolized by the nobility . . . The servile classes mimicked their superiors, and in many instances, improved games that without fail 'carried them away' (from the Latin *desporto*, *deportare)* from their daily drudgery.[9]

Escapism and fun played a negligible role as motivations for participation in athletic training and competition in classical Greece. Sport was far too serious an affair, with its many social, religious, military and educational functions, and classical athletes would have found the sentiment expressed in twentieth-century sports writer Grantland Rice's maxim, 'It's not whether you win or lose, it's how you play the game,' quite alien. For the ultra-competitive Greeks, who left drudgery to their slaves, all that mattered was winning. In contrast, sport in the Middle Ages had two distinct functions: as a mirror of and preparation for war, and as an escape from the harshness of daily life. Carter does mention swimming among medieval pastimes, but as a form of recreation rather than a competitive sport on a par with football, and one which often led to fatalities by drowning.[10]

These two different conceptions of sport – ancient Greek *athlein* and medieval *desport* – began to come together during the European Renaissance, but before they could hybridize to create modern sporting culture, sport underwent a further transformation between the sixteenth and eighteenth centuries when it became fully monetized. This occurred at both ends of the social scale: the elite sport of horseracing was the first to get a national governing body in England, the Jockey Club, founded in 1760; while the commoner pursuits of boxing and wrestling became prizefighting, with gifted athletes winning handsome purses and sponsors and spectators betting large sums on the outcome of fights.[11]

In ancient Greece, sport was something the elites took part in for the greater glory of the gods and the Hellenic race, but in eighteenth-century England, it was something that the elites watched for their own entertainment and sometimes profit, as sport was yet another opportunity for the British aristocracy to engage in its favourite pastime of gambling. Perversely, the spectating gamblers were the ones known as the 'sportsmen', who bet on the outcome of horse races and boxing and wrestling matches, relegating the competitors to the rank of servants and entertainers. In the case of horse racing, the livestock was much more valuable than their human entourage of stable boys, trainers and riders. During this formative period of English sport, swimming underwent the same process of professionalization as prizefighting, with talented swimmers taking on challenges for wagers or races for prize money. Gradually a small group of professional swimmers emerged who made their living from racing, teaching swimming and putting on swimming displays and entertainments.

'Feats in Swimming and Other Aquatic Exertions'

It is one of the serendipitous joys of library research, as compared to the now almost universal Internet variety, that one occasionally comes across an unpublished, unregarded gem, such as John Goulstone's typewritten *A Chronology of British Swimming, 1766– 1837, with Accounts of the Manchester Swimmers Isaac Bedale and Matthew Vipond* (1999) – a collection of press cuttings presented in chronological order that give a snapshot of swimming in England before the advent of official bodies such as the ASA (Amateur Swimming Association) and regulated competitions. I was particularly taken with the entry for 1791 that opens this chapter, which sees the victorious swimmer drinking so much gin after his race that 'he expired in about half an hour after his victory.' Fortunately, prizes for latterday competitions do not run to fatal doses of bathtub gin.

The initial phase of competitive swimming took the form of private challenges and wagers competed for in natural bodies of water. The chronology reveals no restrictions of age or gender. In 1806, a young woman swam a mile in Norwich's river Yare 'for a small wager'. If she swam dressed in female undergarments made of linen or woollen fabrics that would immediately become waterlogged the feat is all the more impressive. But such challenges were not for the unwary: in 1824, a man drowned while attempting to swim across the Serpentine in Hyde Park. Three years later, however, another man bet that he could swim the Serpentine in twelve minutes with his hands and feet tied. Unfortunately, there is no record of weather he won his bet, but at least we can be fairly certain that he did not drown, as this would probably have made the next editions of *Bell's Life* or *The Sporting Magazine*, two publications that regularly reported on sporting wagers and events during the nineteenth century.

There was clearly a public interest in swimming as the 2 September 1832 edition of *Bell's Life* featured the Olympic Festival held at The Stadium, a Thames-side pleasure garden in the grounds of Cremorne House, Chelsea, which included a day devoted to 'feats in swimming and other aquatic exertions'. These events attracted professional swimmers who gave demonstrations, competed in races and accepted challenges for prize money and wagers. One such nineteenth-century swimmer was Matthew Vipond, who had made his name as a prizefighter. His great rival, Isaac Bedale, who styled himself 'Doctor' Bedale and was described as an 'amphibious son of Galen' but who most likely was some kind of quack practitioner selling patent remedies, challenged other swimmers to swim against him for the not inconsiderable prize of 500 guineas (now over £300,000). It is unlikely that he ever had a tenth of that sum to wager, or that he allowed another swimmer to defeat him, using any means at his disposal – be they fair or, most likely, foul. One of his 'aquatic exertions' involved swimming from London Bridge to Greenwich, an event that attracted a large, cheering crowd of spectators that lined the banks of the River Thames. The last of the breed was another self-styled 'Professor', Fred Beckwith

Fred Beckwith, the last of the great Victorian 'professors' – swimming professionals who made their living by teaching, racing for prizes and putting on swimming entertainments that drew large appreciative crowds, who were all the more impressed as most would have been non-swimmers. Although Beckwith himself was not reputed to be a particularly expert swimmer, his four children, both male and female, were all professional champions.

(1821–1898), racer, teacher and swimming impresario. He put on popular entertainments, featuring his four children in the aquatic displays. He was also notorious for making large wagers on the outcome of races and of making sure that he backed the winner.[12]

The Great Divide

The origins of swimming as an amateur competitive sport in England can be traced back to 1837, the year the National Swimming Society (NSS) organized a swimming competition in the Serpentine which was described in *Bell's Life* as 'A final or "grand heat" for prizes swum in the Serpentine'. *Bell's Life* praised the NSS as 'A society to be established for the purpose of teaching youths the necessary art of swimming'. The race was swum by twelve of the 200 boys taught swimming by the society.[13] The NSS was a typical Victorian creation, dedicated to moral improvement, wholesome exercise and empire building. In 1840, a second would-be national governing body, the British Swimming Society (BSS), was established with the more limited aims of promoting 'health and cleanliness by encouraging swimming' and which also organized races.[14] The existence of two rival organizations with differing aims meant that neither was particularly effective in taking control of swimming on the national level.

Despite moral concerns over betting and race fixing among professional swimmers, both the NSS and BSS employed 'professors' to teach swimming at open-water venues such as the Serpentine and the Thames, and later in the new in-ground pools that were being built all over the country. As many of the early pools were only open in the warmer months of the year, professors organized 'benefits' featuring races and entertainments, which were the ancestor of today's swimming galas, to supplement their seasonal income. Without a national governing body, until the mid-1840s, the running of swimming remained in the hands of the professors, who did not make a distinction between amateur and professional swimmers. Until the 1860s swimming was seen not so much as a competitive sport but as a form of commercial entertainment.[15]

The latter half of the nineteenth century was a period of huge investment in swimming infrastructure, after the Baths and Wash-houses Acts of 1846 and 1878, which in turn created a whole new type of swimmer. For the first time, safe swimming in a controlled environment in in-ground, heated pools attracted the Victorian middle classes, who were always on the lookout for new diversions, as long as they were also character building and conformed to that great Victorian obsession, respectability. This sudden interest in swimming meant that it was no longer the province of a small number of professionals, but was fast becoming a mass-participation activity that involved a variety of stakeholders alongside the professors: the municipalities that financed the construction of the pools and the organizers and members of the swimming clubs that were springing up all over the country.

The Clubbing Spirit

It would be impossible to include a comprehensive history of all swimming clubs in England; therefore, I have decided to focus on a single case study, Brighton Swimming Club, to illustrate the role of swimming clubs in the development of competitive swimming. The club may not be able to claim the distinction of being the first to be established in England, but it is the oldest that has remained in continuous operation until the present day. The English are a very clubbable race, though not always in the sociable sense of the term applied to Dr Johnson, 'the most clubbable man in London', but rather that a group of Englishmen and -women pursuing a common interest or hobby – be it restoring vintage cars, gardening, playing bridge or swimming – are almost certain to establish a club, with a committee, a chair, finance officer and membership secretary, who then decide the all-important club rules and membership criteria.

The result can be the exact opposite of sociability, as the club can spawn an 'us-versus-the-rest' mentality, especially where the allocation of scarce resources such as pool time is involved. But on the flipside, the formal structure of a club provides a nucleus of dedicated members, who, while they themselves might have retired from the activity, provide the organizational skills, experience and sometimes the funds to ensure the club's survival during the periodic crises that are bound to affect any organization. This certainly proved to be true in the case of the Brighton Swimming Club, founded 1860, which twice survived the demolition of its club headquarters, the first time because of urban redevelopment and the second due to a major storm, and weathered two world wars and any number of economic recessions.

It is not surprising that Brighton should be the host city of one of the first swimming clubs in England and the world, because its associations with therapeutic bathing were over a century old when a small group of enthusiasts met in a Brighton hotel in 1858 to discuss the establishment of a swimming club in the town. Two years later the club was formed with an initial membership of thirteen, who paid a joining fee of one shilling (approximately £4.50 at today's prices) and a weekly subscription of two old pennies (around 68 new pence). As there was no public swimming pool in Brighton, club members swam in the sea, and sessions had to take place between six and eight in the morning. As it was still the custom for many men to swim in the nude, the city fathers feared that the all-male club might cause public offence if it was allowed to meet at times when respectable ladies were taking their morning constitutionals on the sea front. Despite these restrictions and the absence of any changing facilities in the first year, the club thrived, organizing its first swimming gala in July 1861, which attracted many spectators and competitors despite the early-morning start.

In 1862, the club purchased a shed where members could change – clearly a popular move as by 1863 the membership had more than tripled to 59. The club survived its first major crisis when its sheds were demolished to make way for the new Brighton Aquarium. In 1872 the club moved into its new headquarters, the quaintly named 'Hole in the Wall', in one of the arches below the promenade east of the Palace Pier. Racing was a feature of the club's activities from its earliest years, with a 1,000-yard (914-m) race for adults and a 500-yard (457-m) race for younger swimmers, with small prizes in both cash and kind, and small payments for the officials, practices that would later be outlawed by the Amateur Swimming Association. The club's first gala featured 100-, 150- and 200-yard races (91, 137 and 183 m) and a diving competition for both adults and youths.

By 1875, the club's future was assured when it reached a membership of 115. Henceforth, it helped to establish other clubs on the south coast, including Portsmouth SC, against whom it held regular competitions. The club's annual festival in 1877, held that year at the fashionable Sussex resort of Shoreham, 7 miles east of Brighton, was particularly spectacular and well-attended; it included a swimming gala, competitions in other sports and open-air concerts. In 1885, the club introduced the event that remains one of the highlights of the swimming year, the Christmas Day Swim, instituting the Christmas Day handicap a decade later. Another very popular open-water event, the yearly Pier to Pier Race, was inaugurated in 1936 at the behest of Brighton Council. In 1893, the club's annual fete, held off the West Pier, attracted a record entry of 194 competitors from twenty British clubs who took part in ten 'entertainments'. At the same time, the club was taking a leading role in the formal organization of aquatic sports in England, hosting the headquarters of the Sussex County Amateur Swimming Association and establishing the Sussex Water Polo Association (1893).

Since its earliest years, the club had been lobbying the municipality to build a public swimming pool. Finally, in 1895, the town opened its first swimming baths, in North Road. The club had played an advisory role during the planning of the baths and provided the entertainment for the opening ceremony. Henceforth many of the club's activities moved to the new baths, which shortly afterwards staged the 500-yard and 220-yard Championships of England and which in 1913 hosted a water polo match between England and Wales and the 100-yard Championship of England – all staged under the strict ASA rules that by then excluded professional swimmers from taking part in amateur competition.

The club continued to thrive through the post-war period, opening a sub-aqua section in 1954. It now offers swimming sessions in four pools in the Brighton area for junior, age group and masters swimmers, sea swimming, water polo and synchronized swimming. The club holds yearly championships and takes part in county and national competitions. The Christmas Day Swim and Pier to Pier Race remain popular favourites, drawing large crowds of participants and spectators.[16]

Over my swimming career, I have swum with many similar clubs in England, continental Europe, Australia, New Zealand, Japan and the United States. What all these clubs have in common is the 'amateur ethos': they are associations of like-minded enthusiasts who have full-time jobs and for whom swimming is a hobby – albeit, for many, one that burns up all their spare time and energy on training and competition and accounts for a considerable financial outlay in equipment, membership dues and travel to national swim meets. The amateur ethos, which originated in the second half of the nineteenth century, is the fourth and final component of modern sporting culture (after leisure, fitness and competition).

Organizing Aquatic Sport

The proliferation of public and private pools in the second half of the century led to the establishment of swimming clubs all over England. As competition was an important aspect of these amateur clubs, there was a need for a single overarching body to establish common rules for swimming races and water polo matches and organize, run and validate local and national championships. But progress towards the creation of a national organization to oversee aquatic sport in England was stymied by the existence of two rival would-be governing bodies: the NSS and BSS. In 1868 several London clubs met at a special congress at the German Gymnasium in King's Cross, with the aim of improving the state of competitive swimming in the capital. The next few years saw the foundation of several competing bodies, including the Metropolitan Swimming Association (MSA), founded in 1870 by five London clubs to 'promote and encourage the art of swimming', and the Swimming Association of Great Britain (SAGB), founded in 1874. In 1873 the MSA issued the Laws of Amateur Swimming, establishing the first formal distinctions between amateur and professional swimmers:

1 Persons who have competed for money prizes, for wagers, for public or admission money, or who have otherwise made the art of swimming a means of pecuniary profit, shall not be allowed to compete as amateurs.

2 Any amateur competing against a professional swimmer shall be disqualified from all future amateur contests.

3 Winners of club prizes shall not be disqualified from open competitions.[17]

The rules seem clear and straightforward, but their application at a time when professionals were still a vocal group within swimming was far from easy. For one thing, not all clubs supported so draconian a distinction, and then there was the matter of deciding when someone had infringed laws 1 or 2, and what exactly constituted 'money prizes' – especially as the MSA had established a loophole with clause 3, dealing with 'club prizes'. But by the 1880s, the professors were being squeezed out of competitive swimming. Having lost control of the clubs, and no longer able to organize galas and benefits or to compete against amateurs for prizes, they had to find new livelihoods. Beckwith opened a cigar shop and later a hotel. But it was not the strictures of organized swimming alone that killed off professional swimming. Another major element in the 1880s was the competition from other professional sports, especially football. In-ground pools could accommodate 200–300 spectators at most, while football grounds could hold thousands. Hence the spectators who had flocked to see open-water races and 'entertainments' were going elsewhere, leaving the enthusiastic amateurs and their friends and relations as the main participants and spectators in swimming galas.[18]

In 1886, the existing swimming bodies put aside their differences and merged to form the Amateur Swimming Association – the choice of the name confirming the central role of amateurism in swimming. That same year, the ASA reached agreements with the Amateur Athletics Union and the National Cycling Union about the definition of amateur status, and set out common sanctions for breaches of the rules. Swimming teachers who accepted fees for teaching swimming were barred from membership, and this even included schoolteachers who also taught academic subjects, as well as swimmers who earned fees to take part in entertainments. The professors tried to retaliate by starting the Professional Swimming Association, but they garnered little support among the clubs, which overwhelmingly joined the ASA. By 1888 the ASA had a membership of 65 swimming and water polo clubs; in 1890, this had more than doubled to 135, and in 1894, it reached 300, which were subdivided into the ASA's regional districts. With its position as the governing body of the sports of swimming, diving and water polo assured, the ASA received the ultimate accolade for an English sporting organization when it obtained royal patronage.[19]

The transformation of sport from a business and form of popular entertainment into a respectable Victorian pursuit was also taking place in the U.S. and continental Europe. In the U.S. in 1884, the director of Harvard University's gymnasium thundered against the evils of professionalism:

> The natural tendency of all sports is towards professionalism, and we must regard it as the evil of all evils. A professional athlete in success is praised and paraded before the world until he overestimates his ability, becomes vainglorious and haughty.[20]

The locus of the amateur movement in the U.S. was an institution that I featured in Chapter Seven, the patrician New York Athletics Club (NYAC), which in collaboration with other elite and university sports clubs established the Amateur Athletics Union (AAU), with similar rules defining amateur status to those established by the MSA and SAGB in England.

Organized competition developed rapidly on both sides of the Atlantic. By 1900, the ASA and its member clubs were running six national swimming championships and a further three championships in saltwater swimming, plunging and water polo. In 1901, the ASA instituted the first swimming race for women, the 100-yard championship, followed in 1912 by a 200-yard championship

(91- and 183-m respectively). By 1920, many of the competitive swimming events that we are accustomed to today had been established.[21] In the u.s., taking its lead from the British example, the NYAC hosted the first national championships in the country and the first transatlantic amateur swimming competition in 1883, with competitors from the u.s. and England. The AAU took over the organization of national championships for male swimmers, but when it came to female swimmers, it was more conservative than the ASA, opposing women's participation in official AAU meets until 1915.[22] In continental Europe, Pierre de Coubertin (1863–1937), who was a fervent admirer of English public school team sports as a way of promoting physical health and building moral fibre, led the movement to revive the ancient Olympic Games, which enshrined the cult of amateurism for all the sports that took part, including swimming.[23] Although the Olympic Oath was not instituted until the 1920 Antwerp Games, its wording made clear that amateurism was at the heart of the revived Olympic movement:

> In the name of all the competitors I promise that we shall take part in these Olympic Games, respecting and abiding by the rules which govern them, committing ourselves to a sport without doping and without drugs, in the true spirit of sportsmanship, for the glory of sport and the honour of our teams.[24]

The 1896 Athens games featured 241 athletes from fourteen nations, all men, because de Coubertin felt that the participation of women athletes would be 'impractical, uninteresting, unaesthetic and incorrect'. The founding games included four swimming races: 100, 500 and 1,200 m (328, 1,640 and 3,937 ft) freestyle, open to all qualifying athletes, and a sailors' 100 m freestyle restricted to members of the Greek Navy. As no Olympic pool had been built, the events were held in the Bay of Zea, formerly one of the two military harbours of classical Piraeus.[25] Nineteen swimmers from four nations (Austria, Greece, Hungary and the United States) competed in the races.[26] A foretaste of things to come, the competition drew a crowd estimated to be nearly 20,000 strong. Alfréd Hajós (1878–1955), a Hungarian architecture student from Budapest, won the 100 m and 1,200 m freestyle, and probably would have won the 500 m had there been enough recovery time between events. Instead, the gold went to a Viennese medical student, Paul Neumann (1875–1932), who won with a comfortable ninety-second lead over his nearest rival. Hajós earned little recognition for his double Olympic gold, which would now see him making the headlines of the Hungarian media for weeks. He had had difficulty in getting the university to agree to giving him time off to compete, and on his return, his tutor told him that he was not at all impressed by his victories and was much more interested in seeing his examination results. We know little of Neumann's reception in Austria after his victory in the 500 m, but perhaps tellingly, he emigrated to the u.s. soon after the Athens games.[27]

The Triumph of the Amateur

How do we explain the inexorable rise of the amateur swimmer during the last quarter of the nineteenth century? We have to account for nothing less than the complete redefinition of the nature and role of sporting competition in society within the space of a generation. The English borrowed the word amateur from the French word meaning 'lover of'. It was first used in the sense of 'dabbler' as opposed to professional in 1786 and as an adjective in 1838 – the year after the first amateur races organized by the nss in the Serpentine. Although at that event, small prizes were awarded to the winners (in contravention of later msa and asa rules) there would have been no question of wagers, betting or large purses for the adolescent swimmers.

The pools built after the Baths and Washhouses Acts were a form of social engineering to promote hygiene among the urban poor, but they later became a means of inculcating the middle-class values of hard work, self-discipline, temperance and respectability into the working classes, whose physical uncleanliness and ill-health were associated with sloth and immorality. Physical education and sports were seen as means of reforming the working class, but the problems with the sports of the day were that they fostered a 'degraded athletic atmosphere, of working class athletes who accepted money for their efforts and attracted gamblers and other hooligans'.[28] Prizefighting and football would remain professional sports with paid athletes, and at the other end of the social scale, horseracing remained a professional sport whose *raison d'être* was gambling.

Swimming had followed the same pattern in the first half of the nineteenth century, and we need to account for why it did not develop in the same way as other popular professional sports. In theory, there should have been room for a professional circuit of swimming races, like the contests that sustained professional boxing. But there was a crucial difference between swimming and boxing, as the latter was easy to host in a wide range of indoor venues. In-ground pools were an expensive, limited resource that was under the control of different stakeholders: the municipalities that wanted to see them used for certain social ends (which did not include lining the pockets of professional swimmers with prizes or encouraging the immorality of betting) and the members of swimming clubs set up by enthusiasts, who were interested in swimming for fitness and competition, but did not rely on swimming for their livelihoods.

Swimming provides an enlightening case study of an activity that was not a sport in antiquity; hence, there was no question of swimming as a competitive sport being revived like athletics and Graeco-Roman wrestling. What revival there was, starting during the Renaissance, was for the therapeutic uses of swimming and bathing, and an awareness among Enlightenment educational reformers that physical education in general (though not swimming in particular) was desirable for the development of a healthy child. At first, physical education was modelled on ancient athletic practices, particularly in continental Europe, while English public schools, most famously Rugby School under the nineteenth-century stewardship of Matthew Arnold, favoured the playing of traditional team sports as the preferred means of promoting physical health and inculcating in the sons of the ruling class the virtues of discipline, leadership, team spirit and good sportsmanship.

Unlike their decadent Regency forebears, who had misspent their lives and squandered their fortunes on drinking, gambling and whoring, the Victorian ruling classes saw themselves as the heirs of the military might of Imperial Rome, which they attempted to marry with the democratic values of classical Athens. Victorian interpretations of Graeco-Roman virtues, artistic forms and symbols, along with neoclassical architecture, were co-opted to give legitimacy to the British imperial project, which was otherwise little more than a land grab for economic advantage paid for by slavery and the exploitation of indigenous peoples on five continents. Educated on the playing fields of Rugby, Eton and Harrow, and persuaded of their God-given right to rule, the British set out to 'civilize' the two-thirds of the world that it now controlled. But they could not claim to civilize the globe if their own backyard was populated with a working class that 'let the side down'.

This coincided with another social reform movement within British society: a product of the evangelical movement known as 'Muscular Christianity', which promoted sport as a means to encourage hard work, self-discipline and temperance among the working classes. Before it could serve this purpose, however, sport had to be cleansed of the worst excesses of gambling and cheating. It is likely that Muscular Christianity appealed mostly to the converted, that is, to the respectable middle classes who also aspired to be part of England's grand imperial project. Swimming and water polo, which were relatively untainted by cheating and gambling, especially once they had moved from the increasingly polluted urban waters to new in-ground public pools, were co-opted into the great moral crusade against the perceived immorality and sloth of the working classes.

Christopher Love identifies another reason for the exclusion of the working-class professionals from swimming. As swimming became more popular, the middle and upper classes were less happy about sharing their pool water with what they saw as physically and morally degenerate individuals – a fear of disease justifying the social exclusion of working men. He writes:

Class came to affect all features of English life, and sport was no exception. Exactly what forms of sport, recreation and physical training were appropriate for these various classes became an issue in late Victorian England. Most importantly, sport became a forum for issues of social inclusion and exclusion. The manner in which competitive swimming came to be organized and the ideas underlying the provision of, and the regulations governing, public swimming facilities are but two of the many areas that illustrate these social codes at work.[29]

He supports his claim by examining the way the rules were applied and the exceptions that were made to them. These included the treatment of the issue of 'broken time' – time off work – and of expenses to train and compete. Exceptions were also made on grounds of class. While the strictest interpretation of the rules had initially excluded schoolteachers, this was rescinded in a revision of the ASA laws in 1898. Henceforth, they could retain their amateur status, even though they were paid by their employers to teach swimming to their students. A similar exemption was made in 1901 for lifesaving instructors, when the rules were circumvented by redefining the teaching of lifesaving from 'sport' to 'athletic exercises' and with the further justification that they worked 'for the benefit of the race'. These exemptions led to the appearance in the 1880s and '90s of 'shamateurs', who after 1898 had no trouble getting expenses and winning cash prizes for racing. The rules were reinforced in 1918, Love explains, 'the better to maintain the class divide in organized swimming'.[30]

Going Global

During the fourth modern Olympiad, held in London in 1908, the national swimming associations of Belgium, Denmark, Finland, France, Germany, Great Britain, Hungary and Sweden met to establish the sport's governing body, FINA (Fédération internationale de natation), with the aim of managing competitions at the summer games, establishing unified rules for swimming, water polo and diving and verifying and registering world records. At the next Olympics, held in Stockholm in 1912, FINA approved the participation of women swimmers, despite the reservations of de Coubertin, who was serving out his term as the second president of the IOC (International Olympic Committee), and of the AAU, which held off on sending women swimmers to represent the U.S. at an Olympic Games until 1920.

Today, FINA, in collaboration with the IOC and its 207 national member federations, oversees the development of swimming in the four approved strokes: freestyle, backstroke, butterfly (first included at an Olympic Games in Melbourne in 1956) and breaststroke, medleys and relays; diving: springboard, platform, synchronized, mixed and team and high diving; water polo; synchronized

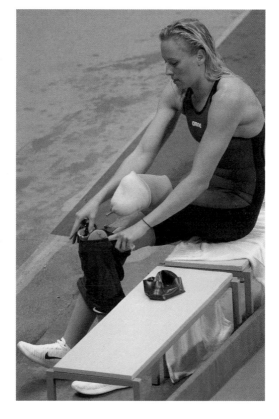

American swimmer Jessica Long was one of the stars of the 2016 Rio Paralympics. The worldwide television coverage of the 2012 London Paralympic Games established Paralympic swimming as a major spectator event, on a par with the Olympics and FINA world championship competitions.

swimming: solo, duet, mixed, team and free (the only remaining women-only discipline); and open-water swimming. In addition to the Olympic Games, FINA runs world championships, cups, grand prix and trophies in the five aquatic disciplines, covering all ages from juniors to masters.[31]

In order to give the reader a complete overview of competitive aquatic sport, I have to mention major international sporting events that feature swimming, including the Deaflympics, held since the first edition of the games in Paris in 1924; the Paralympics, which traces its origins back to the Stoke Mandeville Games, in Buckinghamshire, England, which started as an archery competition for disabled servicemen and -women in 1948 and adopted the Paralympics Games in Rome in 1960; and the Gay Games, first held in San Francisco in 1984.[32] I should mention two sports not overseen by FINA: triathlon, which includes swimming as one of its three disciplines, and competitive free-diving.

Amateurism RIP

Even when the amateur rules were strictly imposed at the elite level, amateurism was always more an ideal than a reality. It was easy to endorse amateurism if you were from a privileged background, like the students of Oxford and Cambridge in the UK and of the Ivy League Universities in the U.S., who did not need to work and could train in the best facilities available with the help of top coaches; likewise, the wealthy members of exclusive clubs such as the New York Athletic Club. The team sent by the U.S. to the Athens Games was made up of college athletes from Harvard and Princeton and members of the Boston Athletic Club. The system did not disbar working-class athletes, unless they received any form of remuneration for participating in the sport they competed in or for any other sport, so a professional footballer would not have been allowed to compete as an amateur swimmer or water polo player. Less fortunate but particularly talented athletes could be helped with university scholarships, as long as they were considered respectable enough to rub shoulders with the sons of the elite.

The system creaked and groaned on, with several causes célèbres such as the Cairns–Blew-Jones case. In 1883, Walter Blew-Jones from London's Otter sc complained to the SAGB that the winner of the 220-yard freestyle championship, Thomas Cairns, was not an amateur because he worked as a bath attendant, and because he had raced for cash prizes in the past. The SAGB ruled that Cairns, despite his employment at a swimming baths, was in fact an amateur when he had swum the race. The SAGB upheld its decision a year later after another attempt by Blew-Jones, who had come second, had failed to disqualify the winner. The case, however, caused Otter SC, the oldest swimming club in London, founded in 1868, to split from the SAGB, and ultimately led to the formation of the ASA.[33]

Until the end of the Second World War, amateur sporting competition was a genteel affair largely practised by members of the world's elite. But everything changed after the war with the entrance into the amateur sporting arena of the nations of the Soviet Bloc, followed by the Communist Chinese a couple of decades later. Communist athletes were notionally employed in factories or offices but were in reality athletes who trained full time and benefited from privileged lifestyles when compared to the rest of the population. This was not very different from the American system of collegiate scholarships for talented athletes, but what was particularly galling to the British was that the Communists were in it not to play the game but to win, and they applied strict, scientific training regimes and did not shy away from giving their athletes chemical advantages.

This was war fought on the athletics field. The Americans were not disadvantaged, though they too had to up their game. But the British – who clung on to their ideas of good sportsmanship and held up the badge of amateurism like a holy icon in a church procession crossing the path of an approaching pagan army – found themselves in a ridiculous situation. Britain provided only the most basic funding for their elite squads going to the Olympic Games and world championships, obliging them to hold down full-time jobs while they were competing against athletes from the U.S. and Soviet Bloc who trained full time. The result was a predictable series of *nul points* at major competitions during the 1970s and '80s, and the extraordinary ruling that elite British athletes could not even claim unemployment benefit for the two weeks of the Olympic Games because they were out of the country and therefore unable to look for work. Something was bound to give, and it was unlikely to be the Americans, Russians or Chinese. In 1988 the ASA and FINA revised the laws governing the funding of amateur swimming and those relating to advertising sponsorship and the payment of expenses. The ban on professionals from other sports competing as swimmers was also quietly dropped.[34]

Although the distinction between amateurs and professionals had effectively disappeared, there was no major professionalization of swimming and the other aquatic sports, though the superstars of the sport were now able to benefit from lucrative sponsorship deals from swimwear and equipment manufacturers. What is particularly striking in the aquatic sports is that in many countries, such as the UK, the superstructure of elite events such as the Olympic Games, the Paralympics and the FINA world championships are sustained by the vast substructure of local clubs that are run by unpaid enthusiasts who, through their dues, help to finance FINA. This is in stark contrast to the case of a professional sport, such as football in the UK, where elite clubs receive millions in TV and sponsorship deals, some of which is fed back into funding for grass-roots, non-professional football. While there are elite swimmers who can earn large sums from commercial sponsors, there is no swimming or water polo equivalent of the highly paid league footballer, and no opportunities for swimming clubs to earn entrance money from or sell broadcast rights to the swim meets they host. At the local and national levels, swimming remains an amateur pursuit, and it is only at the international level that athletes can expect sufficient levels of funding to allow them to train and compete full time, and if very successful at major international competitions, to earn lucrative commercial sponsorship deals from swimwear and equipment manufacturers.

Michael Phelps celebrates winning another of the gold medals at the 2016 Rio Olympics that have put him in the record books as the most decorated Olympian of all time. Although a world superstar worth an estimated $40 million, Phelps is the rare swimming exception to the general earnings' rule, especially when elite swimmers are compared to professional football, basketball and baseball players.

A People's Sport

Competition shaped the development of swimming and played a role in its popularity in the modern period, but could we say that it is currently a truly 'popular' spectator sport? It is certainly not on a par with football, where the professional leagues are the main driver and recruiting sergeants for the amateur levels of the beautiful game. The two work synergistically, with young talent being nurtured by local clubs for the league clubs, which are supported by a large fan base who go to matches, and financed by huge revenues in sponsorship and TV rights. Swimming has a huge constituency of fitness and leisure swimmers, and a large infrastructure of local clubs that host and take part in any number of local and national competitions, but they are divorced from the elite squads because at the very top of the pyramid there is only one squad, with a few dozen swimmers, and they compete infrequently, especially when compared to Premier League footballers.

It might be fairer to compare swimming to professional tennis, where there is a small world elite of players who are also distant from the millions of weekend club and leisure players. But tennis has a much larger TV audience than any of the aquatic disciplines. Even in comparison with athletics, the aquatic sports suffer badly. Swimming is well organized and has a faithful following of enthusiasts, but there is no interplay between elite competition swimming and swimming at the local pool. Contrast this with football: at weekends, in parks and on five-a-side football pitches you will hear the latest professional games analysed forensically, discussed and possibly replayed during matches by players who support rival teams, but I challenge the reader to go to a local public pool and find someone who imagines he is Michael Phelps swimming the 4 × 100 m medley at the Rio Olympics.

Although most kids can imagine themselves playing for Manchester United or the New York Knicks it is the very rare and very gifted few who will ever aspire to swimming at a world championship or an Olympic Games. It is not that there are far fewer places on the national squad, but also a question of the level of natural ability and the amount of training that is required to reach the international level, and the fact that for all that hard work and dedication, you are over the hill and retired by the age of thirty. While Cristiano Ronaldo was at the peak of his playing career, Michael Phelps announced his retirement from international competition after the Rio Summer Games of 2016. For two weeks every four years, aquatic competitions are a glittering spectacle watched by billions all over the world, and swimmers become national heroes and celebrities; but like every one-hit wonder, once the Olympic flag has been furled, they are quickly forgotten. Competitive sport played a central role in the development of swimming into a popular mass-participation pastime, but it is only occasionally a popular spectator sport.

10
Imaginary Swimmers

Then dreadful thoughts of death, of waves heaped on him.
And friends, and parting daylight, rush upon him.
He thinks of prayers to Neptune and his daughters.
And Venus, Hero's queen, sprung from the waters;
And then of Hero only, – how she fares.
And what she'll feel, when the blank morn appears;
And at that thought he stiffens once again
His limbs, and pants, and strains, and climbs, – in vain.
Fierce draughts he swallows of the wilful wave.

LEIGH HUNT, *HERO AND LEANDER* (1819)[1]

In Chapter Two, I examined our ancestors' relationship to swimming through a study of ancient mythology, which revealed a close affinity between the earliest human cultures and the aquatic world. It was a fruitful relationship that ensured humanity's survival but it was also one fraught with danger. Through magic, ritual and sacrifice, humans sought to propitiate and control the personified rivers, seas and oceans on which their lives depended. With the coming of Christianity, the old sea gods passed into legend and the stories remained and gradually morphed into folktales.

As the general population became less dependent on the resources of seas and rivers and their exploitation became the province of specialists, people forgot how to swim, and for the majority of the population that lived in inland cities and villages, the aquatic realm became a dangerous 'otherworld' populated by soulless mermaids who lured men to their deaths and fearful monsters that could rise up from the deep to attack the unwary. The medieval folktales about mermaids and sea serpents were like the urban myths of today, stories that people wanted to believe because they fitted their expectations of the world. After the scientific revolution began to demystify the world, folktales became fairy tales for children, and the plight of the Little Mermaid became a metaphor for Christian redemption rather than an explanation for mysterious sea creatures, drowned sailors and ships wrecked on reefs. Today's saccharine-sweet *The Little Mermaid* has lost any serious moral message and the tragic ending of the original, and Disney's teenage Ariel would be more at home in a Burbank high school than at the bottom of the sea.

Humans continue to explain their existence in the world by telling stories, though we have to broaden the notion of story to include all the narratives, both fictional and non-fictional, with which we delude ourselves. In the case of swimming, it could be a story about subjects that I have covered in earlier chapters, for example a tale of leisure: the story about a little boy who almost drowned during a summer holiday in Spain; one about competition: like the tale of the young Michael Phelps, who started swimming at the age of seven to overcome his ADHD and went on to be the most decorated Olympian of all time; or exploration: like the adventures of the young French naval officer who invented the Aqualung and spent the rest of his days exploring the oceans. This chapter will examine the fictional narratives that humans have created about swimming in the past 500 years.

The Swimming Imagination

Although descriptions of water in all its forms are commonplace in English literature, references to swimming are rare. I am indebted to Nicholas Orme's *Early British Swimming* for his survey of references to swimming in 'Imaginative Literature', which for Orme begins with the Elizabethan poet Edmund Spenser (*c*. 1552–1599), whose *Faerie Queene*, while commonly thought to be a panegyric about the reign of Gloriana, Elizabeth I, contains several references to swimming. Spenser was a pupil of the pedagogue Richard Mulcaster and a friend of Everard Digby, the author of *De arte natandi*. We do not know whether Spenser himself was a swimmer, or merely acquainted with the art through Digby. Spenser's use of swimming is not as a technical description but an otherworldly practice that adds to the magical atmosphere of the piece.

A distraught Hero discovering the lifeless body of Leander, drowned one stormy winter's night when the light she lit to guide him to shore had been extinguished. Marlowe's retelling of the myth is one of several in the English language, including Leigh Hunt's, which is quoted at the head of this chapter.

The first expression in the English language of the sensuality of swimming was penned by Spenser's younger contemporary, the dramatist, poet and Elizabethan *enfant terrible* Christopher Marlowe (*c.* 1564–1593), in his retelling of the classical myth of Hero and Leander, the tragic lovers who lived respectively in Sestos and Abydos on either side of the Hellespont (now the Dardanelles), the strait that separates Asia and Europe. So smitten was Leander with the beautiful Hero that he swam nightly across the kilometre-wide strait to see her, until one fatal winter's night, overcome by the waves and currents, he drowned. Hero, seeing his corpse washed up on the beach the next day, threw herself into the sea to perish with him. Marlowe's version, interrupted by the poet's early death, did not include the couple's tragic deaths, but the passage in which the naked Leander is accosted by an amorous Neptune (Poseidon), who has mistaken him for Zeus' cupbearer and catamite Ganymede, is not just a celebration of the sensuality of swimming but is also unashamedly homoerotic:

> And smiling wantonly, his love bewrayd.
> He watcht his armes, and as they opend wide,
> At every stroke, betwixt them would he slide,
> And steale a kisse, and then run out and daunce,
> And as he turnd, cast many a lustfull glaunce,
> And throw him gawdie toies to please his eie,
> And dive into the water, and there prie
> Upon his brest, his thighs, and everie lim,
> And up againe, and close beside him swim,
> And talke of love: *Leander* made replie,
> You are deceav'd, I am no woman I.[2]

While on his Grand Tour in May 1810, the 22-year-old Lord Byron (1788–1824) re-enacted Leander's fatal swim, though not in December but in the 'genial month of May'. Byron, accompanied by an officer from a Royal Navy ship on which the poet was travelling to Constantinople, succeeded at his second attempt on 3 May 1810, recording:

This morning I swam from Sestos to Abydos, the immediate distance is not above a mile but the current renders it hazardous, so much so, that I doubt whether Leander's conjugal powers must not have been exhausted in his passage to Paradise.

However, the last verse of a poem that he wrote about the event pokes fun at his own achievement, when he compares himself unfavourably with the tragic Leander:

'Twere hard to say who fared the best:
Sad mortals! thus the gods still plague you!
He lost his labour, I my jest;
For he was drown'd, and I've the ague.[3]

Byron was not the usual 'Grand Tourist' of his day. Like other young English gentlemen on their aristocratic gap year in Europe, he was deeply steeped in the Classics and he found meaning in the landscapes he visited through classical references, but he also had something to prove. He had a club foot that made most land sports difficult or impracticable but which did not affect his ability to swim. Unlike many of his contemporaries, not only could he swim but he was clearly an able swimmer and something of a daredevil. Although 1,000 m (over 1,000 yards) is not a challenging distance for an accomplished swimmer in the flat calm of an indoor pool, one has to factor in the temperature of the sea in May and the strength of the currents in the strait that make his time of one hour ten minutes more than respectable for someone attempting the crossing using breaststroke – the stroke favoured by Europeans at the time. At least Byron was spared the presence of modern-day sewage and the oil slicks left by the oil tankers, naval vessels, cruise liners and cargo ships that throng one of the world's busiest commercial and naval waterways.

Byron was not indulging in a half-hearted historical re-enactment and he would not have been satisfied to stand on the coast gazing across the strait and imagining its crossing. He felt compelled to experience Leander's swim, maybe in an attempt to capture some of his burning passion for Hero. Byron enjoyed the swim, relishing its physical challenge. It is something that one recognizes in the swimmers who repeat the crossing in the 'Victory Day' race that commemorates the poet's original swim. Clinton Pascoe, who competed in the race in 2013, summed up the combination of swimming, socializing, tourism and personal challenge offered by the modern-day Hellespont swim:

> This has been one of my favourite swims to do. The water was beautiful and it was really great to make it to the finish. I met some really interesting and inspiring people also, which made the trip even more memorable.[4]

Marlowe's early death deprived us not only of the ending to *Hero and Leander*, finished for him by fellow dramatist George Chapman (*c.* 1559–1634), but of who knows how many other swimming-themed masterpieces.

Orme moves from Marlowe to his great contemporary and rival, William Shakespeare (*c.* 1564–1616), who also includes swimming references in his plays. Orme cites a striking image from *Julius Caesar*, when, contrary to the historical evidence of Caesar's prowess as a swimmer, he has Cassius rescuing him from the Tiber (1.2). In *Macbeth* he likens two combatants to 'two spent swimmers that do cling together / And choke their art' (1.2). But these examples express both the bravado and rashness of the characters and the dangers of swimming. Orme can find only one positive description of swimming from a Shakespearean play, *The Tempest* (2.1), when Ferdinand, the King of Naples' son, feared drowned by his father, is reported to be safe:

> I saw him beat the surges under him,
> And ride upon their backs; he trod the water,
> Whose enmity he flung aside, and breasted
> The surge most swoln that met him; his bold head

> 'Bove the contentious waves he kept, and oar'd
> Himself with his good arms in lusty stroke
> To the shore, that o'er his wave-worn basis bow'd,
> As stooping to relieve him: I not doubt
> He came alive to land.

Swimming existed in the literary imagination of Elizabethan England but, reflecting the state of the art in the country at the time, this was a far from positive depiction.[5] There was little change in the conception of swimming as dangerous between Spenser's version of *Hero and Leander* and that of Leigh Hunt (1819), which I quote at the head of this chapter. In Hunt's poem, the sensuality of the encounter with Poseidon is forgotten, and the swimmer despairs before he succumbs to the chill embrace of the waves, imagining his beloved's reaction when she finds his lifeless corpse.

Exactly a century before Hunt's poem, Daniel Defoe (*c.* 1660–1731) presented a more positive portrayal of swimming in *Robinson Crusoe* (1719), in which the ability to swim saves several of the characters' lives, including that of the two main characters, Crusoe and Man Friday. In the novel, Defoe did not portray the ability to swim as a commonplace skill, practised for leisure, fitness or enjoyment, but it was necessary to a plot that features several shipwrecks that the hapless Crusoe has to survive, as well as for the salvaging of his vessel after he is marooned on the island. Swimming also saves the life of Crusoe's companion, Man Friday, whose skill in the water must be seen in the context of the Enlightenment notion of the 'Noble Savage' who, untrammelled by the constraints of civilization, is endowed with physical abilities far superior to the average white man's, though in every other way he is seen as deficient. Swimming appears as a similar plot device in Jonathan Swift's (1667–1745) *Gulliver's Travels* (1726), as the hero is required to survive a number of shipwrecks during his travels and, on one occasion, to swim for his life when maliciously dropped into a bowl of cream in Brobdingnag by one of his giant hosts.[6]

Watery Allegory

Before I begin the next section, which deals with swimming in science fiction and fantasy, reference must be made to *The Water-babies, A Fairy Tale for a Land Baby* (1863), a Victorian fable written in instalments for *Macmillan's Magazine* by the Reverend Charles Kingsley (1819–1875). The book follows the adventures of Tom, a child chimney sweep, who drowns and is reborn as a 10-cm-long (4-in.) water baby with gills. During his underwater adventures, he completes his moral education, helped by fairies and aquatic animals, and upon attaining redemption is reborn in the human world, where he leads an exemplary life as a scientist. Although a churchman, Kingsley was also a fervent supporter of Charles Darwin's theory of evolution through natural selection. In addition to its scientific polemic, the book touches on other mid-Victorian concerns, including the treatment of the poor and child labour.

Like many other nineteenth-century children's classics, *The Water-babies* fell out of favour because of its Victorian attitudes and prejudices, but it is not the content of the book that interests me as much as its setting. In its Lewis Carroll-like creation of an underwater wonderland, the book is quite unlike Kingsley's other literary output of turgid historical novels. The idea of the water babies is a stroke of imaginative genius, but the underwater location is incidental rather than central to the social and moral concerns of the author. Although by the early 1860s, the aquatic world was already accessible by diving bell and standard diving dress, Kingsley chose it as a setting because, like Alice's rabbit hole, it would have been completely alien to the everyday life of his readers. Rather than counting on their familiarity, he uses their ignorance of the aquatic world as a literary device to astound and charm them, the better to persuade them of the rightness of his moral pronouncements. Kingsley's fantastic novel, therefore, reveals the same alienation from the practice of swimming as in the references from earlier periods.[7]

The Water-babies is a charming Victorian moral fable. The hero, Tom, a drowned child chimney sweep who is reborn as a diminutive water baby with gills, achieves Christian redemption and is reborn in the human world as a 'man of science'. The Reverend Charles Kingsley chose the underwater setting because it would have been so alien to his readers.

The Science Fiction of Swimming

We can date a change in the depiction of swimming in fiction to
the emergence of a new literary genre, science fiction, with the works
of French novelist and visionary Jules Verne (1828–1905). Verne's
Twenty Thousand Leagues under the Sea (1870) – which I first saw in
the 1954 Hollywood version, *20,000 Leagues under the Sea*, starring
James Mason and Kirk Douglas in the lead roles – is prescient in
its vision of a large, self-contained submarine, but when it comes
to diving, Verne has the crew of the *Nautilus* walking on the sea
bottom like the SDD divers of his day. The novel inspired four other
films (including a 1916 version that was the first motion picture
to be filmed underwater), an animated feature, a radio adaptation,
a musical and a ride at Tokyo's Disneyland. Verne's Captain Nemo,
the master of the fantastic *Nautilus*, is a typical Victorian inventor-
engineer. In the luxurious interior of his living quarters, he recreates
the opulent interior of a well-to-do Victorian dwelling. He imposes
himself, his values and lifestyle on an unfamiliar environment rather
than adapting himself to it. The sea remains a dangerous realm, populated by monsters, such as the giant squid that attacks and almost
destroys the *Nautilus*. Verne's novel embodies the notion, which
would endure for another century, that through technology humans
would tame the seas just as they were taming hostile terrestrial
environments.

Since Verne, the underwater world has been the setting for a
number of science fiction films, TV series and graphic novels, though
very few when compared to the genre's favourite setting: outer space.
The two programmes set in the underwater world that I remember
from my childhood were the made-for-TV British 'Supermarionation'
children's series *Stingray* and the American film and TV franchise
The Man from Atlantis. *Stingray* was one of several marionette series
made by producer, director and writer Gerry Anderson (1929–2012)
in the 1960s; it aired in the UK, the U.S. and Canada in 1964–5, just
prior to his more famous *Thunderbirds* (1965–6), which also featured
a submarine, *Thunderbird 4*, though it had far fewer outings than
the much more famous flying *Thunderbirds 1* and *2*.

Based in the fictional coastal city of Marineville, the *Stingray* of the title was a submarine piloted by Captain Troy Tempest and his navigator Phones and the first line of defence against the Aquaphibians, an underwater race hell bent on the destruction of the human race and all its works. Troy and Phones were often assisted in their underwater adventures by the naiad-like Marina, who could breathe underwater and was mute but did not have the traditional mermaid's tail. If *Stingray* were remade today, one could easily imagine that the roles of good and bad guys might be reversed, as they were in *Avatar* (2009), with Tempest – recast as a Cousteau-like marine biologist – fighting to save the exploited sea races from greedy human governments, criminals and international corporations. But in the mid-1960s, it was still possible for children to believe that human heroes could do no wrong, and that science was a solution rather than the cause of the degradation of the aquatic environment.

The *Man from Atlantis* franchise started as four made-for-TV films, starring Patrick Duffy and aired in the U.S. in 1977, whose success ensured the commissioning of a series broadcast in 1977–8.[8] The hero, who had lost his memory, was discovered washed up on a beach, fortuitously near a naval research station in California. Given the name Mark Harris, he turns out to be the sole survivor of the vanished civilization of Atlantis. He possessed extraordinary swimming and diving abilities, which he demonstrated amply in the first film, in which he raced a dolphin and leapt out of the water to seize a fish held out by a trainer standing on a high platform. He had webbed feet and hands, could (of course) swim underwater without scuba gear and was also able to resist the intense pressure and cold that would have proved fatal to an unprotected human diver. Made over a decade after *Stingray*, *Man from Atlantis* had a different take as to who was the real danger to the aquatic world: technology gone bad, aliens, criminals, mad scientists and pirates, and while undersea races such as mermaids featured in the *Man for Atlantis* universe, they were usually portrayed as the victims of humans.

Mark Harris owed a great deal to an earlier aquatic superhero, Aquaman, who made his debut in the DC Comics graphic novel

Illustration from Jules Verne's *Twenty Thousand Leagues under the Sea* (1870). When exploring the sea bottom, the crew of the *Nautilus* walk like the SDD divers of Verne's day, though their suits are self-contained – like the SCUBA designs that would appear in the twentieth century and culminate in Cousteau's Aqualung.

universe in November 1941.[9] Although created much earlier than *Stingray* or *Man from Atlantis*, I have listed him third in my review of the fictional aquatic universe because, as I was never an aficionado of American comics, I only became aware of Aquaman much later, when flicking through the comics of a friend who is an avid collector of graphic novels. Like Superman, Aquaman first went into action projecting American power during the Second World War. He began life as an ordinary human who was altered by his scientist father in order to fight the underwater machinations of the Axis powers. Post-Second World War, like other superheroes, he became a more generalized projection of American power and also an idealized representation of masculinity.[10] Unlike other, better-known superheroes, Aquaman did not play a leading role in the Justice League of America adventures, in which he featured between the 1960s and '80s. Compared to graphic novel giants Superman, Iron Man and Batman, Aquaman was a bit of an 'also-ran', the

Mark Harris, the Man from Atlantis, played by *Dallas* star Patrick Duffy. The sole survivor of the vanished civilization of Atlantis, who has superhuman swimming abilities, Harris is found by the U.S. Navy and agrees to help his human rescuers as they battle a variety of mechanical, alien and human foes.

butt of jokes by U.S. stand-up comedians and derided on comedy shows because of his weaker powers and abilities and because of a general perception that he was not 'cool'.[11]

During the 2000s, Aquaman underwent a major reinvention, gaining both in superpowers and edginess. He took the lead role in the full-length animated feature *Justice League: Throne of Atlantis* (2015), in which he was no longer a human scientifically altered to be able to breathe underwater, but a half-human, half-Atlantean prince who helps the Justice League defeat his evil half-brother, Ocean Master, who plots to take over Metropolis. Aquaman was portrayed by Jason Momoa in the live action *Batman v Superman: Dawn of Justice* (2016), and Momoa will reprise the role in a solo Aquaman movie to be released in 2018.[12] The studio no doubt hopes that Momoa's high profile, and perceived 'coolness' among sci-fi fans, will succeed in finally providing Aquaman with the live-action-movie credibility that have made Superman, Batman, Iron Man and Captain America such successful movie franchises.

Again, as with my examination of earlier aquatic heroes, my interest is not in the rehabilitation of Aquaman but to understand how he and other characters from science fiction and fantasy illuminate the contemporary relationship with swimming. Aquatic heroes like Mark Harris and Aquaman have so far failed to capture the popular imagination in the same way as Superman and Batman. The ability to fly and superhuman strength on the one hand, and on the other, the technical wizardry of the Batmobile, Batcave and Batplane, trump the ability to breathe underwater and survive in the deep oceans. But is that enough to explain why the Man of Steel (who is after all an alien from another planet) is so much more popular than the half-Atlantean Aquaman? There is something quaint and, if you'll excuse the pun, 'wet' about Aquaman in his earlier incarnations. Is it our familiarity with swimming that makes his superpowers less impressive than those of other comic-book heroes?

If Superman and others are the modern versions of the Olympian gods and demi-gods, and graphic novels the modern take on classic mythology, what does Aquaman's popularity tell us about our imaginative relationship with swimming? Our eyes are drawn relentlessly skyward and beyond into outer space, rather than to the inner spaces of our own planet. The ocean deeps may be extraordinary and largely unexplored but we can be pretty certain that they are not home to sunken cities or advanced amphibian civilizations. They are both scary and familiar; all around us but still near-impossible to access. But if swimming does not meet the needs of the modern imagination for escapist excitement and adventure, there is one area of human experience with which swimming is closely associated: sex.

Symbolic Swimming

For the two men who most famously tried to make sense of the human psyche, Sigmund Freud (1856–1939) and Carl Jung (1875–1961), water has powerful meanings. For Jung, it is a symbol of the unconscious. He wrote:

> The lake in the valley is the unconscious, which lies, as it were, underneath consciousness, so that it is often referred to as the 'subconscious' . . . Water is the 'valley spirit',

the water dragon of Tao, whose nature resembles water
– a yang in the yin, therefore, water means spirit that has
become unconscious.

For Jung, the 'swimmer' was exploring the depths of his unconscious mind. Water was a symbol rather than a physical element and
swimming in myth and dream were unrelated to the physical act
of swimming.[13]

The spirituality of Jung's work, however, is in stark contrast
with the materiality of Freud's approach to dreams, which saw water
and swimming as both symbolic and real. In *The Interpretation of
Dreams* (1899), Freud made the following claim for 'People who
dream often, and with great enjoyment, of *swimming*, cleaving the
waves', whom, he claimed, 'have usually been bedwetters, and they
now repeat in the dream a pleasure which they have long since
learned to forgo.' A second example are swimming dreams that

are concerned with passing through narrow spaces or with
staying in the water, are based upon fancies about the embry-
onic life, about the sojourn in the mother's womb, and
about the act of birth.

If Freud's interpretation is correct, then we all have a deep but mostly
forgotten connection to swimming, thanks to the nine months we
spent floating in the womb, which in turns links us to the aquatic
past that Elaine Morgan put forward to explain the evolution of
the genus *Homo*. From bedwetting and the womb, Freud extended
the symbolism of water to include semen; of urination, to include
ejaculation; and of swimming, to include sexual intercourse.[14] Popular culture has absorbed both Jung's notion of water as a potent symbol
of the unconscious mind in which 'troubled waters run deep', and
Freud's characterization of water and swimming as symbolic of
the often murky waters of human sexuality, which are uncovered
in dreams and in the conscious creations of visual artists.

The Eroticized Swimmer

Classical Greek artists had no problem with depicting the naked male form, and though there were more restrictions on the representation of female nudity, there are also many examples of statues of naked goddesses from antiquity, the most famous being the statues of Venus-Aphrodite naked or caught in the act of bathing or disrobing, such as the Louvre Museum's Venus de Milo. Male nudes were both idealized representations of gods and demi-gods and portraits of living men; during the classical period, of victorious athletes and warriors and during the Hellenistic period, of idealized rulers. Sculptural conventions also accorded with the sexual mores of a period when the athletic, youthful male form was the focus of the erotic imagination. Heroic nudity was adopted by the much more prudish Romans to portray their deified emperors, whose nakedness and idealized physiques served as visual symbols of their power and divinity.[15]

The combination of barbarian incursions into the Roman Empire starting in the second century CE and the establishment of Christianity as its state religion in the fourth century CE transformed attitudes to the care and depiction of the human body. It would be a gross oversimplification to claim that the display and representation of the naked form disappeared with the end of paganism, but what vanished from medieval art was any glorification or idealization of the human body. What nudes there were featured in scenes of the Fall and exile from the Garden of Eden and of the Last Judgement and Hell, condemning the naked body as sinful and a danger to one's immortal soul. With the European Renaissance, the idealized nude returned, with depictions of both naked men and women, but by this time, it was the naked female form that had become the focus of the erotic imagination, and therefore the cause of the greatest anxiety among the guardians of public morality.

In depicting male nudes, Renaissance painters and sculptors could cite the many rediscovered Graeco-Roman statues of naked gods, heroes, kings, warriors and athletes as models hallowed by antiquity, but female nudes were much rarer and more sexually charged and continued to be much more controversial. The nudity associated with swimming and bathing, wrapped within an allusion to a well-known classical myth, was one way to make the female nude respectable. The most famous Renaissance nude female is Sandro Botticelli's (1445–1510) *The Birth of Venus* (*c.* 1485) – a *Venus pudica* who hides her breasts and pudenda with her hands. Three centuries later, during the exuberant French Rococo period, François Boucher (1703–1770) painted his own version of *The Birth of Venus* (1740), which shows the naked goddess emerging from the waves surrounded by swimming naiads and tritons. The painting combines the sensuality of water and the orgiastic eroticism of this group of curvaceous eighteenth-century courtesans with the respectability of an academic subject. The true function of the painting was as a kind of decorative soft porn for the mansions of

Édouard Manet's *Le Déjeuner sur l'herbe* (1862–3) parodies the established artistic convention whereby a female nude was considered suitably respectable if it was an allusion to a well-known classical myth, such as the birth of Venus or the judgement of Paris. *Le Déjeuner* strips away the academic respectability of earlier French nudes, leaving an ungainly composition that both shocked and amused contemporary viewers.

France's *Ancien Régime* aristocracy, whose members would never have considered stripping off to perform such a plebeian activity as swimming.

Several republics, two empires and a couple of royal restorations later, the French Impressionist Édouard Manet (1832–1883) used the shock value of the female nude in *Le Déjeuner sur l'herbe* (1862–3) to overthrow centuries of academic convention that had made the female body a respectable artistic subject. The choice of a swimming setting was a direct allusion to classical models, but the naked female subject was not a goddess at her toilet or emerging from the waves. Sitting next to two fully dressed men, she is incongruous, ridiculous, absurd or shocking, depending on the viewer's sensibilities. The painting was considered too shocking to be exhibited at the Paris Salon and was shown instead at the Salon des Refusés in 1863.

Another century on and half a world away, British artist David Hockney (b. 1937) used a series of paintings of swimmers and swimming pools to illustrate his experience of the hedonistic gay lifestyle of southern California in the 1960s and '70s. In *Peter Getting Out of Nick's Pool* (1966) and *A Bigger Splash* (1974), the erotic focus returns unashamedly to the naked male form emerging from or diving into the azure-blue waters of an immaculate Californian pool.

The impact of the fine arts on the practice of swimming, however, has been minimal. Such nudes as there were, were elite works of art, seen only by the privileged few. Boucher's *Venus* would have hung on the walls of Versailles to titillate the jaded libido of Louis XV (1710–1774) and his mistress Madame de Pompadour rather than encourage them to swim. Prior to the nineteenth century, there was no mass-participation swimming for either leisure or competition, and the use of swimming and bathing in works of art was a convention that allowed the depiction of a subject that would otherwise have been condemned as prurient and pornographic. Although there was an association between real-life swimming and nudity, this was male nudity, which would not be problematized until the end of the nineteenth century. It was because women were normally so covered up that the naked female swimmer was charged with so much erotic power. But this would not become manifest until the appearance of the new media that would make the naked female form available to millions of viewers for the price of a few pence or cents: photography and the cinema.

Swimming Comes into Focus

The invention of still photography transformed the individual's perception of his or her body. Fine art portraiture in sculpture or painting had been reserved for the great and the good, representing them in an idealized form. Similarly, public art also made use of idealized bodies as depictions of civic virtues, religious beliefs and political concepts. Photography, by contrast, was the ultimate democratic medium. Once initial technical difficulties had been resolved to make it truly affordable, it showed the subject as he or she was (at least until the invention of retouching), and when combined with printing and the telegraph, an image could be reproduced at will and published worldwide almost instantaneously.

Among the first to exploit photography's power as an advertising and marketing tool were the early pioneers of physical education and bodybuilding: men such as Eugen Sandow in the UK and Bernarr Macfadden in the U.S. (see Chapter Six) used photographs of their own near-naked bodies to promote their health and fitness businesses and publications.[16] Sandow and Macfadden had female counterparts – strongwomen who performed tours de force on stage – but they were more restricted in how much flesh they could show, and their physical strength, which then as now was not considered an attractive feminine attribute, meant that their sexual appeal was at best ambiguous.[17]

Other early adopters of photography were the pornographers, with the predictable consequence that photographic materials considered obscene were quickly made illegal. Measures to stem the production and sale of photographic pornography were just as successful as efforts to control it on the Internet today. In any case, definitions of obscenity were subjective, and the law could be circumvented by how the material was presented. Sandow's photographs of him posing wearing only a fig leaf in the 1890s were deemed acceptable – first, because he was a man; second, because the photographs were 'scientific' and 'educational'; and finally, because they were 'artistic', as they reproduced the poses of famous Graeco-Roman statues.

Humans have always known that 'sex sells'; what photography demonstrated was that realistic depictions of sex sell best of all. The still photographic image, first of the female body and more recently of the male body, have been used to market a wide range of products, but in combination with swimming, it seems to have a particular appeal to manufacturers of high-end fragrances. Current at the time of writing are the campaigns of Dolce and Gabbana's Light Blue, Giorgio Armani's Aqua di Gio and Davidoff's Cool Water, which all use very similar branding and imagery to market their products. The adverts feature swimmers and play on the sensuality of full immersion in water, equating it with the refreshing qualities of splashing the product on the skin while combining this with the erotic display of the body to suggest how the product will increase the wearer's sex appeal. In one Davidoff Cool Water ad campaign, the naked swimmers could be in the throes of aquatic coitus – a visual confirmation of Freud's interpretation of swimming dreams used for commercial purposes, though, one hopes, without the urination that he associated with them.

Million-dollar Mermaid

There was another medium that perfectly understood the power of sex to sell its products to an audience of millions: cinema. But while the still photograph pornographers could ply their trade under plain covers and in brown paper envelopes, the film industry – at least until the home video revolution – needed maximum visibility to sell its offerings. It needed sex but also needed visual conventions to sanitize the obviously erotic and make it, if not respectable, at least acceptable to more conservative audiences and lawmakers. Swimming provided the perfect cover to reveal as much as was permissible in the movies. The early cinema was remarkably permissive in this respect. One of the leading exponents of the genre

Having made her name in amusement park shows and on the vaudeville circuit, Annette Kellerman went to Hollywood, becoming the first actor to appear nude in a commercial motion picture. In this scene from *Neptune's Daughter* (1914), Kellerman's modesty is protected by artfully placed locks of hair.

was someone we have met before, in Chapter Six, the swimmer and diver Annette Kellerman.

Australian by birth, Kellerman began swimming to correct what may have been the consequences of a mild case of polio. A successful competitive swimmer and diver in her home country, in 1904, aged just seventeen, she travelled to England with her ailing father, hoping to make money from her swimming and diving. In order to attract publicity, she swam 27 km (17 miles) in the Thames from Putney Bridge in west London to Blackwall in east London – a not inconsiderable feat considering how polluted and busy with commercial traffic the Thames was in the early 1900s. She gave diving exhibitions and took on men in river races. The *Daily Mirror* hired her to swim the English Channel, and though she failed three times, she became famous as a swimmer, diver and entertainer.

In 1906 she was invited to perform in Chicago. She later moved to Revere Beach, Massachusetts, to work at an amusement park for $300 a week (now about $8,000), performing a gruelling schedule of fourteen shows a week. Her notoriety, after her arrest and trial for indecency on Revere's public beach for wearing a swimsuit that, while modest, showed off her figure, led to her being invited to perform her diving act on Broadway. From New York, she toured the u.s. vaudeville circuit as a 'high diving and stunt swimming artiste', earning the phenomenal salary of $1,500 a week (now about $38,500), making her one of the highest paid entertainers of the period.

Now an established performer, Kellerman decided to capitalize on her fame, and like many other entertainers, headed west to see if she could make her fortune in the burgeoning motion picture business in Hollywood. Between 1914 and 1924, she made seven major silent motion pictures, including *Neptune's Daughter* (1914) and *Daughter of the Gods* (1916), in both of which she appeared naked in and out of the water – in one scene, her breasts and pudenda artfully hidden by her long tresses. Between 1907 and 1941, she starred in nine films as herself, demonstrating swimming, diving and water ballet.[18]

Although practically unknown today, Kellerman left an impressive legacy. She promoted leisure and competitive swimming and diving among women at a time when, as swimming historian Lisa Bier explained, exercise of any kind was seen as 'dangerous to a woman's health and supposedly delicate body'.[19] Her innovative swimsuit design made it much easier for women to swim, and the water ballet she performed in her films was a precursor of the modern sport of synchronized swimming. In 1952 Hollywood released a biopic of Kellerman's life called *Million Dollar Mermaid*, starring her undisputed aquatic heiress, Esther Williams (1921–2013).

Me Tarzan, You Naked

Kellerman's aquatic exploits were the opening act of what would be the golden age of aquatic-themed films, which continued to titillate audiences until the sexual revolution of the 1960s made the need for any justification to show a nude, topless or lightly clad swimmer completely redundant. The imposition of film censorship in the u.s. with the establishment of the Hays Code in 1930 ended the freedom seen in *Neptune's Daughter*. An early victim of the new censor was *Tarzan and His Mate* (1934), starring Johnny Weissmuller and Maureen O'Sullivan. The scene that caused the censors the most concern was the underwater ballet, in which Tarzan, played by Olympic gold medallist Weissmuller, swims with a naked Jane, played in the sequence not by O'Sullivan but by body double and Olympic medallist Josephine McKim. O'Sullivan's revealing costumes and her close physical contact with Weissmuller in other scenes also attracted the censor's attention, but it was the water ballet that was cut from the original release. The sequence was only restored when the film was rereleased in the 1990s.[20] Although the nude scene was cut, it was reshot with McKim in different states of undress to meet the varying requirements of national and international censors. The writers did not have to find a pretext to have Tarzan stripped, as traditionally he wore nothing but a loincloth, but swimming was a suitable pretext to have Jane bare as much flesh as the censors would allow.

There was no problem with the skimpiness of the loincloth worn by the Lord of the Jungle, which was considerably briefer than the swimwear that men were wearing on beaches at the time, and that Weissmuller himself had worn when he medalled at the 1928 Amsterdam Olympics. The Hayes Code would go on to insist that men's genitalia be not just securely contained but that even their shape be hidden, but the double standard about how much flesh the sexes could decently display endured until the code became unenforceable in the 1960s. One of the perverse results of u.s. censorship between the 1930s and 1960s was that women and gay men could thrill at the sight of any number of scantily clad men in Hollywood movies, but American heterosexual men had to go and see foreign films to catch a glimpse of a female nipple.

Aquatic Follies

Just as *Tarzan and His Mate*'s nude swim was failing to meet the stringent criteria of the Hayes Code, water ballet was taking swimming in films to another dimension: forget artfully placed locks of hair or a nude underwater ballet featuring two Olympians; enter 100 chorus girls performing an extraordinary swimming and diving routine, choreographed by Busby Berkeley (1895–1976) for the 'By a Waterfall' sequence of *Footlight Parade* (1933). The sequence employed all of Berkeley's trademark techniques, which had made *42nd Street* and *Gold Diggers of 1933* (both 1933) such hits with the cinema-going public: the movement of both cameras and dancers and multiple-angle, underfloor and overhead shots, which he achieved with a 12 × 24-m (40 × 80-ft) swimming pool with glass sides and floor so that the swimmers could be filmed from every angle.[21]

Berkeley was tapping into the aquatic zeitgeist of the time because that same year a large-scale water show drew audiences of 10,000 spectators to a specially constructed pool in Lake Michigan for the Chicago Century of Progress International Exposition (also known as the Chicago World's Fair), marketed in the event's advertising as 'Performing ten complicated routines in perfect unison, thirty-five modern mermaids are revealing to patrons of the Lagoon Theater at the Chicago World's Fair, the highly modern art of synchronized swimming' – incidentally, the first time the term 'synchronized swimming' was used to describe what was previously referred to as water ballet.

In 1939–40, impresario Billy Rose (1899–1966) staged the Billy Rose Aquacades at the New York World's Fair, headlining Johnny Weissmuller and Olympic gold medallist Eleanor Holm. When the main cast moved on to the Aquacades at the 1940 San Francisco's Golden Gate International Exhibition, swimmer turned actor Buster Crabbe took Weissmuller's spot in the New York shows, and Rose hired an unknown swimmer to replace Holm, picking her from a line-up of 75 hopefuls. Her name was Esther Williams (1921–2013), and the rest, as the Hollywood cliché should run, was box-office gold. Like Kellerman before her, Williams graduated from competitive swimming to live shows to Hollywood. Her first major picture in which she figured as a swimmer was *Bathing Beauty* (1944), which featured a now iconic swimming and diving finale choreographed by Busby Berkeley.

The days of the aquatic spectacular, however, were numbered. During the counter-cultural 1960s explosion, the Hays Code became unenforceable, and female nudity became much more common in movies, which now received an age-graded rating. In the 1970s, the introduction of the VHS video recorder created a whole new mode of distributing pornographic films that no longer required them to be shown in public cinemas. Swimming was no longer necessary to make female nudity or near-nudity acceptable to the censors, and it pretty much vanished from cinema screens outside of the sci-fi and fantasy genres that I have covered earlier in the chapter. There were, of course, a few exceptions, such as the charmingly vapid *Splash* (1984), with Daryl Hannah taking the role of Madison the mermaid. And who could forget Shelly Winters swimming her way through the *Poseidon Adventure* (1972), and of course, the chilling swimming scenes in the *Jaws* four-movie franchise (1975–83), which not only scared sea swimmers witless for a decade but also led to the slaughter of many harmless species of shark that posed no real threat to swimmers.

Ars Natatoria

Sport and the visual arts have a very ancient relationship in Europe dating back to classical Greece. The connection established the 'Grecian ideal' as a standard of masculine beauty during the Renaissance – a standard that continues to influence our own conception of masculinity and male beauty. After the Renaissance, when artists sought to justify their use of female nudes, which lacked ancient precedents when compared to male nudes, they turned to the retelling of ancient myths such as the birth of Venus and the triumph of Amphitrite, which gave them licence to cover their canvases with acres of naked flesh – a convention that endured for centuries and was so entrenched in academic painting that rebellious artists in the late nineteenth century were able to subvert it to challenge established styles. Early modern literature and poetry, with a few notable exceptions, had very little to say about swimming, but merely reflected the prejudices of the day that swimming was dangerous and only practised in the extremis of shipwreck and other like dangers to save one's life.

At the end of the nineteenth century, science fiction used the strangeness and mystery of the aquatic world as a setting for escapist fantasies in which characters were freed of the limitations of ordinary swimmers and divers by advanced technology or superhuman powers. But when compared to other sci-fi settings, water comes a distant fourth after land, sky and outer space. Many still cling to the belief that there are aliens and UFOs waiting to be discovered in the depths of space, but few still believe that there is an Atlantis on the ocean floor or underwater races, benign or sinister. Sci-fi and fantasy have had limited success in using swimming as a vehicle for escapism. Rather than giving a positive representation of swimming, these modern myths hark back to pre-modern fears of the dangers that lurk beneath the water.

The modern visual arts, photography and cinema initially used the same conventions as academic painting in using swimming as a justification to show women in the nude or lightly clad. The imposition of stricter censorship rules in the U.S. between 1930 and 1960 ensured a central role for swimming in Hollywood, as it was the perfect excuse to have actresses disporting themselves in swimwear. As is often the case, strict censorship promoted an extraordinary burst of creativity. With the water spectaculars starring Esther Williams and choreographed by Busby Berkeley, Hollywood had hit upon the perfect formula, using swimming to make the erotic display of the female body a respectable form of popular entertainment. The relaxation and then abolition of censorship meant that the makers of movies and TV programmes no longer needed to find elaborate excuses for nudity. In our hyper-permissive age, when pornography of every stripe is just a few mouse clicks away, the eroticism of the naked body in water, suggestive of sensual and sexual pleasure, has been retained in advertising campaigns.

If asked to say how much the arts, literature and popular media have contributed to the popularity and practice of swimming, I would have to answer very little, because the depictions of swimming are so mixed. It is swimming that has been a useful device for artists, whose depictions were usually of the before and after the swim, when the model is fully exposed to the gaze of the lascivious onlooker. An exception to that statement could be made about the swimming extravaganzas from Kellerman to Williams, which demonstrated beyond doubt that women could excel at sport without becoming over-masculine or collapsing from exhaustion. It is an advertising cliché that sex sells, but for decades, it has been swimming, masquerading as sex, that has sold a wide range of products – swimwear, holidays, suntan cream, cosmetics and fragrances, to name a few – but strangely, not itself. Again, as in my conclusion about the influence of competition on the practice of swimming, I have found a strange disconnect between the uses of swimming in the arts, literature and popular media and the reality of leisure and fitness swimming experienced by the vast majority of swimmers.

11
The Aquatic Human

Great things are going on down at the bottom of the sea.
Even greater things are in store. Man's age-old dream of
living on the ocean floor with fish and other sea creatures
for neighbors is no longer a dream but a reality.

TERRY SHANNON AND CHARLES PAYZANT,
PROJECT SEALAB (1966)[1]

We now reach the end of a journey that began several million years before our species existed, when swimming may have played a key role in our evolution into the upright, bipedal and hairless *Homo sapiens*, so it is fitting that this closing chapter should examine what role swimming might play in the future of humanity. Through 5,000 years of recorded history, the human connection with the aquatic realm and swimming has undergone several complete transformations. Humans, who owed their very survival to their ability to swim and dive, gradually turned away from the water and forgot how to swim. The seas, rivers and lakes that were once sources of life and the abodes of gods and benign spirits turned into fearful, mysterious otherworlds populated by monsters and sinister humanoid races.

In the eighteenth century, the pendulum swung back and humans dipped their toes back into the water in spas and seaside resorts in search of cures for the woes of affluence and civilization. In doing so, they accidentally discovered two much more powerful therapies for humanity's *mal de vivre*: leisure and tourism. Meanwhile, Victorian science and engineering were opening up the underwater world, with diving bells, submersibles and standard diving dress. At first divers were tied to the surface by life-sustaining umbilical hoses, but in the post-Second World War period, Cousteau's invention of the Aqualung gave humans the keys to Poseidon's kingdom. We have now gone further and deeper, disturbing the abyssal layers of the oceans where blind phosphorescent fish dance to Darwin's tune in the pitch darkness.

But with all our boldness, enterprise and scientific curiosity, we have not been kind to our planet, using its oceans as a huge septic tank for all the waste that spews from our towns and factories and the garbage for which we no longer have room in landfills. But the seas are not just under threat from raw sewage and billions of tons of non-biodegradable plastic but from acidification – the evil and still lesser-known twin of global warming. And as if to pay us back for those centuries of misuse, the seas may prove to be the undoing of human civilization, if the worst fears of climate scientists come to pass and the most populous and productive regions of the globe, the coastal plains, are submerged by rising sea levels. If the seas do vengefully rise like a second biblical flood, will this be the end of civilization and of our species, or merely the end of civilization as we currently know it? Shall we be able to adapt technologically and physically to a much warmer, wetter world, and shall we finally colonize the continental shelf in a second great human migration that takes us back to the original home of life on earth?

Back to the Future

Back in 1943, it was all going to be different. After the *Mousquemers* had finished their surprise banquet of lobster following Cousteau's first sortie wearing the Aqualung, he recalled in *The Silent World*,

> Tailliez pencilled on the tablecloth and announced that each yard of depth we claimed in the sea would open to mankind three hundred thousand cubic kilometres of living space.[2]

The future that they foresaw was a great second colonization – like the dispersals of early humans from Africa across the planet – only this time of the continental shelf that stretches up to 1,500 km (930 miles) from the coast but averages a much more modest 80 km (50 miles), at a depth that does not exceed 150 m (490 ft).

The Bathyscaphe *FNRS-3*. The small spherical crew cabin is suspended beneath a much larger arrangement of float tanks and iron-shot ballast hoppers that allowed the craft to descend to record depths and ascend again under its own power.

Beyond the continental shelf are the ever deepening waters of the abyssal plain that are between 3,000 m (9,800 ft) and 6,000 m (20,000 ft) and of the oceanic trenches from 5,000 m (16,400 ft) to 11,000 m (36,000 ft).

The record for open-circuit scuba diving is 1,080 ft (330 m) but it required the diver to wear a battery of air tanks to be able to survive the long decompression back to the surface. While this is twice as deep as the average depth of the continental shelf, it falls far short of the abyssal plane, and gets nowhere near the deep trenches. Commercial saturation divers breathing a special mixture of gases can work at 600 m (2,000 ft), and the Atmospheric Diving System (ADS) – an armoured one-man suit that looks like Robbie the Robot in *Forbidden Planet* (1956) – can descend to 700 m (2,300 ft), but the ADS is a throwback to the diving bell and SDS, with the diver unable to swim: he either walks on the sea floor or uses the suit's built-in propulsion systems. In any case, the vast majority of divers, who dive for leisure, will never be able to reach those depths, as they are limited by regulation to 40 m (130 ft), and many never make it even to that depth.[3]

Exploration beyond the continental shelf began long before the invention of the Aqualung. Between 1930 and 1934, the Bathysphere, a spherical unpowered submersible, was lowered down into the ocean by cable in a series of deep dives off the coast of Bermuda. The Bathysphere was designed to study deep-sea animals that had never been observed in their natural habitats. The pre-Second World War depth record that it set was 923 m (3,028 ft). There was no question of the crew leaving the sphere, which was bolted shut to avoid leaks. Even if the Bathysphere had been equipped with some kind of airlock, divers wearing the diving suits of the day would have been instantly crushed by the pressure at those extreme depths.

The Bathysphere was succeeded by Professor Auguste Piccard's (1884–1962) Bathyscaphe *FNRS-2*, designed and built between 1946 and 1948, which was the first of three independent, self-propelled deep-sea submersibles of the same design. The U.S. Navy purchased the third bathyscaphe, *Trieste*, from Italy in 1957. In 1960, the *Trieste*, carrying a two-man crew in its cramped spherical cabin, reached the deepest point on earth, the Challenger Deep in the Mariana Trench of the northwest Pacific, south of the island of Guam. The Deep is 10,920 m (35,827 ft), and the descent in a manned craft was not repeated until 25 March 2012, when film director James Cameron (b. 1954) reached the bottom of the trench in the *Deepsea Challenger*. It is telling to note that while there have been six manned landings on the Moon, with a total of twelve astronauts visiting the lunar surface, which is 384,550 km (239,000 miles) from earth, only four aquanauts have ever reached the lowest point of the Mariana Trench, which is a mere 10 km (6 miles) down. While the Moon, planets and other celestial objects within our solar system have been bombarded with probes, and we have a permanent space station in orbit and over 2,000 artificial satellites in orbit at the time of writing, we only have one undersea research station, which is crewed for part of the year. It is true that any number of submarines sail beneath the oceans at any one time, but most of these are military rather than deep-ocean submersibles. The working depth of the present generation of u.s. nuclear submarines and of the other powers with nuclear fleets is 490 m (1,600 ft), which makes most of the ocean floor inaccessible.[4]

Living in the Sea

Although there was no more question of a diver descending to the deep oceans in a Bathyscaphe and going out for a swim with a wetsuit and Aqualung than for an astronaut on the Moon to go out onto the lunar surface wearing a lounge suit, the 1960s saw the first human attempts to colonize the shallower waters of the continental shelf, starting with the u.s. Navy's Man-in-the-Sea programme, established in 1957, and the European Conshelf project, pioneered by Jacques Cousteau in the early 1960s and part-funded by the French petrochemical industry. The funding arrangements of the two projects illuminate three very different agendas. Man-in-the-Sea was backed by the u.s. military, and at the height of the Cold War was primarily concerned with keeping the Soviet Union in check rather than exploring the bottom of the sea. This was an 'undersea habitat race', another aspect of the scientific and military contests between the two superpowers. For Conshelf, there were the very different aims of Cousteau, whose interests were the exploration and conservation of the marine ecosphere, and of the petrochemical industry that wished to use it to evaluate the commercial possibilities of exploiting oil and gas reserves from permanent undersea bases.

The two projects were broadly similar in their aims and in the capabilities of the six underwater habitats they deployed during the 1960s. Where the American and French projects differed was in the designs of the habitats. The u.s.'s three Sealabs looked like uninspiring metal blimps, but Cousteau, with his usual visual flair, decided on much more futuristic designs. Built in 1962, Conshelf I was placed at a depth of 10 m (30 ft) off the French port of Marseilles, and was home to two aquanauts for seven days. Conshelf II, built in 1963 and deployed in the warm waters of the Red Sea, was a more ambitious test of saturation diving. It had a main starfish-shaped habitat sunk at the same depth as Conshelf I, where six aquanauts

The futuristic design of Conshelf II was visually much more striking than the rather pedestrian design for the Sealab missions. A born showman, Cousteau understood that design was a way to attract public interest in and backing for Conshelf. Located in the Red Sea, Conshelf II consisted of three buildings: the main starfish-shaped habitat, the deep cabin and the underwater garage for the 'Diving Saucer' submersible.

spent one month. Unlike Sealab, which consisted of one habitat, Conshelf II had two other underwater installations: a smaller deep cabin where two aquanauts spent a week at 30 m (100 ft), allowing their bodies to become fully saturated with the breathing gas, and a garage for Cousteau's 'Diving Saucer', making it the first time a submersible had been operated from an underwater base.

The u.s. Navy's Sealab I, II and III operated in 1964, 1965 and 1969 respectively and set records for the aquanauts' lengths of stay underwater. NASA teamed up with the Navy, the Department of the Interior and General Electric in 1969 to launch Tektite I, off the coast of the u.s. Virgin Islands, in which a research team stayed for a record-breaking 58 days. In 1970, Dr Sylvia Earle led the first all-female team to stay in an underwater habitat to Tektite II. Tektite was the first undersea habitat to employ scientists to explore the ocean rather than focus entirely on the physiology of diving and undersea living. To date, more than 65 undersea marine habitats have been built and operated by different nations around the world, but the only habitat still fully functional at the time of writing is Aquarius, located within the Florida Keys National Marine Sanctuary. Operated by Florida International University, Aquarius hosts teams of researchers who stay for two weeks at a time between April to November, or for as long as the hurricane season allows.[5]

Watching the two u.s. Navy-made films about Sealab I and II and Cousteau's *World without Sun* about Conshelf II, one can recapture some of the excitement of the 1960s, when humans were setting off to explore both inner and outer space, convinced that technology would solve every problem and that in just a few decades, we would be holidaying on the Moon and living in ocean-bed cities, commuting to work in submarine cars to undersea offices, factories, mines and farms. Sealab and Conshelf demonstrated that it was possible for humans to live and work at the bottom of the sea through a technique known as saturation diving. In saturation

The u.s. Navy's Sealab I was part of the Man-in-the-Sea Programme, one of the many military and scientific 'races' the u.s. engaged in with the Soviet Union during the Cold War. Unlike Cousteau's futuristic Conshelf designs, Sealabs I and II were functional metal blimps.

Decompression chambers used in saturation diving. Once the diver's tissues are saturated, he remains within a pressurized environment on the surface and is transported to and from his working depth in a diving bell. In this way, the diver only requires one single decompression once he has completed his allotted task.

diving, the mixture of gases that the divers breathe is altered so that they can remain exposed to much greater pressures than normal without any major risk of injury. Once their tissues are completely saturated with the gas mixture, the time it takes them to decompress to return safely to the surface is the same whether they remain at depths for one day or several weeks.

This opened up the possibility of humans being able not only to live in underwater habitats but to exit them to explore and work on the sea bottom. During the Conshelf III experiment of 1965, located in the Mediterranean between Nice and Monaco, six aquanauts spent 22 days at a depth of 102.4 m (336 ft), living in a two-storey sphere 5.5 m (18 ft) in diameter, mounted on a barge that contained ballast, an air reservoir and two emergency decompression chambers that could be used as escape pods. While aquanauts from Sealab II were simulating the salvage of a crashed fighter plane, their counterparts from Conshelf III were simulating the installation of an underwater wellhead known as a 'Christmas tree' for the French petrochemical industry. But there were limitations: they had to remain within their saturation depth; they had to wear specially heated suits as the gas mixture they were breathing meant that they lost heat much faster than in normal diving; and their range was limited by the length and sturdiness of the umbilical hoses that provided them with power for their suits and the breathing mixture.[6]

Although the first-generation habitats did not develop into permanent undersea communities, they led to the development of the commercial saturation diving industry in the 1960s and '70s, which did not employ costly fixed underwater bases but instead used mobile ship-based saturation diving facilities. Divers would travel by ship and use on-board pressurized chambers to saturate their body tissues with the gas mixture approximate to their working depth. The chambers would serve as their accommodation for the duration of the dive and be used to decompress them once the job was completed. They were ferried to and from the sea floor in diving bells that often also provided breathing gas and power to the divers' suits.[7] While ship-borne systems have the advantage of being mobile, they are costly and still comparatively dangerous. Since the 1980s, the trend has been to replace divers with deep-sea submersibles, atmospheric diving systems and increasingly by remotely operated underwater vehicles – the drones of the sea.[8]

Sealab and Conshelf demonstrated how difficult and expensive it was to maintain even a handful of aquanauts at relatively shallow depths for a few weeks at a time. Although the underwater habitats themselves were fairly robust, the surface installations and ships that ensured their survival were at the mercy of storms. Even with the resources of the u.s. military, nasa and major corporations behind them, the projects proved too costly. Although it would have been possible to build major undersea facilities and populate them with trained divers, as with the Apollo Moon shots, what was possible and what was practical and useful were two very different things. In *Living and Working under the Sea*, James Miller and Ian Koblick observed, a little wistfully:

At the risk of shattering the dreams of some readers, we think that the likelihood of even small underwater communities is an idea whose time has not yet come nor will it in the foreseeable future. The reasons? Cost, the lack of a real need, and the priorities of a world faced with health, economic, and political issues affecting our survival.[9]

Plastic Not So Fantastic

Although we are very infrequent visitors to the undersea world beyond the near continental shelf, this does not mean that our impact on the oceans is limited to coastal waters. Of course, what disturbs leisure swimmers most, as anyone who has swum in the sea near populated regions such as the English Channel and the Mediterranean knows, is the amount and variety of refuse and rubbish that comes floating your way or is washed up on a beach after a storm. A group of friends who swam the Channel as a relay team reported that it was far preferable to swim with your mouth closed, because if you saw something floating towards your open mouth, you had to hope that it was seaweed.

But once you are in the open sea, you would think that the water should be in its pristine state. For one, there is so much of it: 360 million km^2 (139 million sq. miles), with most of it incredibly deep; it is salty, and everyone knows salt is a natural antiseptic; and finally the sea is full of useful organisms large and small that can eat or digest almost any manmade waste. While this is true of all biodegradable materials, there is one ubiquitous material that is non-biodegradable – or at least not in the timescales that humans would usually employ: plastic. Many of the plastics that we take for granted today were invented between the First and Second World Wars, but they only became commercialized in the post-Second World War period. Plastics are synonymous with the throwaway consumer society that has beguiled humanity since the 1960s, and therein lies the main problem. They are cheap to manufacture, and though recyclable, they are much cheaper to discard. We manufacture millions of tons of plastic and much of it ends up in the marine environment, where it can take up to 1,000 years to degrade.

In the late 1980s researchers predicted that much of the non-biodegradable plastic waste that we had been dumping in the ocean since the Second World War would drift to the North Pacific Gyre, a huge marine vortex created by the rotation of the earth and ocean currents. Confirmation of such waste's existence was not long in coming, when Charles Moore, a yachtsman and oceanographer, sailed into it in 1997 when returning home across the north Pacific after taking part in a yachting race. He wrote:

> I often struggle to find words that will communicate the vastness of the Pacific Ocean . . . Yet as I gazed from the deck at the surface of what ought to have been a pristine ocean, I was confronted, as far as the eye could see, with the sight of plastic. It seemed unbelievable, but I never found a clear spot. In the week it took to cross the subtropical high, no matter what time of day I looked, plastic debris was floating everywhere: bottles, bottle caps, wrappers, fragments.

Estimates of the size of the Great Pacific Garbage Patch vary from 700,000 km^2 (270,000 sq. miles) to 15 million km^2 (5 million sq. miles). According to Moore, 80 per cent of the garbage originated on land and the remainder was dumped by ships, either on purpose or accidentally. A high concentration of this debris is plastic. In a study in 2001, researchers found that the concentration of plastic debris in parts of the patch had reached one million pieces per 2.5 km^2 (1 sq. mile). The problem is not restricted to the Pacific; similar garbage patches exist in the other major oceans and seas. The busiest coastal areas of the Mediterranean revealed in excess of 4,000 items of debris per square mile (2.5 km^2) in the early 2000s, 77 per cent of which was plastic, of which 93 per cent was accounted for by plastic carrier bags.

Plastic will degrade over time, but all that happens is that it is broken down into smaller and smaller pieces, which remain suspended in the upper layers of seawater, until they are small enough to be ingested by aquatic organisms. These floating plastic particles, known as 'nurdles', or more romantically 'mermaid's tears', are small enough to look like plankton or fish eggs. But any fish, bird or marine reptile unfortunate enough to eat them will either starve, as the nurdles obstruct its digestive tract, or die of poisoning from the chemicals leaching from the plastic. Larger marine animals can eat bigger items, such as whole plastic bags, which can also cause starvation through obstructions of their digestive tracts.[10]

A Bad Case of Acid Reflux

The second problem that we have unwittingly created in the oceans is a change in the acidity of the ocean caused by an increase in the carbon dioxide (CO_2) in our atmosphere. Global warming's lesser-known evil twin, ocean acidification, is a by-product of the large quantities of CO_2 that have been released into our atmosphere by the burning of fossil fuels. The uptake of CO_2 is changing the pH of the oceans and gradually changing the chemical properties of seawater. Unlike dumped plastic objects and sewage, which pollute our inshore waters and discourage people from swimming, acidification has no direct impact on humans. Unchecked, however, it is having a significant impact on marine life such as corals and plankton. Although some species may benefit from the altered pH of the oceans, others will undoubtedly suffer. Giving the oceans a bad case of acid reflux may cause a major upset in the marine food chain, causing scarcities of certain species of fish and shellfish in an already food-poor world. Along with the other changes that are being brought about by global warming, acidification may prove to be a significant threat to the health of the marine ecosphere, and therefore to the survival of humanity.

Waterworld

If pollution and acidification are not threat enough to the health of the planet and the future of the human race, there is an even greater danger to the long-term viability of human civilization: global warming leading to the melting of the ice caps and a rise in sea levels. In 1995, the movie *Waterworld*, starring Kevin Costner, imagined the earth in the year 2500, when the sea level has risen a cataclysmic (but totally unrealistic) 7,600 m (25,000 ft), until the water covers nearly the entirety of the planet's surface. Costner plays a lone mariner who is revealed to be a mutant with superhuman swimming abilities – another completely unlikely occurrence in a mere 500 years of human evolution. Despite a multi-million-dollar budget and some of the most expensive sets ever built, the film was a prize turkey – though in this case, some kind of waterfowl might be more appropriate. The plot was so thin as to be transparent, the acting wooden and the whole premise of the movie – that any portion of the human race could survive the near total flooding of the earth for several centuries in ramshackle floating communities made up of recycled oil tankers – was so unbelievable that the film was universally panned. According to the best estimates of the U.S. Geological Survey, even the worst case scenario if all the ice on earth contained in the ice caps and glaciers melted would be a sea level rise of 80 m (262 ft).[11]

A world map showing the effects on Europe of a much more realistic sea-level rise of 65 m (216 ft) demonstrates the disappearance of several northern European countries, the flooding of half of the British Isles and large chunks taken out of the Mediterranean,

An atoll, a floating refuge for humans in a world covered in water after the melting of the ice caps and a cataclysmic sea level rise of 7,600 m (25,000 ft). A kind of aquatic *Mad Max* (1979), *Waterworld* (1995) failed to impress the critics or the paying public.

Black Sea and Caspian Sea coasts. Similar destruction would be wrought on the other continents, resulting in the flooding of most of the world's major population and economic regions that are located on or near the coast.[12]

The oceans already cover 71 per cent of the earth's surface. Would it make so much difference if we lost another 10 per cent of our landmass to the seas? It might not sound like a lot, but the land we would lose is currently the most populous and economically productive on the planet: the low-lying coastal plains that are the locations of the world's premier population centres, including New York, Los Angeles, London, Amsterdam, Rome, Dhaka, Rio de Janeiro, Sydney, Cape Town, Alexandria, Mumbai and Shanghai, to name just a handful of cities at risk. Recent extreme flooding events in Europe, Australia, Japan and the U.S. might be a foretaste of what might overtake the world in the next century. But rather than a global catastrophe, could this be an incredible opportunity for the human race?

In 1984, Miller and Koblick asked, 'Can humans be transformed into aquatic animals unfettered by steel suits, submersibles, and sophisticated breathing equipment?' and then reviewed research into artificial gills and other methods that would allow humans to extract oxygen directly from the water as they now do from the air. Experiments on animals have shown that terrestrial mammals such as rats can breathe underwater, but only in water that has much higher concentrations of oxygen than natural fresh- or seawater.[13] It is an intriguing possibility but one that seems as far away as the flying car and the domestic robot. Breathing underwater would not be the only problem if we were forced to migrate en masse to the oceans by a climate catastrophe: before we can set out to conquer the oceans like the Man from Atlantis or Aquaman, we would have to alter our physiology to be able to survive the pressure and cold of the deep oceans. While this remains science fiction, the manipulation of the human genome and its combination with the genes of marine mammals, could provide a solution to the human colonization of the seas. Even if we did not evolve from aquatic apes, might we not one day, through desire or necessity, evolve into aquatic humans?

Epilogue

When I started writing this book, as a lifelong swimmer whose introduction to water was a headlong dive into the Round Pond in Kensington Gardens at the age of two, I took it for granted that the vast majority of humans were by nature and nurture deeply engaged with swimming – how else to explain the proliferation of urban pools and the yearly summer exodus to the world's beaches? But upon researching and writing the previous ten chapters, I gradually became shaken by moments of self-doubt. What if I were deluding myself, and I was in fact a member of a minority of aquatic eccentrics? A trawl through the Internet netted several worrying articles about the numbers of people who cannot swim, as well as about a decrease in swimming numbers across the Western world. An American Red Cross survey revealed that 44 per cent of Americans do not know basic water-safety skills, a proportion that goes up among African and Hispanic Americans.[1] In England, a 2015 survey carried out by the ASA (Amateur Swimming Association) reported that up to 9 million people over the age of fourteen had never learned to swim. More disturbingly, the same survey found that half a million women had stopped swimming between 2005 and 2015 because they were too self-conscious to appear in public in a bathing suit.[2]

I enquired among my friends who were not habitual fitness swimmers or competitors. Though not a representative sample, the vast majority had a positive attitude to swimming, and most swam on their yearly summer holidays and many frequented their local pool throughout the year. A small number confirmed the ASA findings: they no longer swam, and if pressed to explain why, said that pools were too crowded or that they felt embarrassed to wear swimwear in public – though this seemed to apply to pools more than to beaches. I was further reassured by the finding in the ASA survey that swimming is the sport with the highest number of participants in England, with some 2.6 million adults swimming for thirty minutes at least once a week.

To this statistical reassurance, I added a more personal one. When I undertook my first course to become a swimming teacher, I was entrusted with a class of primary schoolchildren at a local swimming baths for one of my practical exams. I cannot recall their exact age, but they were too young to go into the main pool, so I supervised the session in the shallow teaching pool. What I could achieve in terms of teaching a group of twenty or so children in a thirty-minute session was pretty limited, my inexperience notwithstanding, but what I remember most of all was their boundless enthusiasm and sheer joy at being in the water. Kept afloat with water wings and noodles, though their feet easily reached the bottom, they screamed with delight and screeched with laughter as I tried (and failed miserably) to make them perform simple swimming drills across the narrow teaching basin. There were probably a few timid swimmers among them, but once they saw their friends splashing happily in the water, they forgot all their misgivings and joined in. The tutor supervising my practical smiled benevolently through the session and passed me, allowing me to graduate to teaching and coaching more committed teenagers and adults.

I have managed to reassure myself that I was not wrong and that humans do have a strong emotional attachment to swimming, though it is probably far more complex than I imagined when I started writing this book. At one end of the swimming continuum, we have the ecstatic sensualists who would happily grow gills and abandon land altogether, and at the other, the terrified hydrophobics, but most of us float somewhere in the middle, sometimes enthralled and sometimes frustrated. If our emotional connection to swimming is complex, our social, artistic and economic connections to it are even more varied and nuanced. If I can draw some kind of conclusion, it is that most people have a positive attitude to swimming but that we cannot take that positivity for granted. In the past we have gone from being majority swimmers to majority non-swimmers and back again. I can foresee a number of factors that could seriously reduce participation in swimming: the closure of swimming facilities because of economic pressures; a reluctance to swim in the sea because of increasing levels of pollution and the threat of pathogens in the water; and a decrease in the popularity of resort holidays in certain regions of the world because of terrorist threats. However, as a leisure and fitness swimmer, and occasional coach and competitor, I remain optimistic that we have come too far, learned too much and enjoyed ourselves for far too long ever to turn away from water once more.

References

Introduction

1 Swimming, synchronized swimming, open-water swimming and water-polo are the four swimming-based sports regulated by FINA (Fédération internationale de natation); the fifth sport, which only involves swimming as a secondary activity used to leave the water, is diving.

2 Dir. Stanley Kubrick, based on a short story by Arthur C. Clarke, 'The Sentinel of Eternity'.

1 The Aquatic Hominin

1 From Alister Hardy, 'Was Man More Aquatic in the Past?', *New Scientist* (17 March 1960), pp. 642–5.

2 For example, adult humans are composed of 57 per cent water.

3 The taxonomic terminology has changed in the past few decades; hominid includes humans and the great apes; hominine is similar but excludes the orang-utans; hominin includes modern humans and their extinct relatives; and human comprises the members of the genus *Homo*, both extinct and the one extant species, *Homo sapiens*.

4 Of the three extant species of great apes, the orang-utans (genus *Pongo*) split first, followed by the gorillas (genus *Gorilla*) and then, last of all, the chimpanzees (genus *Pan*), between 5 and 7 million years BP.

5 Three possible hominin ancestors, *Sahelanthropus tchadensis* (7 million years BP), *Orrorin tugenensis* (6 million years BP) and *Ardipithecus ramidus* (4.4 million years BP), have been identified

since the mid-1990s, but none are definitely accepted as human ancestors. Interestingly, all three show features indicating that they might have been bipedal.

6 Hardy, 'Was Man More Aquatic?'

7 Attenborough produced two two-part radio documentaries on the AAH, entitled *Scars of Evolution*, broadcast on the BBC on 12 and 19 April 2005, and *The Waterside Ape*, broadcast on 14 and 15 September 2016. The programmes were still available on the BBC's iPlayer service at the time of writing.

8 Elaine Morgan, *The Aquatic Ape Hypothesis* (London, 2001), p. 18.

9 Ibid., pp. 26–7.

10 Colin Groves, *Bones, Stones and Molecules* (London, 2004), p. 68.

11 'Elaine Morgan Obituary', *The Guardian* (29 July 2013).

12 Elaine Morgan, 'Why a New Theory Is Needed', in Machteld Roede, Jan Wind, John M. Patrick and Vernon Reynolds, eds, *The Aquatic Ape Theory: Fact or Fiction? The First Scientific Evaluation of a Controversial Theory of Human Evolution* (London, 1991), p. 9.

13 The great apes can and do stand on two legs and walk bipedally; for example, in aggression displays to make themselves look larger and when walking on branches; but their preferred mode of locomotion and the one their body is adapted to is knuckle-walking on all fours.

14 Morgan, *The Aquatic Ape Hypothesis*, pp. 64–6; Darren Naish, 'The Amazing Swimming Proboscis Monkey', *Scientific American* Blog, (29 November 2012).

15 David Attenborough, *Scars of Evolution*, programme two, originally broadcast on 19 April 2005.

16 Carsten Niemitz, 'The Evolution of the Upright Posture and Gait: A Review and a New Synthesis', U.S. National Library of Medicine, National Institutes for Health, see www.ncbi.nlm.nih.gov (accessed 12 March 2015).

17 Genetics has also identified 'Mitochondrial Eve' and 'Y-chromosomal Adam' – our oldest common male and female *Homo sapiens* ancestors, who lived in Africa between 200,000 and 140,000 years BP, though not necessarily contemporaneously.

18 Michael Marshall, 'Neanderthals Were Ancient Mariners', *New Scientist* (29 February 2012).

19 Heather Pringle, 'Primitive Seafarers', *National Geographic Magazine* (17 February 2010); Marshall, 'Neanderthals Were Ancient Mariners'.

20 Spencer Wells and Mark Read, *The Journey of Man: A Genetic Odyssey* (Princeton, NJ, 2002).

21 Douglas Oliver, *Polynesia in Early Historic Times* (Honolulu, HI, 2002), pp. 6–7.

22 Rick Torben, John Erlandson, René Vellanoweth and Todd Braje, 'From Pleistocene Mariners to Complex Hunter-gatherers: The Archaeology of the California Channel Islands', *Journal of World Prehistory*, 19 (2005), pp. 169–228.

23 Matthieu Paley, 'We Are What We Eat: Diving for Dinner with the Sea Gypsies', www.nationalgeographic.com (accessed 26 February 2015).

2 Divine Swimmers

1 Theodore Gachot, *Mermaids: Nymphs of the Sea* (San Francisco, CA, 1996), pp. 15–16.

2 *The Little Mermaid* (1989), dir. Ron Clements and John Musker.

3 Claude Lévi-Strauss, 'The Structural Study of Myth', *Journal of American Folklore*, LXVIII/270 (1955), pp. 428–44.

4 Tim Dietz, *The Call of the Siren: Manatees and Dugongs* (Golden, CO, 1992), p. 17.

5 Eric Chaline, *History's Greatest Deceptions, and the People Who Planned Them* (London, 2009), pp. 78–81.

6 Usually thought to start in the 'Fertile Crescent' (Egypt and the Near East), followed by China, India, New Guinea, Central and South America, sub-Saharan Africa and, finally, North America.

7 Gwendolyn Leick, *Mesopotamia: The Invention of the City* (London, 2001), p. 3.

8 Ibid., p. 2.

9 The temple of Enki was rebuilt on the same spot eighteen times. Each time the temple was renewed and enlarged, the old building was partially demolished and infilled, becoming part of the foundations of the new structure. This has allowed archaeologists to reconstruct the different stages of the temple's development and has also preserved cult objects and the remains of the feasts that took place there from the earliest times.

10 Leick, *Mesopotamia*, p. 25.

11 In the Bible, God sends the flood to punish humanity, which has become evil, saving only the righteous Noah and his family. In the Mesopotamian version, the gods, forgetting that they are

dependent on humans, decide to destroy them because they are disturbed by the noise they make. Enki foils their plan by saving Utnapishtim and his wife, and the gods, realizing their mistake when there are no humans left to serve them, grant the survivors immortality, transporting them to the earthly paradise of Dilmun.

12 Gwendolyn Leick, *A Dictionary of Near Eastern Mythology* (London, 1991), pp. 71–6.

13 The Greeks had their own version of the flood myth in which Zeus decided to punish humanity for waging constant wars. As in the other flood myths, one man is forewarned, in this case Deucalion, who, forewarned by his father, the Titan Prometheus, survived the flood in a wooden chest accompanied by his wife. After the flood had subsided, the couple repopulated the earth by casting stones over their shoulders: those thrown by Deucalion became men, and those cast by his wife, women.

14 A region now occupied by Ukraine, southern Russia and western Kazakhstan, thought to be where the horse was originally domesticated around the fourth millennium BCE; see Eric Chaline, *Fifty Animals that Changed the Course of History* (London, 2011), pp. 76–81.

15 Robin Hard, *The Routledge Handbook of Greek Mythology* (London, 2004), pp. 98–107.

16 Eric Chaline, *Traveller's Guide to the Ancient World: Greece in the Year 415 BCE* (London, 2008), pp. 86–7.

17 Hard, *The Routledge Handbook of Greek Mythology*, pp. 106–7.

18 Ibid., pp. 221–2.

19 They are most famously described in Homer's *Odyssey*, when Odysseus, anxious to hear the sirens' song, has himself lashed to the mast of his ship, while he orders his crew to stop their ears with wax so that they cannot hear the songs themselves or heed his orders to untie him.

20 Eric Chaline, *The Temple of Perfection: A History of the Gym* (London, 2015), pp. 15–50.

21 Ibid., pp. 24–30.

22 Aliette Geistdoerfer, Jacques Ivanoff and Isabelle Leblic, *Imagi-mer: créations fantastiques, créations mythiques* (Paris, 2002), p. 11.

23 'The Little Mermaid', www.andersen.sdu.dk (accessed 1 March 2015).

24 For the different versions of the story see 'Melusina', www.pitt.edu (accessed 21 March 2015).

25 'Mermaid of Zennor', www.en.wikipedia.org (accessed 14 February 2015).

26 Geistdoerfer et al., *Imagi-mer*, pp. 115–19.

27 Frédéric Laugrand and Jarich Oosten, *The Sea Woman: Sedna in Inuit Shamanism and Art in the Eastern Arctic* (Fairbanks, AK, 2008), pp. 17–19.

28 Gachot, *Mermaids*, pp. 15–16.

29 Geistdoerfer et al., *Imagi-mer*, p. 171.

3 Harvesting the Treasures of the Sea

1 Gwendolyn Leick, *Mesopotamia: The Invention of the City* (London, 2001), pp. 46–50.

2 The Sumerian terms *en*, *ensi* and *lugal* are translated as 'king' or 'queen' but it is unclear what their functions were or how they were appointed.

3 The fossilized sap of ferns and trees, amber was initially found on the beaches of the Baltic Sea and was later mined in the same area. See '*Anbar*', in Eric Chaline, *Fifty Materials that Changed the Course of History* (London, 2012), pp. 34–7.

4 John Wilford, 'Artifacts in Africa Suggest an Earlier Modern Human', *New York Times*, www.nytimes.com (2 December 2001).

5 For various articles concerning the widespread use of Spondylus shells, see 'Spondylus Studies', spondylus.wordpress.com.

6 Eric Chaline, '*Bolinus brandaris*', in *Fifty Animals that Changed the Course of History* (London, 2011), pp. 26–7.

7 Eric Chaline, '*Nakara*', in *Fifty Minerals that Changed the Course of History* (London, 2012), pp. 110–13, and '*Pinctada radiata*', ibid., pp. 168–73.

8 Robin Donkin, *Beyond Price: Pearls and Pearl-fishing, Origins to the Age of Discoveries* (Philadelphia, PA, 998), pp. 42–79.

9 Ibid., pp. 45–6.

10 Ibid., p. 48.

11 Although usually referred to in the singular, the Silk Road included a number of different overland and maritime routes between East and West.

12 Donkin, *Beyond Price*, pp. 66–8.

13 Ibid., pp. 57–65.

14 Although Erythraean Sea translates as 'Red Sea', in the *Periplus* it encompassed the Red Sea, Persian Gulf and the Indian Ocean as far east as the Bay of Bengal.

15 See '*Periplus*', www.depts.washington.edu (accessed 1 May 2015).

16 Donkin, *Beyond Price*, p. 80.

17 Ibid., p. 251.

18 Ibid., p. 121.

19 Ibid., p. 127.

20 Ibid., pp. 157–9.

21 Ibid., p. 198.

22 Chaline, '*Nakara*', p. 112.

23 Quoted in Donkin, *Beyond Price*, p. 314.

24 Ibid., pp. 313–14.

25 See '*De la costa de las Perlas y de Paria y la Isla de la Trinidad*, www.eumed.net (accessed 7 May 2015).

26 Donkin, *Beyond Price*, p. 277.

4 The Art of Swimming

1 Flavius Vegetius Renatus, 'To Learn to Swim', *The Military Institutions of the Romans*, digitalattic.org (accessed 19 May 2015).

2 Eric Chaline, '*Homo Sapiens*', in *Fifty Animals that Changed the Course of History* (London, 2011), pp. 214–15; www.catalhoyuk.com (accessed 11 May 2015).

3 Known to Layard and other nineteenth-century archaeologists as Nimrud.

4 Lesley Adkins, *Empires of the Plain: Henry Rawlinson and the Lost Languages of Babylon* (London, 2004), pp. 193–211.

5 Arnd Kruger, 'Swimming and the Emergence of the Modern Spirit', in John McClelland and Brian Merrilees, eds, *Sport and Culture in Early Modern Europe* (Toronto, 2009), p. 409.

6 Herodotus, *The Persian War*, Book VIII 'Urania', www.mcadams.posc.mu.edu (accessed 18 May 2015).

7 Pausanias, *Description of Greece*, Book X, www.perseus.tufts.edu (accessed 18 May 2015).

8 Thucydides, *The Peloponnesian War*, Book VII, www.perseus.tufts.edu (accessed 18 May 2015).

9 Howard Larson, *A History of Self-contained Diving and Underwater Swimming* (Washington, DC, 1959), pp. 5–6.

10 Flavius Vegetius Renatus, *The Military Institutions of the Romans*, digitalattic.org (accessed 19 May 2015).

11 Plutarch, 'Julius Caesar', in *Parallel Lives*, penelope.uchicago.edu (accessed 20 May 2015).

12 Kruger, 'Swimming and the Emergence of the Modern Spirit',
   p. 409.
13 Nicholas Orme, *Early British Swimming, 55 BC–AD 1719. With the
   First Swimming Treatise in English, 1595* (Exeter, 1983), pp. 11–15.
14 Eric Chaline, *The Temple of Perfection: A History of the Gym* (London,
   2015), pp. 55–6; Kruger, 'Swimming and the Emergence of the
   Modern Spirit', pp. 410–11.
15 Orme, *Early British Swimming, 55 BC–AD 1719*, p. 33.
16 Orme, *Early British Swimming, 55 BC–AD 1719*, pp. 22–38; *Les Très
   Riches Heures du Duc de Berry*, www.christusrex.org (accessed
   21 May 2015).
17 Chaline, *The Temple of Perfection*, pp. 58–63.
18 *The Boke Named the Governour*, Book III, section XVII, www.luminari-
   um.org (accessed 21 May 2015).
19 Richard Mulcaster, *Positions*, Chapter 23, www.archive.org (accessed
   22 May 2015), and *The Four Bookes of Flauius Vegetius Renatus*,
   www.quod.lib.umich.edu; Orme, *Early British Swimming*, pp. 52–4.
20 'The Way Things Were', www.queens.cam.ac.uk (accessed 23 May 2015).
21 Orme, *Early British Swimming*, pp. 69–70; Kruger, 'Swimming and
   the Emergence of the Modern Spirit', pp. 414–16.
22 Ibid., pp. 71–80.
23 Kruger, 'Swimming and the Emergence of the Modern Spirit',
   p. 419.
24 Ibid., p. 422.
25 Doing the backstroke with a breaststroke kick is still legal under
   FINA rules, but it is much slower than using the flutter kick.
26 Orme, *Early British Swimming*, pp. 81–8.
27 Ibid., pp. 111–208; Orme provides a full facsimile version of
   Middeleton's translation of *De arte natandi*, complete with
   woodcut illustrations.
28 Ibid., p. 104.
29 Ibid., pp. 104–7.
30 Phokion Heinrich Clias, *Elementary Course of Gymnastic Exercises
   Intended to Develope and Improve the Physical Power of Man, and
   A New Complete Treatise on the Art of Swimming* (London, 1825),
   pp. 145–73.
31 Chaline, *The Temple of Perfection*, pp. 82–6.
32 Johann Guts Muths, *Gymnastics for Youth, or, A Practical Guide
   to Healthful and Amusing Exercises* (London, 1800), p. 343.
33 Ibid., p. 347.

34 Ibid., pp. 353–4.

35 See 'First Visit to London', *Autobiography of Benjamin Franklin*, www.gutenberg.org (accessed 8 October 2016).

36 Chaline, *The Temple of Perfection*, pp. 87–91.

37 Thomas A. P. van Leeuwen, *The Springboard in the Pond: An Intimate History of the Swimming Pool* (Cambridge, MA, 1998), pp. 21–40.

38 Christopher Love, *A Social History of Swimming in England, 1800–1918* (Abingdon, 2008), pp. 78–9. 'The Autobiography of Benjamin Franklin', www.gutenberg.org (accessed 8 October 2016).

39 Love, *A Social History of Swimming in England*, pp. 88–9.

40 *Au xixe siècle l'enseignement de la natation se faisait à terre*, www.liberation.fr (accessed 8 June 2015).

41 Love, *A Social History of Swimming in England*, pp. 100–104; and see www.rlss.org.uk (accessed 9 July 2015).

42 Robert Baden-Powell, *Scouting for Boys: A Handbook for Instruction in Good Citizenship* (London, 1908), p. 138; Love, *A Social History of Swimming in England*, pp. 115–23.

5 Pure, Clean and Healthy

1 Pliny the Elder, *Natural History*, Book XXXI, www.loebclassics.com (accessed 10 June 2015).

2 'Great Bath', www.harappa.com (accessed 8 June 2015).

3 Wendy Doniger, *The Hindus: An Alternative History* (Oxford, 2010), p. 79.

4 Mary Douglas, *Purity and Danger: An Analysis of Concepts of Pollution and Taboo* (London, 1966).

5 Originally a large secular building used to conduct business and legal matters. Many Roman basilicas were later converted into Christian churches.

6 Pliny the Elder, *Natural History*, Book XXXI.

7 Ralph Jackson, 'Waters and Spas in the Classical World', in *The Medical History of Waters and Spas*, ed. Roy Porter (London, 1990), pp. 1–13.

8 See www.szechenyifurdo.hu and www.gellertbath.com (accessed 12 June 2015).

9 Flavius Vegetius Renatus, *The Military Institutions of the Romans*, digitalattic.org (accessed 19 May 2015).

10 Ian Gordon and Simon Inglis, *Great Lengths: The Historic Swimming Pools of Britain* (Swindon, 2009), pp. 20–21.

11 Jules Michelet was the first historian to use the term Renaissance. He made this comment about bathing in *La sorcière* (Paris, 1862).

12 Although the doctors of the day did not understand how waterborne diseases such as cholera and typhoid fever were spread, in the case of spas and bathhouses, they were correct in associating them with contaminated water. However, they also believed that communal bathing was responsible for non-waterborne diseases such as plague and leprosy.

13 'A Brief History of Spa Therapy', http://ard.bmj.com (accessed 22 June 2015).

14 Thomas A. P. van Leeuwen, *The Springboard in the Pond: An Intimate History of the Swimming Pool* (Cambridge, MA, 1998), p. 20; and see 'Bains flottants', www.nicolaslefloch.fr (accessed 7 October 2016).

15 'Centuries', www.scarboroughspa.co.uk (accessed 21 June 2015), and 'Dr Robert Wittie', www.thescarboroughnews.co.uk (accessed 21 June 2015).

16 Roy Porter, *The Greatest Benefit to Mankind: A Medical History of Humanity from Antiquity to the Present* (London, 1997), pp. 267–8.

17 Julia Allen, *Swimming with Dr Johnson and Mrs Thrale: Sport, Health and Exercise in Eighteenth-century England* (Cambridge, 2012), pp. 254–5.

18 'Royal Leamington Spa: Royal Pump Rooms and Baths', www.victorianturkishbath.org (accessed 23 June 2015).

19 www.suleymaniyehamami.com.tr (accessed 28 June 2015).

20 'The Russian Bania', www.cyberbohemia.com (accessed 28 June 2015).

21 'Temazcal', www.tlahui.com (accessed 28 June 2015).

22 'Onsen', www.japanguide.com (accessed 28 June 2015).

23 Allen, *Swimming with Dr Johnson and Mrs Thrale*, p. 1.

24 Ibid., p. 5.

25 Ibid., p. 224.

26 Ibid., pp. 244–54; Fred Gray, *Designing the Seaside: Architecture, Society and Nature* (London, 2006), pp. 20–23.

27 Quoted in John Goulstone, 'A Chronology of British Swimming, 1766–1837, with Accounts of the Manchester Swimmers Isaac Bedale and Matthew Vipond', unpublished chronology (1999).

28 Nicolas Meynen, 'La Rochelle, One of the First French Nineteenth-century Seaside Resorts: A Dream that Failed to Come True', in *Spas in Britain and France in the Eighteenth and Nineteenth Centuries*, ed. Annick Cossic and Patrick Galliou (Newcastle, 2006), pp. 455–68.

29 Christopher Love, *A Social History of Swimming in England, 1800–1918* (Abingdon, 2008), p. 128.

30 Jeff Wiltse, *Contested Waters: A Social History of Swimming Pools in America* (Chapel Hill, NC, 2007).

31 Ibid., p. 4.

32 George A. Cape, *Baths and Wash Houses: The History of Their Rise and Progress: Showing Their Utility and Their Effect on the Moral and Physical Condition of the People* (London, 1854), p. 58.

33 Love, *A Social History of Swimming in England*, pp. 135–6.

34 Ibid., pp. 54–70.

35 The fifth world cholera pandemic killed 50,000 people in North America between 1866 and 1873.

36 Wiltse, *Contested Waters*, pp. 16–22.

37 In addition to class and gender, race has been a major cause of socio-cultural conflict in the U.S. As Wiltse's study shows, however, in the early development of swimming pools in the northern U.S., race was not the issue that it would become in later stages when pools changed into recreational facilities. Wiltse, *Contested Waters*, pp. 25–6.

38 Ibid., p. 22.

6 Bathing Beauties

1 Alain Corbin, *The Lure of the Sea: The Discovery of the Seaside in the Western World, 1750–1840* (Cambridge, 1994), p. 62.

2 Jeremy Bentham, *Selected Writings on Utilitarianism* (Ware, Herts, 2001), p. 120.

3 Corbin, *The Lure of the Sea*, pp. 1–26.

4 Ibid., pp. 38–42.

5 Ibid., p. 39.

6 Jan Hein Furnée, 'A Dutch Idyll? Scheveningen as a Seaside resort, Fishing Village and Port, *c.* 1700–1900', in *Resorts and Ports: European Seaside Towns since 1700*, ed. Peter Borsay and John K. Walton (Bristol, 2011), pp. 33–49.

7 Corbin, *The Lure of the Sea*, pp. 40–42; John Urry, *The Tourist Gaze* (London, 2002), p. 4.

8 Urry, *The Tourist Gaze*.

9 *The Modesty Machine: The Seaside Bathing Machine from 1735*, exh. cat., Towner Art Gallery and Local History Museum, Eastbourne (1992).

10 Michael Colmer, 'Bathing Beauties: The Amazing History of Female Swimwear', *After Lunch*, I/I (Summer 1976), pp. 5–144.

11 Ibid., pp. 7–10 (Fiennes and Smollett).

12 Ibid., pp. 11–12.

13 Ibid., p. 12; for the Hollywood retelling of her story, see *Million Dollar Mermaid* (dir. Morgan LeRoy, 1952), starring Esther Williams as Annette Kellerman.

14 Jeff Wiltse, *Contested Waters: A Social History of Swimming Pools in America* (Chapel Hill, NC, 2007), p. 5.

15 Chaline, *The Temple of Perfection*, pp. 138–9.

16 Kate Rew, *Wild Swim: River, Lake, Lido and Sea: The Best Places to Swim in Britain* (London, 2008), and Roger Deakin, *Waterlog: A Swimmer's Journey through Britain* (London, 1999).

17 Deakin, *Waterlog* (London, 1999), p. 3.

18 Ibid., p. 4.

19 Douglas Oliver, *Polynesia in Early Historic Times* (Honolulu, HI, 2002), p. 132.

20 Ibid., p. 54.

21 Cecil Colwin, *Breakthrough Swimming* (Champaign, IL, 2014).

22 David Thomas, *Advanced Swimming: Steps to Success* (Champaign, IL, 1990), p. 116.

23 Rew, *Wild Swim*, p. 19.

24 Ibid., p. 29.

7 Temples of Neptune

1 William Hone describing the Peerless Pool, London, 1826. See 'The Peerless Pool', www.janeaustensworld.wordpress.com (accessed 21 June 2015).

2 Cassius Dio, *Roman History*, vol. VI, www.penelope.uchicago.edu (accessed 25 May 2015).

3 'Pool', www.emma.cam.ac.uk (accessed 31 July 2015).

4 Ian Gordon and Simon Inglis, *Great Lengths: The Historic Swimming Pools of Britain* (Swindon, 2009), p. 21.

5 Thomas A. P. van Leeuwen, *The Springboard in the Pond: An Intimate History of the Swimming Pool* (Cambridge, MA, 1998), p. 48.

6 See www.londonaquaticscentre.org (accessed 4 August 2015).

7 Leeuwen, *The Springboard in the Pond*, pp. 21–2.

8 'The Peerless Pool'.

9 Gordon and Inglis, *Great Lengths*, pp. 22–3.

10 Leeuwen, *The Springboard in the Pond*, pp. 21–3.

11 Ibid., pp. 40–44.

12 Gordon and Inglis, *Great Lengths*, pp. 24–8.

13 Ibid., p. 31; See 'Lidos, Oasis', www.homepage.ntlworld.com (accessed 4 August 2015).

14 Leeuwen, *The Springboard in the Pond*, p. 44; 'Dianabad', austriaforum.org and www.dianabad.at (in German, accessed 5 August 2015).

15 Ibid., p. 48; 'Undosa', www.de.wikipedia.org (in German; accessed 5 August 2015).

16 'Piscines', www.paris.fr (in French; accessed 5 August 2015).

17 In chronicling recreational swimming in America, I am again indebted to Jeff Wiltse's excellent study of municipal pools in the northern U.S., *Contested Waters: A Social History of Swimming Pools in America* (Chapel Hill, NC, 2007).

18 Wiltse, *Contested Waters*, p. 9.

19 Ibid., pp. 11–29.

20 Ibid., pp. 46–8.

21 Ibid., pp. 87–90.

22 Ibid., p. 78.

23 Ibid., pp. 152–3.

24 Ibid., pp. 29–30; see www.nyac.org and www.chicagoathletichotel.com (accessed 11 August 2015).

25 Ibid., pp. 180–84.

8 The Silent World

1 Jacques Cousteau, *The Silent World* (London, 1954), p. 3.

2 Eric Chaline, *History's Lost Treasures: And the Secrets Behind Them* (London, 2013), pp. 181–2.

3 Howard Larson, *A History of Self-contained Diving and Underwater Swimming* (Washington, DC, 1959), pp. 4–5.

4 Ibid., pp. 7–8.

5 Sir Francis Bacon, *Novum Organum* (London, 1620), pp. 271–2.

6 Carl Edmonds et al., *Diving and Subaquatic Medicine*, excerpt in archive, p. 4, rubicon-foundation.org (accessed 20 January 2016).

7 Cousteau, *The Silent World*, p. 16.

8 Larson, *A History of Self-contained Diving and Underwater Swimming*, pp. 12–14.

9 Ibid., p. 23.

10 Ibid., pp. 24–6.

11 Ibid., pp. 29–30.

12 'Belloni, il genio dei sommergibili', www.storiain.net (Italian; accessed 8 February 2016).

13 Larson, *A History of Self-contained Diving and Underwater Swimming*, pp. 37–9.

14 Ibid., pp. 40–42. Free-divers use no or minimal equipment; skin-divers use more equipment including a mask or snorkel, flippers, weight belt and wetsuit; scuba divers carry their own source of oxygen and make use of all the clothing and equipment required for the longer and deeper dives that are impossible for free- or skin-divers.

15 United States Naval Academy, *Naval Forces Under the Sea: A Look Back, A Look Ahead* (Flagstaff, AZ, 2002).

16 Larson, *A History of Self-contained Diving and Underwater Swimming*, pp. 33–4.

17 Axel Masden, *Cousteau: An Unauthorized Biography* (London, 1986).

18 Cousteau, *The Silent World*, pp. 28–30.

19 Ibid., pp. 30–31.

20 Ibid., p. 16.

21 Masden, *Cousteau*, pp. 251–3.

22 *Épaves* is available on several sites. I accessed it on Vimeo.com (28 March 2016).

23 Masden, *Cousteau*, pp. 97–8.

24 *The Brighton Swimming Club, 1860–1960: One Hundred Years of Swimming. A Short History of the Brighton Swimming Club* (Brighton, 1960), p. 18.

25 See www.cmas.org, www.naui.org and www.padi.com.

9 This Sporting Life

1 John Goulstone, *A Chronology of British Swimming, 1766–1837, with Accounts of the Manchester Swimmers Isaac Bedale and Matthew Vipond*, unpublished chronology (1999).

2 Short-course races are swum in a standard 25-m (82-ft) pool, and long course, in a standard Olympic or 50-m (164-ft) pool. I would include the swimming element in triathlon in open-water swimming though the sport is regulated by its own separate governing body. The fifth aquatic discipline, diving, though it requires competitors to know how to swim, does not use the skill as part of competition.

3 A mix of wrestling and fighting not unlike modern-day cage fighting but with fewer rules.

4 Athens' Panathenaic Games, for example, held a night-time torch race and a foot race in full armour.

5 Eric Chaline, *The Temple of Perfection: A History of the Gym* (London, 2015), pp. 15–49.

6 Ibid., pp. 16–17.

7 For a detailed treatment of sports played during this period, see Sally Wilkins, *Sports and Games in Medieval Culture* (Westport, CT, 2002).

8 John M. Carter, *Medieval Games: Sports and Recreation in Feudal Society* (Westport, CT, 1992), pp. 34–5.

9 Ibid., pp. 72–3.

10 Ibid., p. III.

11 For a full treatment of the transformation of prizefighting into boxing, see Kasia Boddy, *Boxing: A Cultural History* (London, 2008).

12 Christopher Love, *A Social History of Swimming in England, 1800–1918* (Abingdon, 2008), pp. 38–41.

13 Goulstone, *A Chronology of British Swimming*.

14 Ian Keil and Don Wix, *In the Swim: The Amateur Swimming Association from 1869 to 1994* (Loughborough, 1996), pp. 8–9.

15 Love, *A Social History of Swimming in England*, pp. 37–8.

16 I am indebted to the Brighton Swimming Club, which produced a short history of the club on the occasion of its centenary: *1860–1960: One Hundred Years of Swimming, A Short History of the Brighton Swimming Club* (Brighton, 1960), and also to the 'history' section of www.brightonsc.co.uk (accessed 20 April 2016).

17 Ibid., p. 10.

18 Love, *A Social History of Swimming in England*, p. 44.

19 Keil and Wix, *In the Swim*, pp. 15–17.

20 Lisa Bier, *Fighting the Current: The Rise of American Women's Swimming, 1870–1926* (Jefferson, NC, 2011), p. 41.

21 Keil and Wix, *In the Swim*, pp. 21–32.

22 Bier, *Fighting the Current*, p. 94.

23 De Coubertin's efforts must be seen in the wider context of concerns about the decline in physical and moral health of the populations of the industrialized nations in the late nineteenth century. For a full treatment of this subject, see Chaline, 'The Health of Nations', in *The Temple of Perfection*, pp. 77–107.

24 Taken on behalf of all competitors by Victor Boin (1886–1974), a Belgian freestyle swimmer, water polo player and fencer.

25 Eric Chaline, 'Piraeus', in *Traveller's Guide to the Ancient World: Greece in the Year 415 BCE* (London, 2008), pp. 78–81.

26 Austria and Hungary then formed part of the Austro-Hungarian Empire, leading to disputes as to the total number of countries taking part.

27 See 'The 1896 Olympic Games Results for All Competitors in All Events', with Commentary by Bill Mallon and Ture Widlund, library.la84.org (accessed 27 April 2016).

28 Bier, *Fighting the Current*, p. 40.

29 Love, *A Social History of Swimming in England*, p. 36.

30 Ibid., pp. 45–50.

31 'History' and 'Overview', www.fina.org (accessed 27 April 2016).

32 See gaygames.org (accessed 27 April 2016).

33 Love, *A Social History of Swimming in England*, pp. 44–5.

34 Keil and Wix, *In the Swim*, pp. 110–11.

10 Imaginary Swimmers

1 Leigh Hunt, *Hero and Leander* (London, 1819).

2 *Hero and Leander*: 'The Argument of the Second Sestyad' (published posthumously in 1598), www.perseus.tufts.edu (accessed 5 May 2016).

3 'Written after Swimming from Sestos to Abydos', www.readytogoebooks. com (accessed 5 May 2016).

4 'Hellespont and Dardanelles Swim', www.swimtrek.com (accessed 5 May 2016).

5 Nicholas Orme, *Early British Swimming, 55 BC–AD 1719. With the First Swimming Treatise in English, 1595* (Exeter, 1983), pp. 54–62.

6 The full texts of *Robinson Crusoe* and *Gulliver's Travels* are available in a variety of formats at www.gutenberg.org (accessed 13 May 2016).

7 The full text of *The Water-babies* is available in a variety of formats at www.gutenberg.org (accessed 14 May 2016).

8 Duffy would go on to achieve much greater fame as Bobby Ewing in *Dallas* (1978–91).

9 'The Submarine Strikes', *More Fun Comics* no. 73, www.comics.org (accessed 18 May 2016).

10 Eric Chaline, *The Temple of Perfection: A History of the Gym* (London, 2015), pp. 140–41.

11 'In Defense of Aquaman', www.diamondbackonline.com (accessed 19 May 2016).

12 Momoa is famous from roles in such hit sci-fi series as *Game of Thrones* and *Stargate Atlantis.*

13 Quoted from Carl Jung, *Collected Works*, 9i, para 40, www.carljungdepthpsychology.wordpress.com (accessed 21 May 2016).

14 Sigmund Freud, *The Interpretation of Dreams*, Chapter Five, www.bartleby.com (accessed 21 May 2016).

15 Chaline, *The Temple of Perfection*, pp. 24–30 and pp. 52–6.

16 Ibid., pp. 117–28; p. 141.

17 Ibid., pp. 179–82.

18 Dawn Pawson Bean, *Synchronized Swimming: An American History* (Jefferson, NC, 2005), pp. 4–5, and Lisa Bier, *Fighting the Current: The Rise of American Women's Swimming, 1870–1926* (Jefferson, NC, 2011), pp. 47–51.

19 Bier, *Fighting the Current*, p. 3.

20 The nude swimming sequence is available on www.youtube.com (accessed 31 May 2016).

21 Bean, *Synchronized Swimming*, pp. 9–12. The sequence is available on www.youtube.com (accessed 2 June 2016).

11 The Aquatic Human

1 Terry Shannon and Charles Payzant, *Project Sealab: The Story of the Navy's Man-in-the-Sea Program* (San Carlos, CA, 1966), p. 11.

2 Jacques-Yves Cousteau, *The Silent World* (London, 1954), p. 18.

3 See www.scubarecords; and 'Commercial Diving; and How Deep is Deep?', www.skin-diver.com (accessed 6 June 2016).

4 A nuclear submarine can descend beyond this depth, but not beyond its 'collapse' or 'crush' depth of 730 m (2,400 ft).

5 There is a wide range of materials available about underwater habitats. Books: Frank Ross Jr, *Undersea Vehicles and Habitats: The Peaceful Use of the Oceans* (New York, 1970), James W. Miller and Ian G. Koblick, *Living and Working under the Sea* (New York, 1984), and Shannon and Payzant, *Project Sealab*. Online video: *World without Sun* (1964), about Conshelf II (www.youtube.com, accessed 12 March 2016) and *Story of Sealab I* (1965) and *Story of Sealab II* (1966), archive.com (accessed 12 March 2016).

6 James W. Miller and Ian G. Koblick, *Living and Working under the Sea* (New York, 1984), pp. 65–71.

7   Ibid., pp. 72–4.
8   Ibid., pp. 399–417.
9   Ibid., p. 417.
10 Eric Chaline, *History's Worst Inventions, and the People Who Made Them* (New York, 2009), pp. 141–5.
11 'Sea Level and Climate', pubs.usgs.gov (accessed 13 June 2016).
12 'Rising Seas', ngm.nationalgeographic.com (accessed 10 June 2016).
13 Miller and Koblick, *Living and Working under the Sea*, p. 415.

Epilogue

1   'Red Cross Swimming Campaign', www.time.com (accessed 10 June 2016).
2   'One in Five Adults Cannot Swim, Survey Warns', www.telegraph.co.uk (accessed 10 June 2016).

Select Bibliography

Allen, Julia, *Swimming with Dr Johnson and Mrs Thrale: Sports, Health and Exercise in Eighteenth-century England* (Cambridge, 2012)

Banse, Karl, 'Mermaids: Their Biology, Culture, and Demise', *Limnology and Oceanography*, XXXIV/1 (1990), pp. 148–53

Bean, Dawn Pawson, *Synchronized Swimming: An American History* (Jefferson, NC, 2005)

Beck, Horace, *Folklore of the Sea* (Middletown, CT, 1973)

Bier, Lisa, *Fighting Current: The Rise of American Women's Swimming, 1870–1926* (Jefferson, NC, 2011)

Borghese, Junio, *The Sea Devils*, trans. James Cleugh (Milan, 1950)

Brighton Swimming Club, *One Hundred Years of Swimming, 1860–1960: A Short History of the Brighton Swimming Club* (Brighton, 1960)

Chaline, Eric, *The Temple of Perfection: A History of the Gym* (London, 2015)

Colmer, Michael, 'Bathing Beauties: The Amazing History of Female Swimwear', *After Lunch*, I/1 (Summer 1976), pp. 5–144

Corbin, Alain, *The Lure of the Sea: The Discovery of the Seaside in the Western World, 1750–1840* (Cambridge, 1994)

Cossic, Annick, and Patrick Galliou, eds, *Spas in Britain and France in the Eighteenth and Nineteenth Centuries* (Newcastle, 2006)

Cousteau, Jacques-Yves, *The Silent World* (New York, 1953)

—, *The Ocean World of Jacques Cousteau: Man Re-enters the Sea* (New York, 1974)

—, *Jacques Cousteau's Calypso* (New York, 1983)

Culver, Lawrence, *The Frontier of Leisure: Southern California and the Shaping of Modern America* (Oxford, 2010)

Dalley, Stephanie, *Myths from Mesopotamia* (Oxford, 2008)

Davies, Caitlin, *Downstream: A History and Celebration of Swimming the Thames* (London, 2015)

Deakin, Roger, *Waterlog: A Swimmer's Journey through Britain* (London, 2000)

Dietz, Tim, *The Call of the Siren: Manatees and Dugongs* (Golden, CO, 1992)

Donkin, Robin, *Beyond Price: Pearls and Pearl-fishing, Origins to the Age of Discoveries* (Philadelphia, PA, 1998)

Finamore, Daniel, and Stephen Houston, *Fiery Pool: The Maya and the Mythic Sea* (New Haven, CT, 2010)

Gachot, Theodore, *Mermaids: Nymphs of the Sea* (San Francisco, CA, 1996)

Geistdoerfer, Aliette, Jacques Ivanoff and Isabelle Leblic, eds, *Imagi-mer: créations fantastiques, mythiques* (Paris, 2002)

Gordon, Ian, *Great Lengths: The Historic Indoor Swimming Pools of Britain* (Swindon, 2009)

Goulstone, John, *A Chronology of British Swimming, 1766–1837, with Accounts of the Manchester Swimmers Isaac Bedale and Matthew Vipond* (1999)

Gray, Fred, *Designing the Seaside: Architecture, Society and Nature* (London, 2006)

Hard, Robin, ed., *The Routledge Handbook of Greek Mythology* (London, 2004)

Keil, Ian, and Don Wix, *In the Swim: The Amateur Swimming Association from 1869 to 1994* (Loughborough, 1996)

Kuliukas, Algis, and Elaine Morgan, 'Aquatic Scenarios in the Thinking on Human Evolution: What Are They and How Do They Compare?', in *Was Man More Aquatic in the Past? Fifty Years after Alister Hardy*, ed. M. Vaneechoutte, A. Kuliukas and M. Verhaegen (Sharjah, 2011), pp. 106–19

Larson, Howard, *A History of Self-contained Diving and Underwater Swimming* (Washington, DC, 1959)

Laugrand, Frédéric, and Jarich Oosten, *The Sea Woman: Sedna in Inuit Shamanism and Art in the Eastern Arctic* (Fairbanks, AK, 2008)

Leeuwen, Thomas van, *The Springboard in the Pond: An Intimate History of the Swimming Pool*, ed. H. Searing (Cambridge, MA, 1998)

Leick, Gwendolyn, *Mesopotamia: The Invention of the City* (London, 2001)

Love, Christopher, *A Social History of Swimming in England, 1800–1918: Splashing in the Serpentine* (London, 2008)

Massett, Derek, *The Western Counties Amateur Swimming Association: The First Hundred Years, 1901–2001* (Wellington, 2001)

Miller, James W., and Ian G. Koblick, *Living and Working under the Sea* (New York, 1984)

Morgan, Elaine, *The Descent of Woman* (London, 1972)

—, *The Aquatic Ape Hypothesis* (London, 1997)

Orme, Nicholas, *Early British Swimming, 55 BC–AD 1719: With the First Swimming Treatise in English, 1595* (Exeter, 1983)

Parr, Susie, *The Story of Swimming* (Stockport, 2011)

Phillips, Murray G., *Swimming Australia: One Hundred Years* (Sydney, 2008)

Porter, Roy, ed., *The Medical History of Waters and Spas* (London, 1990)

Rew, Kate, *Wild Swim: River, Lake, Lido and Sea: The Best Places to Swim in Britain* (London, 2008)

Roede, Machteld, Jan Wind, John M. Patrick and Vernon Reynolds, eds, *The Aquatic Ape Theory: Fact or Fiction? The First Scientific Evaluation of a Controversial Theory of Human Evolution* (London, 1991)

Ross, Frank, Jr, *Undersea Vehicles and Habitats: The Peaceful Use of the Oceans* (New York, 1970)

Shannon, Terry, and Charles Payzant, *Project Sealab: The Story of the Navy's Man-in-the-Sea Program* (San Carlos, CA, 1966)

Sprawson, Charles, *Haunts of the Black Masseur: The Swimmer as Hero* (New York, 1993)

Thomas, Ralph, *Swimming: Theory, Practice and History* (1904)

Urry, John, *The Tourist Gaze* (London, 2002)

Waltz, George H., Jr, *Jules Verne* (New York, 1943)

Warren, C.E.T., and James Benson, *The Midget Raiders* (New York, 1954)

Wiltse, Jeff, *Contested Waters: A Social History of Swimming Pools in America* (Chapel Hill, NC, 2007)

Photo Acknowledgements

The author and publishers wish to express their thanks to the below sources of illustrative material and/or permission to reproduce it. Some locations of artworks are also given below.

Library of Congress Prints and Photographs Division Washington, DC: pp. 67, 81, 83, 120, 132, 165, 188, 209, 274; Shutterstock: pp. 60, 135, 286; Shutterstock/Adnan Buyuk: p. 220; Shutterstock/Getmilitaryphotos: p. 207; Shutterstock/Hanafi Latif: p. 37; Shutterstock/Marzolino: p. 90; Shutterstock/Nattanan726: p. 28; Shutterstock/Tateyama: p. 167; Shutterstock/Tropical Studio: p. 30; Shutterstock/HUANG Zheng: p. 128; The Wellcome Library, London: pp. 106, 107, 119, 131, 138, 142, 158, 159, 200.

Cristian Chirita, the copyright holder of the image on p. 35, has published this online under the conditions imposed by a Creative Commons GNU licence; Daderot, the copyright holder of the images on pp. 71, 227, has published these online under the conditions imposed by a Creative Commons CC0 1.0 Universal Public Domain Dedication; Carole Raddato, the copyright holder of the image on p. 174, and Christiaan, the copyright holder of the image on p. 185, have published them online under the conditions imposed by a Creative Commons Attribution-Share Alike 2.0 Generic licence; Mauro Cateb, the copyright holder of the image on p. 68, Roger Culos, the copyright holder of the image on p. 73, Saliko, the copyright holder of the image on p. 121, Kleuske, the copyright holder of the image on p. 125, Petr Vilgus, the copyright holder of the image on p. 126, Myrabella, the copyright holder of the image on p. 151, Juerg.hug, the copyright holder of the image on p. 180, and Fernando Frazão/Agência Brasil, the copyright holder of the images on pp. 247, 251, have published these

Index